On the Shoulders of Giants

UMBERTO ECO

ON THE SHOULDERS OF GIANTS

Translated from the Italian by Alastair McEwen

THE BELKNAP PRESS OF HARVARD UNIVERSITY PRESS

Cambridge, Massachusetts • 2019

Printed in the United States of America

English translation copyright © 2019 La Nave di Teseo Editore, Milano

Originally published in Italian as *Sulle spalle dei giganti : lezioni alla Milanesiana, 2001–2015*
Copyright © 2017 La Nave di Teseo Editore, Milano

Published in the United States by Harvard University Press, 2019

Library of Congress Cataloging-in-Publication Data is available from loc.gov
ISBN: 978-0-674-24089-6 (alk. paper)

We are dwarfs on the shoulders of giants.

—BERNARD OF CHARTRES

Contents

Publisher's Note

The texts published here were written by Umberto Eco, in the years shown at the end of each chapter, expressly for La Milanesiana, a cultural festival held annually since 2000 in Milan. Accepting the invitation to present a *lectio magistralis* twelve times between 2001 and 2015, Eco prepared these to be read aloud. Since 2008, every Milanesiana has had a theme, and Eco held to these themes—and in some cases, inspired them.

The first of his lectures, "On the Shoulders of Giants," serves as apt premise to this book. Presented in 2001, it shares his vision of how the classics contribute to our own time and to the ongoing work of intellectuals. The last lecture printed here, "The Representation of the Sacred," was conceived and prepared for the Milanesiana, but Eco was unable to present it. It strikes a fitting final chord.

It is fascinating to note the recurring themes in Eco's speeches—more leitmotifs than repetitions. Their recurrence across the years bears witness to his enduring interest in the topics dearest to his heart.

On the Shoulders of Giants

1. On the Shoulders of Giants

I have always been fascinated by the historic tension of dwarfs and giants. At the same time, the famous argument about dwarfs and giants is only one chapter of the age-old struggle between fathers and sons, which, as will become clear, still very closely concerns us. We needn't consult any psychoanalysts to know that sons lean toward killing their fathers—and I use the masculine terms here only to match the literature on the subject, not meaning to ignore the fact that it is also a time-honored custom, from the bad blood between Nero and Agrippina to some sensational crimes in today's news, to murder mothers.

The puzzle is rather that, mirroring the attacks by sons on their fathers, there have also always been attacks by fathers on their sons. Oedipus kills Laius, however blamelessly, but meanwhile Saturn devours his own children—and Medea is hardly someone who will have a nursery school named after her. Let's not even mention poor Thyestes, who unknowingly downed a Big Mac made of his own sons' flesh. For every heir to the throne of Byzantium who blinds his father, there are just as many sultans guarding against an overly rapid succession in Constantinople by killing the children of their first marriages.

The conflict between fathers and sons can also take on non-violent forms and be no less dramatic for that. Imagine opposing one's father by mocking him, as Ham did when he couldn't overlook Noah's having a little wine after all that water—upon which, we know, Noah reacted with a kind of racist exclusion, exiling his disrespectful son to the developing world. Let's admit that consigning a line of descendants to thousands of years of endemic hunger and slavery just for making fun of dad after he'd had a few too many does seem truly excessive. And even if we consider Abraham, prepared to sacrifice Isaac, to be a sublime example of submission to the divine will, I would say that, in acquiescing, Abraham treated his son as a thing that was his to dispose of. (Believing the son would die of a slit throat while the father earned the benevolence of Yahweh—you cannot tell me the man was behaving according to our moral canons.) Luckily, Yahweh was joking—but Abraham did not know that. Isaac was especially unlucky, as can be seen by what happens to him after he in turn becomes a father. His son Jacob does not kill him, but he does rob Isaac of his right to name his heir, and with a low trick taking advantage of his blindness—a stratagem arguably more outrageous than a good old parricide.

Every *querelle des anciens et des modernes* involves a struggle parallel to these. To come to the seventeenth-century debate that gave us that phrase, it involved, on one side, Charles Perrault and Bernard Le Bovier de Fontenelle maintaining that the works of their contemporaries were more mature than those of their forebears and therefore better (and so the *poètes galants* and the *esprits curieux* favored the new forms of the story and the novel). The controversy arose and escalated when these advocates of the new were opposed by extremely authoritative figures, such as Boileau, who favored the imitation of the ancients.

When there is a dispute of this kind, the innovators are always opposed by the *laudatores temporis acti* (praisers of times past). And frequently, praise for the new and a breach with the past arises precisely as a reaction to rampant conservatism. While in our day we have had the Novissimi poets, at school we all learned that the *poetae novi* came two thousand years before them. In Catullus's time, the word *modernus* had yet to be invented, but the word *novi* was applied to those poets who looked to Greek lyrical poetry to oppose the Latin tradition. Ovid, in *The Art of Love* (III, 121 ff.), declares that *prisca iuvent alios* (ancient times delight others): *ego me nunc denique natum / Gratulor: haec aetas moribus apta meis* (I celebrate having been born now; this time suits my nature). It is a time of civilization, he explains, when none of the crudity of ancient ancestors remains. Horace (*Epistles* II, 1,75 ff.) reminds us that, even then, the advocates of the new irritated those who praised times past. Instead of "modern," he uses the adverb *nuper* to say that he resents it when a book is deemed unworthy not for lack of elegance *sed quia nuper* (but because it has only been written lately). We encounter that same attitude from those today who, on critiquing a young writer, complain that novels are no longer what they used to be.

The term *modernus* makes its entry right at the end of what we call antiquity—that is to say, around the fifth century AD, when all of Europe plunged into those truly dark centuries that preceded the Carolingian Renaissance—centuries that strike us as the least modern times of all.

It was precisely in those "dark" centuries, in which the memory of past greatness was fading, leaving only burnt-out, dilapidated vestiges, that innovation set in, even though the innovators were unaware of it. In fact, it was then that the new European languages began to prevail, perhaps the most innovative and overwhelming cultural event of the last two thousand years. At the same time, classical Latin was becoming medieval Latin. This period marked the emergence of signs of pride in innovation.

The first act of pride was the recognition that a Latin was being invented that was no longer that of the ancients. After the fall of the Roman Empire, the old continent witnessed an agricultural crisis and the destruction of the great cities, Roman roads, and aqueducts; living in a land covered with woods, the monks, poets, and miniaturists saw the world as a dark forest inhabited by monsters. As early as 580, Gregory of Tours declared the end of literature, and the Pope (I do not remember which one) wondered about the validity of baptisms performed in Gaul, where they were baptizing *in nomine Patris et Filiae et Spiritus Sancti*—that is, in the name of the father, the *daughter*, and the holy spirit—because even the clergy no longer knew Latin. But the period between the seventh and tenth century marked the development of what has been called the "Hisperic aesthetic," a style that spread from Spain to the British Isles, and partly to Gaul, too.

The classical Latin tradition had described (and condemned) this style by labeling it first "Asian" then "African," in contrast with the harmony of the "Attic" style. The Asian style was criticized for what classical rhetoric called *kakozelòn*, or *mala affectatio* (ill affectation). For an example of just how deeply the fathers of the church of the fifth century were scandalized by cases of *mala affectatio*, consider this philippic by Saint Jerome (in *Adversus Jovinianum* I):

These days there are so many barbarous writers and so many discourses rendered so muddled by stylistic vices that one can understand neither who is talking nor what he is talking about. Everything expands and contracts like a diseased serpent that falls apart as it vainly essays to make its coils. All is entangled in inextricable verbal knots, and one has to agree with Plautus: "Here no one can understand anything except the Sybil." What's the point of this verbal witchcraft?

But what was a vice for the classical tradition became a virtue for Hisperic poetics. Hisperic writing no longer complied with traditional syntactic and rhetorical norms; the rules of rhythm and meter were broken to produce lists of a baroque flavor. Long series of alliterations that the classical world would have deemed cacophonic now produced a new music; Aldhelm of Malmesbury (*Letter to Eahfrid*, PL 89.159) enjoyed himself hugely by constructing long phrases in which (almost) every word begins with the same letter: "Primitus pantorum procerum praetorumque pio potissimum paternoque praesertim privilegio panegericum poemataque passim prosatori sub polo promulgantes . . ."

The lexicon was enriched with incredible hybrids, the use of loan words from Hebrew and Greek, and the discourse became dense with cryptograms. Where classical aesthetics saw clarity as an ideal, the Hisperic aesthetic strove for obscurity. Where classical aesthetics saw proportion as an ideal, the Hisperic aesthetic favored complexity, the abundance of epithets and periphrasis, the gigantic, the monstrous, the uncontrollable, the fathomless, and the prodigious. The waves of the sea were described as *astriferus* or *glaucicomus*, and other neologisms such as *pectoreus, placoreus, sonoreus, alboreus, propriferus, flammiger, gaudifluus* were much appreciated.

These sixth-century lexical inventions are the same ones honored by the seventh-century grammarian Virgil in his *Epitomae* and *Epistolae*. This mad grammarian served up passages from Cicero and Virgil (the other Virgil, the real one) that those authors would never have written. It has been surmised that he belonged to a group of rhetoricians who all adopted names of classical authors and, under their false names, exulted in writing in a Latin that was anything but classical. The linguistic universe that Virgil the Grammarian created looks as if it sprang from the imagination of a modern surrealist, perhaps the Italian poet Edoardo Sanguineti, even though it would have to be the other way around. He maintained that there were twelve types of Latin, and thus twelve different words for, say, fire: *ignis, quoquinhabin, ardon, calax, spiridon, rusin, fragon, fumaton, ustrax, vitius, siluleus, aeneon* (*Epitomae* 1.4). Likewise there were various words for battle, including *praelium* because it can take place at sea (called *praelum* because its immensity earns it the primacy, or *praelatum*, of the marvelous). On the other hand, he questions the very rules of Latin, and reports that two rhetoricians he calls Galbungus and Terrentius debated for fourteen days and fourteen nights about the vocative case of *ego*—a problem of the utmost importance, because it was a question of how to refer emphatically to oneself ("Oh, I, have I done well?" *O egone, recte feci?*)

But let's move on to the vulgar tongues. Toward the end of the fifth century, people had already dropped Latin in favor of Gallo-Roman, Italo-Roman, Hispano-Roman, and Balkano-Roman. These were spoken, not written, languages. Yet, even before the Serment de Strasbourg and the Charter of Capua, this looks like a celebration of linguistic novelty. With this proliferation of tongues people were harking back to the tale of the tower of Babel, a story usually seen as a sign of a curse or catastrophe. But in the birth of the new vulgar languages some now dared to see a sign of modernity and improvement.

In the seventh century, some Irish grammarians attempted to describe the advantages of vulgar Gaelic over Latin grammar. In a work titled *The Precepts of the Poets*, they referred to the structure of the tower of Babel: just as eight or nine materials (depending on the version) had been used in the construction of the tower—clay and water, wool and blood, wood and lime, pitch, linen, and bitumen—so Gaelic had been formed from nouns, pronouns, verbs, adjectives, adverbs, participles, conjunctions, prepositions, and interjections. The parallel is revealing: we must wait for Hegel for the legend of the tower to be cast again as a positive model. The Irish grammarians maintained that Gaelic was the first and only case in which the confusion of tongues had been overcome. Its creators, by means of an operation we might now call cutting and pasting, chose the best features of every language. When there was something for which no language had found a name, they produced one—and in such a way as to reveal an identity between the form, the word, and the object.

Centuries later, with a completely different awareness of his own exploit and his own dignity, Dante saw himself as the inventor of a new vernacular. Faced with the plethora of Italian dialects, which he analyzed with the precision of a linguist but the condescension and occasional disdain of a poet (and one who never doubted he was the greatest of all), Dante concluded that there was a need for a language that was illustrious (in the sense of spreading light), cardinal (serving as a mainstay and a rule), regal (worthy of a place in the royal palace of the national realm, if the Italians were ever to have one), and courtly (the language of government, the law, and wisdom). In his *De Vulgari Eloquentia*, he outlined the rules of composition of the only true illustrious vernacular, the poetic language he proudly felt he had founded—and which he contrasted with the tongues of the Babelic confusion, as one who had rediscovered the primordial affinity with things that was proper to the Adamitic language. This illustrious vernacular, to which Dante gave chase as if it were a "perfumed panther" (hidden from the eye but leaving its heavy scent to track), represented a restoration of the Edenic language, hence a tongue capable of healing the post-Babelic wound. This bold concept of his own role as the restorer of the perfect language explains the fact that, rather than criticize the multiplicity of tongues, Dante emphasized their quasi-biological power to renew themselves and change over time. It was precisely on the basis of this claimed linguistic creativity that he was able to set himself the task of inventing a modern, natural, perfect language without chasing after such lost models as the original Hebrew. He set himself up as a new (and more perfect) Adam. Compared to Dante's pride, Rimbaud's far more recent assertion, *il faut être absolument moderne*, looks dated. In the struggle between fathers and sons, the *Inferno* is far more patricidal than the *Saison en enfer*.

Perhaps the first episode of the generational clash in which the word *modernus* makes an explicit appearance occurs not in the literary sphere but in that of philosophy. Whereas the early medieval period found its primary philosophical sources in late Neoplatonic texts, in Augustine, and in those Aristotelian writings called the *Logica Vetus*, scholastic circles in the twelfth century were gradually introduced to the other Aristotelian texts (such as the *Prior* and *Posterior Analytics*, the *Topics*, and *On Sophistical Refutations*) that came to be known as the *Logica Nova*. This stimulus led to a shift from a merely metaphysical and theological discourse to an exploration of all those subtleties of reason that modern logic sees as the liveliest inheritance of medieval thinking, and hence to what was defined (clearly with the pride common to all innovative movements) as *logica modernorum*.

The nature of the *logica modernorum's* novelty as compared to the theological thinking of the past is made clear by the fact that the Church has canonized Anselm of Aosta, Thomas Aquinas, and Bonaventure, but has not done the same for any proponent of modern logic. It is not that these men were heretics. Simply, with respect to the theological debates of past centuries, they were interested in other things. Today we would say that they dealt with the workings of the mind. These men were more or less consciously killing their fathers, just as the humanist philosophers would later try to kill them—outdated modernists that they were by then—but all the humanist philosophers succeeded in doing was to sentence them to hibernation in the university lecture halls, where contemporary (by which I mean today's) universities would eventually rediscover them.

In the cases I have mentioned, it nevertheless appears that every act of innovation, and of protest against the fathers, always occurs with some recourse to an ancestor, who is recognized as better than the father one is trying to kill. The *poetae novae* challenged the Latin tradition by imitating the Greek lyricists; the Hisperic poets and Virgil the Grammarian created their linguistic hybrids by adopting loan words from Celtic, Visigothic, Greek, and Hebrew; the Irish grammarians celebrated a language that was opposed to Latin because it was a collage of far more ancient tongues; Dante needed a strong forefather like Virgil (the classical Latin poet); and the *logica modernorum* was modern thanks to the rediscovery of lost Aristotelian texts.

A very frequent *topos* in the Middle Ages argued that the ancients were taller and better looking, a position that would be completely untenable today: we need only look at the length of the beds Napoleon slept in. But in those days, perhaps, it was not entirely unreasonable, not only because the image people had of antiquity derived from commemorative statuary, whose sculptors added many centimeters to their subjects' heights, but also because the fall of the Roman Empire had been followed by centuries of famine and depopulation. Those towering crusaders and knights of the Holy Grail we see in contemporary cinema were very likely much shorter than their equivalents of our day. Alexander the Great (326–323 BCE) was notoriously short, but Vercingetorix (82–46 BCE) was probably taller than King Arthur (480–550 CE). For the sake of symmetrical contrast, another *topos*, frequently found in the Bible and through late antiquity and beyond, was that of the *puer senilis*, a youngster who, along with the virtues of youth, had all those typical of the old man. Eulogizing the stature of the ancients may seem a conservative foible, and the model of the *senilis in iuvene prudentia* (elderly and young wisdom combined) celebrated by Apuleius (*Florida* IX, 38) may seem to favor the novel. But this is not the case. Praise of the ancients was a way for innovators to justify their modern ways as approaches drawing on traditions their fathers had forgotten.

Apart from the few cases mentioned, Dante's arrogance above all, in the Middle Ages, people assumed that the truth of things lay in the extent to which they were backed up by an earlier authority. If it was suspected that the authority in question did not really support the new idea, his writings were promptly manipulated until they did. "Authority has a nose of wax," Alain de Lille noted in the twelfth century: "it can be twisted in different ways."

We must try to grasp this point because, from Descartes on, a philosopher was one who wiped the slate of previous knowledge clean and—as Jacques Maritain said—presented himself as a *débutant dans l'absolu* (absolute beginner). Any thinkers of our day (not to mention any poets, novelists, or painters) who want to be taken seriously must somehow show that they are saying something different from their immediate predecessors, or if they are not doing so, they must pretend that they are. Well, the Scholastics did exactly the opposite. They committed their most dramatic patricides, so to speak, by claiming and trying to show that they were only restating what their fathers had said. Considering the times he lived in, Thomas Aquinas revolutionized Christian philosophy, but he would have promptly replied to anyone who criticized him (and some did) that he was only repeating what St. Augustine had taught eight and a half centuries before him. This was neither mendacious nor hypocritical. The medieval thinker simply believed it was right to correct the opinions of his predecessors here and there when, thanks to them, he thought he had a clearer idea. Which brings us to the aphorism that inspired the title of this address, that of the dwarfs and giants. The philosopher John of Salisbury gives this account of where it started:

Dicebat Bernardus Carnotensis nos esse quasi nanos gigantium humeris insidentes, ut possimus plura eis et remotiora videre, non utique proprii visus acumine, aut eminentia corporis, sed quia in altum subvehimur et extollimur magnitudine gigantes.

(Bernard of Chartres used to say that we are like dwarfs standing on the shoulders of giants, and so we can see farther than they, not because of our sharper sight or greater stature but because we have been raised higher by their great size.)

To explore the medieval period origins of this aphorism, you might like to track down a copy of Édouard Jeauneau's 1969 book *Nani sulle spalle di giganti*, but a more joyously crazy and exciting romp is *On the Shoulders of Giants*, published in 1965 by one of the greatest contemporary sociologists, Robert Merton. Merton was quite taken by the way Isaac Newton expressed the thought in a letter to Robert Hooke, dated 1675: "If I have seen further it is by standing on ye sholders of Giants." Merton started tracing the history of the aphorism, and his book documents its vicissitudes with a series of erudite divagations that grew from edition to edition as he added notes and other material. Having published an Italian edition (titled *Sulle spalle dei giganti*, 1991) and having been so good as to ask me to write an introduction, he reissued it in English in 1993 as "the post-Italianate edition."

When John of Salisbury, in his *Metalogicon* (3.4), credited Bernard of Chartres with the dwarfs and giants metaphor, it was the twelfth century. Bernard may not have felt he invented it, however, because the concept (if not the image of the dwarfs) was contained in the monumental exposition of grammar produced by Priscian six centuries earlier which served as the standard work for teaching Latin—and, just thirty-six years before John of Salisbury, an intermediary voice, William of Conches, had talked of dwarfs and giants in his *Commentaries on Priscian*. But what interests us is that, after John of Salisbury, the aphorism was picked up pretty much all over: in 1160 it appears in a text attributed to the school of Laon; around 1185 it was used by the Danish historian Sven Aagesen, then by Gerard of Cambrai, Raoul de Longchamp, Gilles de Corbeil, and Gerard of Auvergne; and in the fourteenth century, Alexandre Ricat, physician to the kings of Aragon, invoked it again. It cropped up two centuries later in the works of Ambroise Paré, again in those of seventeenth-century scientist Daniel Sennert, and then in Newton. Tullio Gregory notes a use of the aphorism by the seventeenth-century philosopher Gassendi (*Scetticismo ed empirismo: Studio su Gassendi*, 1961), and the line extends to José Ortega y Gasset, who in his 1947 essay "Entorno a Galileo" writes that men stand "on one another's shoulders, and he who is highest enjoys the impression of dominating the others, but he should feel at the same time that he is their prisoner." On the other hand, in Jeremy Rifkin's 1980 book *Entropy*, I find a quotation from anthropologist Max Gluckman, who defines a science as "any discipline in which the fool of this generation can go beyond the point reached by the genius of the last generation." Eight centuries divide this quotation from that attributed to Bernard, and note what has happened along the way: a saying that referred to the relationship with the fathers in philosophy and theology has become a saying that marks the progressive nature of science.

At the time of its medieval origin the aphorism became popular because it offered a way to resolve generational conflict in an apparently non-revolutionary way. The ancients are certainly giants compared to us, but although we are mere dwarfs seated on their shoulders ready to take advantage of their wisdom, we can see better than they. Was this statement originally humble, or was it proud? Did it mean to say that we merely know, albeit a little better, what the ancients taught us—or that, acknowledging our debt to the ancients, we know far more than they?

Since one of the recurring themes in medieval culture is the progressive senescence of the world (*mundus senescit*), one might interpret Bernard of Chartres's aphorism to mean that we younger ones are aging with respect to the ancients, but at least, thanks to them, we can understand and do a bit more than they managed to understand or do. Bernard made use of his metaphor in the context of a debate on grammar, engaging with the concept of knowledge and whether the style of the ancients should be imitated. But, according to John of Salisbury, Bernard criticized those pupils who slavishly copied the ancients, saying that the point was not to write like them but to learn from them how to write well; he thought that people in the future should be inspired by his pupils as the pupils themselves had been inspired by the ancients. It might not have been in terms we would use today, but Bernard's aphorism contained a call for autonomy and the courage to innovate.

The aphorism said that "we can see farther" than the ancients. The metaphor is clearly a spatial one, implying a march toward a horizon. We should not forget that the concept of history as a progressive movement toward a better future is an invention of the Fathers of the Church—as in, from creation to redemption and then to the coming of Christ triumphant. Whether we like it or not, without Christianity (albeit with Jewish messianism behind it) neither Hegel nor Marx would have been able to talk about what the Italian poet Leopardi saw skeptically as "magnificent and progressive fate."

Again, use of the dwarfs and giants metaphor takes off in the early twelfth century. Only a century before, a key debate had finally subsided, one that had run through the Christian world from the first interpretations of the Book of Revelation to the terrors of the year 1000. *Millenarianism*—that neurotic expectation of the end of days—had been an idea that had grown up through an extensive millenarian literature and in many more or less subterranean schools of heretical thought. Certainly legendary as far as mass movements are concerned, it was still an active inheritance of many heretical movements at the time that the aphorism was coined, but it had disappeared from orthodox debate. The movement was toward a final *parousia* (Second Coming of Christ), but it became the ideal end to a story seen as a positive one. The dwarfs were a symbol of this march to the future.

The medieval appearance of the dwarfs marked the beginning of the history of modernity as innovation that involves rediscovering models forgotten by the fathers. Let us take, for example, the curious situation of the first humanists, and of philosophers like Marsilio Ficino and Pico della Mirandola. They were the leading lights—as we were told at school—in a battle against the medieval world, and it was more or less in this period that the word *gothic* appeared, with not entirely favorable connotations. Yet what did Renaissance Platonism do? It set Plato against Aristotle, discovered the *Corpus Hermeticum* or the Chaldean Oracles, and built a new knowledge upon an ancient wisdom that antedated Jesus Christ. Humanism and the Renaissance were cultural movements commonly seen as revolutionary, but their strategy was one of the most reactionary *coups de main* ever, if we define reactionary as a return to an atemporal tradition. So we are witness here to a patricide that eliminates the fathers by turning to the grandfathers; it was from the latter's shoulders that they attempted to advance the Renaissance vision of man as the center of the cosmos.

It was probably with seventeenth-century science that western culture succeeded in standing the world on its head, thereby truly revolutionizing knowledge. But the starting point of that science, the Copernican hypothesis, referred back to the thinking of Plato and Pythagoras. When the Jesuits of the Baroque period tried to counter the Copernican model by constructing an alternative modernity their opposition took the form of rediscovering the ancient writings and civilizations of the Far East. Isaac de la Peyrère, an out-and-out heretic, tried to show (by killing off biblical chronology) that the world began long before Adam, in the China seas, and consequently that the Incarnation was merely a secondary episode in the history of our world. Giambattista Vico saw all of human history as a process that takes us from the giants of the past to the point of finally being able to reflect with clear minds. The Enlightenment saw itself as radically modern, and as a side effect it really did kill its own father, with Louis Capet serving as physical proxy.

But here, too—just read the *Encyclopédie*—frequent reference was made to the giants of the past. Even as the *Encyclopédie* celebrates the new manufacturing industry by including woodcuts illustrating a wide variety of machines, it is not above printing "revisionist" articles (in the sense that, like an energetic dwarf, it reinterprets history) in which ancient doctrines are revisited.

The great Copernican revolutions of the nineteenth century always refer to previous giants. Kant needs Hume to awaken him from his dogmatic slumbers; the Romantics engage with the Storm by rediscovering the mists and castles of the Middle Ages; Hegel explicitly sanctions the primacy of the new over the old, seeing history as a perfective movement without waste and nostalgia; Marx, reinterpreting human history in its entirety, works out his materialism starting with the Greek atomists, the subjects of his degree thesis; Darwin kills off his biblical parents by making giants of the great anthropomorphic apes, on whose shoulders men came down from the trees to manage, still full of wonder and ferocity, that marvel of evolution that is the opposable thumb. The second half of the nineteenth century witnessed a movement of artistic innovation that was almost entirely a reappropriation of the past, from the Pre-Raphaelites to the decadents. The rediscovery of remote fathers served as a rebellion against the actual fathers, who had been corrupted by mechanical looms. And Carducci, who made himself the herald of modernity with his "Hymn to Satan," continually sought inspiration and ideals in the myths of Italy's earliest "commune" city-states.

The historic avant-garde of the early twentieth century represents a peak expression of this parricide by modernism, which claims to free itself of all homage to the past. This is the speed-smitten Marinetti calling the racing car more beautiful than the *Victory of Samothrace*; the futurists' slogan of "down with moonlight"; their glorification of war as the world's only hygiene; the cubists' fracturing of forms; the progression from abstraction to blank canvas; the substitution of music with noise, or with silence, or at most with the tonal scale; the architects' "curtain wall" that does not dominate but absorbs the environment, and buildings as steles, pure parallelepipeds, minimalist art; and in literature, the destruction of the flow of discourse and narrative tenses, the Burroughs-like collage and blank page. Yet here, too, as the new giants reject the legacy of the old giants, the dwarf's deference also asserts itself. I am not speaking here so much of a Marinetti, who would later atone for murdering the moonlight by becoming a member of the Accademia d'Italia—a body that had a considerable affection for moonlight—but of a Picasso, who only began to disfigure the human face after meditating on classical and Renaissance models, and who ended up revisiting ancient minotaurs. Duchamp stuck a moustache on the *Mona Lisa,* but first needed a *Mona Lisa* to stick the moustache on. Magritte, to deny that he was painting a pipe, had to go to the effort of meticulously painting a realistic pipe. Finally, the great parricide of the novel's historic body was committed by James Joyce—who took the Homeric narrative form as his model. Even the ultramodern *Ulysses* sailed farther thanks to the shoulders, or in this case the mainmast, of an ancient tradition.

This brings us to postmodernism. *Postmodern* is an all-purpose term, which can be applied to many—perhaps too many—things. But the various activities we describe as postmodern are all reacting, perhaps unconsciously, to a shared concern. Nietzsche names it in the second of his *Untimely Meditations* ("On the Use and Abuse of History"), where he denounces our excess of historical awareness. If the oppressive influence of this awareness cannot be eliminated even by the revolutionary activities of the avant-garde, the postmodern stance is that we might as well accept the past, revisit it as a form of apparent tribute, and reconsider it from the distance permitted us by irony.

The last episode of generational rebellion I will offer is a clear example of protest on the part of the "new" youth against adult society, coming from those young people who warned one another not to trust anyone over thirty. This was 1968. Setting aside the American flower children, who drew inspiration from Herbert Marcuse's writings, the slogans chanted during Italian demonstrations (Viva Marx!, Viva Lenin!, Viva Mao Tse-tung!) tell us just how much the rebellion needed to summon earlier giants to fight the betrayal of their immediate fathers on the parliamentary left. There was even a comeback for the *puer senilis*, seen in the iconic figure of Che Guevara, who died young but was transformed by death into the bearer of all ancient virtues.

But something has happened between 1968 and today. This can be seen when we look closely at a phenomenon that some, superficially, see as the new 1968. I am referring to today's anti-globalization movement. While the press often gives most visibility to this movement's younger members, they are not the entire movement; it includes even elderly prelates. The year 1968 was a true generational phenomenon, even if a few adult misfits did adapt by abandoning ties and donning sweaters, throwing away their razors and opting for a liberating proliferation of hair. The old slogan had it that no one over thirty was to be trusted. But the anti-globalization movement is led by mature adults like José Bové and veterans of other revolutions. It does not represent a clash between generations, or even between innovation and tradition—otherwise, one would have to cast the technocrats of globalization (equally superficially) as the innovators, and see the demonstrators as merely *laudatores temporis acti* with Luddite propensities. What is happening from

Seattle to Genoa on the occasion of the G8 conference in 2001 certainly represents a new form of political struggle, but this struggle is wholly transversal with regard to both generations and ideologies. It contains two opposing aspirations, two visions of the world's destiny, I would like to say two forces, one based on possession of the means of production and the other based on the invention of new means of communication. In the battle between the globalizers and their antagonists, young and old are equally distributed, and the rampant thirty-year-olds of the new economy are lined up against the thirty-year-olds of the left-wing social centers, each camp backed by older sympathizers.

The fact is that in the thirty-odd years between 1968 and the battle of the G8, a process begun many years before came to fruition. Let's try to understand its internal mechanism. For a dialectic between fathers and sons to be established, it must always be the case that a strong paternal model exists, and the provocation of the son also has to be so strong that the father cannot accept it, and nor can the father accept the resurrection of forgotten giants. The new poets cannot be accepted *quia nuper*, as Horace puts it; in his time, the vernacular was unacceptable to the pompous Latinists of the universities. Aquinas and Bonaventure innovated in the hope that no one would notice, but enemies of the mendicant orders, in the University of Paris, spotted this and tried to have their teachings banned. And so it went, all the way down to Marinetti's racing car, which could be held up as superior to the *Victory of Samothrace* because and only because his elders saw motor cars as heaps of snarling scrap iron.

The model has to be generational, therefore. Fathers had to worship Cranach's anorexic Venuses as young men to be moved to call Rubens's chubby Venuses an insult to beauty; fathers had to love Alma Tadema before they could demand of their sons what the devil that daub by Miró or that piece of African art was supposed to mean; fathers had to rave about Greta Garbo before, scandalized, they could ask their sons what they saw in that little ape Brigitte Bardot.

The mass media of today, and the mediatization of museums, also visited by the uncultivated of old, have brought about the compresence and the syncretistic acceptance of all models, indeed of all values. When the Australian supermodel Megan Gale appears in an ad in which she dons rollerblades to swoop across the curves and ledges of the Guggenheim in Bilbao, both the sexual and the artistic aspects appeal to all generations: the museum is as sensuously desirable as Megan, and Megan is as much a cultural object as the museum, since both exist in the amalgam of a cinematic fiction that unites the sex appeal of the ad and the aesthetic boldness of vision that in the past could only been the stuff of art-house films.

Between its new concepts and its exercises in nostalgia, television has made transgenerational models out of Che Guevara and Mother Teresa, Lady Diana and Padre Pio, Rita Hayworth, Brigitte Bardot, and Julia Roberts, not to mention the macho John Wayne of the 1940s and the meek Dustin Hoffman of the 1960s. The slender Fred Astaire of the 1930s dances alongside the stocky Gene Kelly of the 1950s, while the cinema makes us dream simultaneously about the sumptuously feminine outfits seen in *Roberta* and the epicene fashion of Coco Chanel. For those who do not go in for the refined masculine beauty of Richard Gere, there is the sensitive appeal of Al Pacino or the blue-collar charm of Robert de Niro. When you cannot afford the majesty of a Maserati, there is always the elegant utility of the Mini Morris.

The major media no longer present any unified model. Even in an advertisement created to air for only a week, they can draw on all the experimental work of the avant-garde and at the same time rediscover nineteenth-century iconography; they can offer the fairy-tale realism of role-playing games and Escher's mind-boggling perspectives, the opulent curves of Marilyn Monroe and the gamine grace of the latest top models, the dusky beauty of Naomi Campbell and the Nordic beauty of Claudia Schiffer, the charm of traditional tap dancing, as in *A Chorus Line*, and the chilling futuristic architectures of *Blade Runner*; the androgynous Jodie Foster and squeaky-clean Cameron Diaz, not to mention Rambo and Ru Paul, George Clooney (whom any father would embrace as his son, perhaps only adding a brand-new degree in medicine), and neo-cyborgs who paint their faces in metallic shades and transform their hair into forests of colored spikes.

Amid this orgy of tolerance, this absolute and unstoppable polytheism, where is the watershed that separates fathers from sons, driving the latter toward patricide (both as rebellion and as tribute) and the former toward the anthropophagy of Saturn?

We are barely at the dawn of this new trend, but think for a moment about the arrival, first, of the personal computer and then of the internet. The computer comes into the home thanks to the fathers, for economic reasons if for nothing else. The sons, far from rejecting it, go on to master it, soon surpassing the fathers in ability. But neither sees it as a symbol of rebellion or resistance of the other. The computer has not divided the generations; if anything, it has united them. No one lays a curse on his son because he surfs the net, and likewise, no son opposes his father's doing so.

We are not lacking for innovation, but today's innovation is almost always technological, it is normally imposed by an international production center run by older people, and it creates fashions accepted by the younger people. We talk today of a new youth language of SMS texting and email, but I could show you essays written ten years ago in which the very people who created the new instruments, and the older sociologists and semioticians who studied them, foresaw the language and formulas that would result and that they in fact made popular. Bill Gates was young when all this began (now he is a mature gentleman who tells young people which language they will have to use), but as a young man he did not advocate generational revolt. He came up with a shrewd offer designed to interest both fathers and sons.

Some people think that young social misfits are opposing their fathers by turning to drugs, but drug abuse is a model that generations have made use of ever since the days of the artificial paradises of the nineteenth century. The new users receive their supplies from international drug traffickers, who are adults.

It might be said that there is no clash of models but merely an accelerated turnover of them. But this changes nothing. For a brief space of time, a certain youth model (whether spotted in a Pasolini film or in Nike footwear) strikes fathers as outrageous, but the speed of its diffusion in the media ensures that it will soon be absorbed by the fathers, too—perhaps even at the risk that, after an equally brief time, it will come to strike the sons as ridiculous. But no one will have time to notice this relay race, and the overall result will always be that absolute polytheism and syncretistic compresence of all values. Was the set of beliefs and practices labeled *New Age* a generational invention? As far as its content goes, it is a collage of age-old esoteric elements. It may be that young people were the first to turn to these elements, as young cohorts in the past turned to new hosts of rediscovered giants, but the diffusion of typical New Age images, sounds, and beliefs, and New Age recording, publishing, cinematic, and religious paraphernalia, was immediately taken over and run by the wily old foxes of the mass media. If some youngsters now run off to India, it is only to throw themselves into the arms of an elderly guru with many lovers and a fleet of Cadillacs.

Things that looked like the last frontier of nonconformity, such as nose rings, tongue studs, and blue hair, in the sense that they are no longer the inventions of a few individuals but universally accepted, were proposed to young people by the gerontocratic centers of the international fashion business. Soon the influence of the mass media will impose them on the parents, too—unless the moment comes when both young and old, perhaps on discovering that ice cream is not as enjoyable with a metal stud in one's tongue, together abandon them.

Why, then, should fathers still devour their sons, and why should sons still dispatch with their fathers? The risk, for everyone, though the fault of no one, is that constant innovation constantly accepted by everybody will lead to ranks of dwarfs sitting on the shoulders of other dwarfs. And, at the same time, let's be realistic: in normal times, there *ought* to be generational turnover. By now, I *ought* to be a pensioner.

That's great, you will say: we are entering a new era in which, along with the decline of ideologies and the blurring of the traditional divisions between left and right and between progressives and conservatives, generational conflict is clearly diminishing. But is it biologically advisable for sons' rebellions to add up to no more than superficial adjustments to the models produced by their fathers' rebellions—or for fathers' devouring of their sons to go no further than giving them a bit of room for some colorful form of social marginalization? When the very principle of patricide is in crisis, *mala tempora currunt*. Bad times are upon us.

But the worst diagnosticians of every epoch are its contemporaries. My giants taught me that there are transitional spaces where the coordinates are lacking, the future cannot be seen clearly, and we still do not understand the chicaneries of reason or the imperceptible plots of the zeitgeist. Perhaps the good old ideal of patricide is rising again, but in different forms. In future generations, cloned sons might rebel against their legal fathers (or sperm donors) in ways we cannot predict.

And perhaps giants we know nothing about are even now lurking in the shadows, ready to climb onto the shoulders of us dwarfs.

[La Milanesiana, 2001]

2. Beauty

In 1954, I graduated in aesthetics with a thesis on the problem of beauty, albeit only as I could explore it in a few pages of Thomas Aquinas. In 1962, I began work on a project for an illustrated book on the history of beauty, a project that the publisher dropped for banal financial reasons, even though a quarter or at least a fifth of the work had already been done. I picked up that project again a few years ago and created a CD-ROM, and after that a book, for the simple reason that I do not like leaving things half done. Considering the span of fifty years across which I have found myself thinking about the concept of beauty from time to time, I realize that, then as now, I could repeat the answer Augustine gave when asked about the nature of time: "If no one asks me, I know what it is; if I wish to explain it to him who asks me, I don't know."

I consoled myself about my uncertainties concerning the definition of beauty when, in 1973, I read the definition of art that Dino Formaggio provided in a booklet written for the *Enciclopedia filosofica* ISEDI: "Art is everything people call art." So likewise I would say: "Beauty is everything people have called beautiful."

This, of course, is a relativistic approach: what is held to be beautiful depends on the period and the culture. This is not a matter of modern heresy. There is a famous passage in Xenophanes of Colophon: "But had the oxen or the lions hands, / Or could with hands depict a work like men, / Were beasts to draw the semblance of the gods, / The horses would sketch them to look like horses, / The oxen, like oxen, and their bodies make / in accordance with their own shape" (Clement of Alexandria, *Stromata*, V, 110). In other words, *le crapaud est beau pour sa crapaude*. Beauty is in the eye of the beholder.

But while beauty has never been absolute and immutable it has taken on different aspects depending on the historical period and the country: and this does not hold only for physical beauty (of men, of women, of the landscape) but also for the beauty of God, or the saints, or ideas.

It should suffice to quote this passage from Guido Guinizelli's sweet poetry (as I invite the Milanesiana audience to gaze on a Gothic statue from more or less the same period of the beautiful Uta of Naumburg):

I have seen the shining morning star,
So bright it might appear the day has dawned,

. . .

Snow white face with rosy blush,
Shining eyes, glad and full of love;
I do not believe in the whole Christian world there is
A woman so full of beauty and virtue.

Let's look now at a nineteenth-century image from Odilon Redon, *The Apparition*, and with it, I offer a passage from Jules Barbey d'Aurevilly's 1832 novel *Léa*:

"Yes, yes, my Léa, you are beautiful, you are the most beautiful of creatures. I would not give you up for the beauty of the angels in heaven." And her defeated eyes, her pallor, her diseased body, he pulled these images into his entwining sensual and agitated dreams of her.

Another problem involves not giving in to our contemporary taste. For some youngsters with earrings or maybe pierced noses, a Botticellian beauty may appear attractive because they are delightfully and perversely high on cannabis, but it certainly was not like that for Botticelli's contemporaries, who admired the face of Venus in the *Primavera* for other reasons.

Meanwhile, what is it that we are talking *about* when we speak of beauty? We in the contemporary world, or at least we Italians influenced by the idealist aesthetic, almost always identify beauty with artistic creations. But for centuries people talked of beauty above all with regard to the beauty of nature, objects, the human body, or God. Art was *recta ratio factibilium*, a way of doing things well, but *techne* or *ars* was applied both to the work of painters and shipbuilders, and even barbers (and, in fact, people began referring to the "fine arts" only much later).

Regarding the ideal of beauty of a given historical period, we have only three types of evidence today, and they all come to us from "cultivated" sources. An alien visitor landing on Earth today, or a thousand years from now, who wanted to discover what kind of beauty—of human bodies, clothes, or objects—was favored by the humble and unrefined of our day, could deduce this from films, illustrated magazines, and television programs. But imagine if that traveler coming from outer space to determine our prevailing idea of female beauty had only Picasso's portraits to go by. With respect to past centuries, we find ourselves in this kind of situation.

We also have written texts at our disposal. But, here too, how much do words tell us? When Proust, in *À La Recherche du Temps Perdu*, describes Elstir's painting, a careful reader might think of the Impressionists—but biographers tell us that, in a questionnaire Proust filled in at age thirteen, he named his favorite painter as the classicist Meissonier, and that he continued to admire him even when older. As he wrote about the nonexistent Elstir's concept of artistic beauty, the kind of beauty he was thinking about was perhaps different from the kind his words suggest to us.

This example also suggests a third type of evidence that we might call (if we wanted to bring some semiotics into our work—something which, on this occasion, I wish I could spare the great and the good), in a Peircean sense, the *interpretant sign*. Charles Sanders Peirce claimed that the meaning of a sign is always made clear by another sign that interprets it in some way. And thus we can compare some texts that talk of beauty with some contemporaneous images that were presumably intended to represent beautiful things. This comparison might clarify our ideas on the aesthetic ideals of a certain period.

Sometimes, however, comparison can be brutally disappointing. Let's take the description of an overwhelmingly seductive beauty, or at least so the narrator tells us: Cecily, a Creole in a novel serialized from 1842 to 1843, Eugène Sue's *The Mysteries of Paris*:

> The Creole uncovered her magnificent head of thick black hair which, parted in the center of her brow and naturally curly, did not fall below the point where her neck met her shoulders. . . .
>
> Cecily's features were the kind that remain engraved in the memory forever. A bold forehead . . . dominated the perfect

oval of her face; her matte white complexion had the velvety freshness of a camellia petal brushed by a ray of sunlight. Her . . . straight, narrow nose ended in two quivering nostrils that flared at the slightest emotion. Her mouth, insolent and sensual, was of a bright red . . .

How would we portray this splendid Cecily today, if we had to translate these words into images? Like a Brigitte Bardot, or a femme fatale of the Belle Époque? Well, the novel's original illustrator (and probably his readers, too) saw Cecily in a certain way. So we must resign ourselves and fantasize about *their* Cecily, at least if we are to understand—according to Sue and his readers—the particular ideal of beauty that caused the notary Ferrand to be consumed with satyriasis.

The comparison of written texts and images is often productive because it allows us to understand how the same linguistic term, in the passage from one century to another, and sometimes from one decade to another, can correspond to different musical or visual ideals. Let's take a classical example, that of proportion. Since antiquity, beauty has been identified with proportion. Pythagoras was the first to maintain that the principle of all things is number. With Pythagoras an aesthetical-mathematical vision of the universe came into being: all things exist because they are ordered and they are ordered because they are the realization of mathematical and musical laws, which are together the conditions of existence and beauty. This idea of proportion ran through all of antiquity and was transmitted to the Middle Ages through the works of Boethius between the fourth and fifth century AD. Boethius says that one day Pythagoras observed how, in striking the anvil, a blacksmith's hammers produced different sounds, and he realized that the ratio between the sounds of the range thus produced was proportional to the weight of the hammers. The ratios governing the dimensions of Greek temples, the intervals between the columns, or the ratios between the various parts of the façade correspond to the same ratios that govern musical intervals. In *Timaeus*, Plato was to describe the world as consisting of regular geometrical bodies.

Between Humanism and the Renaissance, the Platonic regular bodies were studied and celebrated as ideal models, by Leonardo, by Piero della Francesca in *De perspectiva pingendi* (before 1482), and by Luca Pacioli in *De divina proportione* (1509). The divine proportion that Pacioli discusses is the golden ratio, the relationship that exists, for example, between two rectangles, where the smaller is to the larger as the larger is to the sum of the two. This ratio is wonderfully exemplified in Piero della Francesca's painting *The Flagellation of Christ*.

But, in the ten centuries that separate Boethius from Pacioli, did those who used the term "proportion" all mean the same thing? Not at all. In commentaries produced by early medieval scholars on Boethius, images were deemed to be perfectly proportioned and put on manuscript pages even though they did not adhere to the golden ratio in the slightest.

In the thirteenth century, Villard d'Honnecourt, who certainly knew how to draw very well, supplied highly intuitive and quantitative rules for proportion—nothing to do with the more mathematically rigorous rules that had previously inspired the sculpture of Polyclitus and would later inspire Dürer.

On the other hand, when in the thirteenth century Thomas Aquinas spoke of proportion as one of the three criteria of beauty, he was no longer speaking only in terms of mathematical ratios. He believed that proportion was not just a correct arrangement of matter, but a perfect adaptation of matter to form, in the sense that a human body that was well adapted to the conditions of humanity should be considered proportionate. This made proportion also an element of virtue, in the sense that spiritual beauty consists of a person's conduct or actions being well-proportioned with respect to what reason dictates, and so we must also allow that there is such a thing as moral beauty (or moral turpitude). Because, to be beautiful, a thing must be suited to its intended purpose, Aquinas would not have hesitated to define a glass saw as ugly. Despite the superficial beauty of the material of which it was made, it would be unable to perform its proper function. Proportion also applied to the collaborative interaction of things, so it is possible to call "beautiful" the reciprocal action of stones that, by propping and pushing against each other, solidly hold up a building. It also results from having the correct relationship between the intelligence and the thing the intelligence understands. In short, proportion becomes a metaphysical principle that explains the very unity of the cosmos.

Much of the art of Aquinas's day therefore tells us only part of what he meant by proportion, because our interpretative effort is made more difficult by what we might call disparities of development between art and philosophy, or among various aspects of art from the same period. Regarding those Renaissance treatises offering mathematical rules for proportion, for example, theory and reality seem to come together only for architecture and perspective. Looking at a series of men and women held to be beautiful by different artists, are there any criteria of proportion common across them?

The same problems come into play for light, or *claritas*, another traditional attribute of beauty. Considering the origins of this, *claritas* was certainly valued due to the fact that numerous civilizations have associated God with light, and often with the sun.

Through Neoplatonism these images entered the Christian tradition via the sixth-century works of Pseudo-Dionysius the Areopagite. In his *Celestial Hierarchy* and *Divine Names*, he represents God as "light," "fire," and a "fountain of light." The same images are employed by the greatest exponent of medieval Neoplatonism, John Scotus Eriugena.

But here, too, what did medieval man mean by the beauty of light and of color? One thing we know for certain. Even though we always talk of the Dark Ages, and while the rooms and corridors of castles and monasteries and the peasants' huts must have been dark, medieval people saw themselves (or at least represented themselves in poems and paintings) as living in an extremely bright environment.

The Middle Ages play on elementary colors, on well-defined chromatic zones that shun nuance, and on the juxtaposition of colors that generate light from their overall agreement, instead of being determined by a light that envelops them in chiaroscuro or causes color to seep beyond the edge of a figure. If we look at a baroque painting, such as Georges de La Tour's *Magdalene with the Smoking Flame*, everything in the scene is struck by the light of a candle on the right, and in a stack of books can be seen both light and dark areas. In medieval miniatures, by contrast, light seems to radiate out from objects in the scene. They, being beautiful, are luminous in themselves.

The Middle Ages were in love with light and it was in that period that the figurative technique was developed that best exploited the vivacity of simple color combined with the vivacity of the light that filled it: the stained-glass windows of Gothic cathedrals. The Gothic church is built as a function of a burst of light through a tracery of structures.

Dazzling images of light appear in the mystical writings of Hildegard of Bingen, and are wonderfully interpreted in the miniatures that accompany them:

> Then I saw an extremely bright light and in the light the figure of a man the color of sapphire, and it was all burning in a delightful red fire. And the bright light flooded through all the red fire, and the red fire through all the bright light, and the bright light and the red fire shone together through the whole figure of the man so that they were one light in one strength and power.

And then there are the visions of light that blaze in Dante's *Paradiso*, which, oddly, were rendered in their greatest splendor by a nineteenth-century artist, Gustav Doré. Yet, looking at Doré's illustrations, it seems to me that the Dante he interprets must have written one or two centuries before Dante did, or else that Doré was thinking of Neoplatonic texts that had inspired him—because the miniatures of Dante's era are far more restrained. They do not show us explosions of light, arrays of theatre spotlights; rather, their bright colors seem to belong to the bodies themselves.

The fact is that Dante followed a theological tradition that celebrated light as a mystical, cosmological phenomenon, but he was writing after Thomas Aquinas and, between the twelfth and the thirteenth century, there had been profound changes in the way *claritas* was understood. Consider the twelfth-century cosmology of light proposed by Robert Grosseteste, who conceived of the universe as formed by a single flux of luminous energy that was at once the source of beauty and being—an image that, for us, summons the notion of a Big Bang. Through a progressive process of rarefaction and condensation, the heavenly bodies and the natural zone of the elements, and consequently the infinite nuances of color and the volume of things, all derive from this single light. The proportion of the world, therefore, is none other than the mathematical order in which light, in its creative diffusion, materializes according to the various forms of resistance imposed upon it by matter.

Now let us move on to a different vision of heavenly glory—namely, Giotto's. In Giotto's *Last Judgment*, the light is no longer received, so to speak, from on high. The light is proper to the bodies, which are physically well built—healthy, I would say. It so happened that, in the meantime, Thomas Aquinas had spoken. For him, *claritas* did not come from a cosmic explosion from above, as Grosseteste would have it, but from below, or from the interior of the object—a sort of self-manifestation of the form that organizes it. Aquinas's master, Albertus Magnus, had previously said that beauty was " a resplendence of form, whether in the duly-ordered parts of material objects or in men," and the form he was referring to was not a Platonic ideal, but whatever it was on the inside which ordered the matter to take its certain concrete shape in the proper proportions. Thus we have moved from giving beauty a Neoplatonic foundation to giving it an Aristotelian one. The *claritas* of the bodies of the blessed consists in the luminosity of the glorified soul that shines through their corporeal aspect—and this is why in Giotto's work we see light that emanates from the human core of the characters, represented through a corporeality that is far more solid and less abstract.

So, across centuries, there has always been talk of light and *claritas*, but the vision of the world and of beauty to which these terms referred was not the same from era to era.

The play of contrasts between texts and images also allows us to respond to some fairly complex questions. Let's tackle the vexed question of an aesthetic of ugliness, or—to remain in a single historical period—of the beauty of monsters in the Middle Ages.

Apart from proportion and luminosity, the third characteristic of beauty for medieval man was integrity: to be considered beautiful, a being had to possess everything befitting an individual of his species. So a mutilated body was not beautiful and neither was a dwarf. (There was no political correctness in the Middle Ages.) Yet medieval man was fascinated by monsters.

In the first instance people admitted the principle whereby, although ugly things and beings exist, art has the power to portray them in a beautiful way. We think this is a modern criterion, but Saint Bonaventure said that "the image of the Devil is beautiful when it portrays the Devil's turpitude well."

Contacts with distant lands had increased since Hellenic times and this led to the spread of descriptions, sometimes overtly legendary and sometimes with pretensions to scientific accuracy, of unknown lands and beings, from the *Natural History* of Pliny the Elder (c 77 CE) to the *Romance of Alexander* (third century CE) down to the bestiaries (starting with the renowned *Physiologus*, written between the second and fifth century CE). And the exotic always took the form of the monstrous. Medieval people were fascinated by descriptions of the Blemmyae, headless beings with mouths in their bellies, Sciapods with only one foot that they also used to shield themselves from the sun, dog-headed Cynocephali, unicorns, and all kinds of dragons. Such monsters not only adorned the capitals in churches, but filled the margins of manuscripts, even the devotional sort, which dealt with entirely different topics. In some portrayals of Noah's Ark, there were even monsters saved from the flood.

The Middle Ages needed monsters. At least we can say the followers of "negative theology" did. They considered it impossible to represent God with suitable names, given his absolute and unknowable transcendence, and therefore used only terms that would obviously not even pretend to describe perfect goodness, such as bear, worm, panther, even monster. So the mystical and theological thought of the time had to justify in some way the presence of these monsters in creation, and it took two paths. From one side, it inserted them into the great tradition of universal symbolism, in which every worldly thing, animal, vegetable, and mineral, had a significance that was moral (teaching something about virtues and vices) or allegorical, meaning that through its form or its behavior it symbolized the reality of the supernatural. In the "moralized" bestiaries, for example, unicorns prized chastity. This is why, it was said, a hunter would have to set a virgin in the forest as bait: the animal would be attracted by the girl's scent and go to lay its head in her lap, enabling it to be captured. Thus offering itself as prey to men, the unicorn symbolizes the Savior, who dwelt in the womb of an immaculate virgin.

As the second path, from Augustine onwards, mystics, theologians, and philosophers also said that monsters were somehow part of the natural order ordained by heaven and, in the great symphonic concert of cosmic harmony, they contributed—albeit purely by contrast (like shading and chiaroscuro in paintings)—to the beauty of the whole. Because the orderly whole was beautiful, according to this point of view, whatever monstrosity contributed to the equilibrium of that order was redeemed.

But did the faithful who entered the abbey or cathedral and gazed upon these representations from the ridiculous to the teratological to the disturbing really think about the cosmic order? For ordinary people, were these monsters (independent of any theological reflections) pleasing to look at, or disgusting and fearful? Or did they give rise to ambiguous feelings of disorientation?

The answer comes to us indirectly from Saint Bernard. A mystic and also a rigorist if ever there was one (being an enemy of his Cluniac rivals' love of sumptuous ornamentation in churches), Bernard inveighed against the excessive numbers of monsters appearing on abbey capitals and in cloisters. But while his words are of condemnation, his description of this evil also betrays his fascination—as if not even he could resist the seductiveness of those *portenta*. He describes what he denounces with an almost sensual appeal, with the hypocrisy of a moralist who, in complaining about a striptease, gives a detailed description of the dancer's moves:

> What place is there in the cloisters . . . for that ridiculous monstrosity, that strange kind of deformed shapeliness or shapely deformity? What are foul apes doing there? Or ferocious lions? Or monstrous centaurs? Or half-men? Or striped tigers? Or soldiers in battle? Or hunters with their horns? You can see many bodies beneath a single head and many heads atop a single body. On the one side you can see a four-footed beast with a serpent's tail, and on the other a fish with a quadruped's head. Here, a beast that looks like a horse with the hindquarters of a goat, and there, a horned animal with the hindquarters of a horse. In short, there is everywhere such a great and strange variety of heterogeneous forms that there is more pleasure to be had in reading the marbles than the codices, and more in spending the whole day gazing at these images than in meditating on God's law.

And so Bernard, talking in annoyance about a wondrous but perverse delight (*mira sed perversa delectatio*), confesses to us that these monstrous portrayals were pleasing to look at, at least as much as portrayals of likeable aliens in science-fiction films are to

us, and perhaps even as much as we are satisfied by representations of horror in all its hair-raising magnificence. The late Middle
Ages and Renaissance centuries showed a real taste for what has
been defined in art as the *demoniacal.*

The fact is that, deep down, even in classical or classically
inspired periods, people were not totally convinced that the criteria of beauty came down to just proportion and light. But the
only ones brave enough to admit this were theorists and pre- and
proto-Romantic artists, the celebrators of beauty's sibling: the sublime. The idea of the sublime is associated above all with an experience bound up not with art but with nature, and this experience
tended toward the formless, the painful, and the terrible. Consider
Lord Shaftesbury's vivid words in his *Moral Essays* of the early
eighteenth century: "Even the rude rocks, the mossy caverns, the
irregular unwrought grottos and broken falls of waters, with all
the horrid graces of the wilderness itself, as representing nature
more, will be the more engaging and appear with a magnificence
beyond the mockery of princely gardens."

A taste arose for Gothic architecture that, in comparison with
Neoclassical measures, can only seem disproportionate and irregular, and it was precisely this taste for the irregular and the formless that led to a new appreciation of ruins.

With an authentic *coup de théâtre*, Edmund Burke (in his
1757 *Philosophical Enquiry into the Origin of Our Ideas on the
Sublime and Beautiful*) challenged the idea that beauty resides in
proportion:

The neck, say they, in beautiful bodies, should measure with
the calf of the leg; it should likewise be twice the circumference of the wrist. And an infinity of observations of this kind
are to be found in the writings and conversations of many.

But what relation has the calf of the leg to the neck; or either of these parts to the wrist? These proportions are certainly to be found in handsome bodies. They are as certainly in ugly ones; as any who will take the pains to try may find. . . . You may assign any proportions you please to every part of the human body; and I undertake that a painter shall religiously observe them all, and notwithstanding produce, if he pleases, a very ugly figure. The same painter shall considerably deviate from these proportions, and produce a very beautiful one.

Happily disproportionate, the sublime prospers in the shadows, in night, in storm, in darkness, in emptiness, in solitude, and in silence.

If we really wish to continue reflecting on the relativity of the concept of beauty, we must not forget that the same century that witnessed the birth of the modern notion of the sublime also witnessed the celebration of the Neoclassical style. But in the Middle Ages, too, the taste for monsters on capitals coexisted with the taste for the architectonic proportions realized in the naves of churches, and Hieronymus Bosch (1450–1516) was a contemporary of Antonello da Messina (1430–1479). Nonetheless, if we look back at the preceding centuries, at bottom there is always the feeling, on looking "from afar," that every century had unitary characteristics, or at most one single fundamental contradiction.

It may be that, if future interpreters (or the usual Martian who comes to visit us after two hundred years) also look back "from afar," they might identify something as truly characteristic of the twentieth century, and hence prove Marinetti right by finding that the century's equivalent of the *Victory of Samothrace* really *was* a beautiful racing car, and never even considering Picasso and Mondrian. We cannot look at things from that far away, but we can content ourselves with noting that the first half of the twentieth century was the stage for a dramatic struggle between the beauty of provocation or the arts of the avant-garde and the beauty of consumption.

The avant-garde did not pose itself the problem of beauty, and it violated all the aesthetic canons respected until then. With its arrival, art no longer set out to provide an image of natural beauty, nor did it intend to procure the pleasure to be had from contemplating harmonious forms. On the contrary, its goal was to teach us to interpret the world through different eyes, to enjoy the return to archaic or exotic models and the worlds of dream and hallucination, to rediscover matter and accept the slightly mad notion of taking everyday objects and presenting them in improbable contexts. Abstract art, which seemed to represent a "Neo-Pythagorean" return to the aesthetics of proportions and number, ran counter to the common man's idea of beauty. Finally, there are many trends in contemporary performance art (events, for example, where artists cut or mutilate their own bodies, or audiences participate in light or sound phenomena) in which it seems that, in the name of art, people hold ceremonies with a ritual flavor not unlike the ancient mystery rites. There is an element of mystery in the musical events enjoyed by huge crowds in discos or at rock concerts where, amid strobe lights and deafeningly loud music, people experiment with ways of "being together" that are "beautiful" (in the traditional sense of circus games) to those looking on from the outside, in ways that are not perceived or experienced by those involved in the event.

Our visitor from the future, moreover, will be unable to avoid making another curious discovery. Those who visit an exhibition of avant-garde art, buy an "incomprehensible" sculpture, or take part in a happening are dressed according to the canons of fashion. They wear jeans or designer clothes and make themselves up in accordance with a model of beauty proposed by mass media. They follow ideals of beauty proposed by the world of commercial consumerism—the very world that avant-garde art has been battling against for fifty years and more.

At this point, the visitor from the future would naturally seek next to understand what the model of beauty proposed by the mass media was. And he would discover that, within the same era, the media proposed the model of the femme fatale as personified by Greta Garbo or Rita Hayworth, and that of the "girl next door" as played by Doris Day. The same media gave us the virile appeal of big John Wayne as well as the meek and vaguely effeminate Fred Astaire and Dustin Hoffman. The visitor would discover that the mass media were totally democratic; women who could not be Anita Eckberg could flaunt the anorexic grace of Twiggy.

Which of all these, and other possible candidates, would our visitor from the future recognize as the ideal of beauty typical of our day?

He would have to yield before the orgy of tolerance, of total syncretism, and the absolute, unstoppable polytheism of beauty.

But now I would like to halt this relativistic drift that has permitted us to reflect upon the variability and occasional incomparability of the vastly different notions of beauty. Is there really *nothing* that in some way, even a very subtle one, is common to the various experiences of beauty, or whatever was thought to be beautiful at any given historical moment?

I think that if we were to put together an anthology of the various texts that deal with beauty, we would get at least one common element. "Beautiful"—or for that matter, "graceful," or "sublime," or "marvelous"—appears as an adjective always used to indicate something that we like (recall that Aquinas said that *pulchra dicuntur quae visa placent*, we call those things beautiful that have been seen and which please us) and that we might desire, but that will not cease to be pleasing even if we know it cannot be ours. Naturally, in everyday language, we also use *beautiful* or *marvelous* to define what we consider good, and so we might speak of a beautiful erotic experience or run through the woods. But across centuries, a formal distinction has been made between what is beautiful and what is *good to have*. If what is considered to be good (a food, a fine house, the recognition and admiration of my fellows) is not mine, I feel as though impoverished. Instead, with regard to beauty, it seems that the joy in beautiful things is definitely separate from the possession of them. I find the Sistine Chapel beautiful even though I am not the owner, and in the window of a patisserie I find beauty in a cream-filled wedding cake, even though my dietician forbids me to eat it.

The experience of beauty always has an element of disinterest. I can consider a human being (man or woman) to be beautiful, even though I know I can never have a relationship with him or her. But if I desire a human being (who might even be ugly) and I cannot have a relationship with him or her, I feel bad.

Naturally, all this holds for the western tradition. We see beauty in the bison of Altamira, but we do not know why they were carved and painted (probably as propitiatory magic), whether people went to look at them or instead left them respectfully in the darkness of the cave, or whether those who had made them were pleased afterwards at having drawn them so well. It is the same thing with many objects we see as the works of art of primitive societies. We do not have sufficient documents to compare an object to a text, which usually does not exist or which we cannot understand, or to know whether the ritual mask that fascinated painters and sculptors of the European avant-garde was first fashioned to inspire fear or give pleasure, like the monsters in medieval miniatures. All we know is that Saint Bernard had no fear of monsters, that he found them fascinating, and that he condemned them. As for the rest, even without venturing into societies with no history or no writing, to this day specialists debate whether the Indian term *rasa* can be translated with our term and concept of *taste*, or whether it refers (instead or also) to something else that eludes us.

In an ethnographic museum in Bamako, Mali, I saw some very well made female dressmaker's models, in the western style, which were draped in wonderful traditional costumes. One of the dummies looked agile and sinuous, while another was incredibly fat. Our Malian guide, a professor at the local university who had studied in France, winked at us and said that the thin dummy was put there for western tourists. For the locals (or at least for their fathers immune to the lures of the West) the beautiful woman was the fat one. Our guide could negotiate two concepts of beauty with critical awareness, but I still wonder if, after studying in Paris and having seen our films and television, he might have thought that the fat woman was beautiful and the thin one sexually desirable, or vice versa.

However, surely he would have been able to say what he wished to possess and what he was prepared to admire disinterestedly.

I would like to conclude by pointing out that perhaps the greatest statements of aesthetic detachment were made in a period when, along with the experience of the sublime, we seemed to celebrate proximity to natural phenomena of great enormity and majesty. Even the terrifying can be enjoyable provided it does not get too close to us. Sublime beauty is reserved for those things that *placent* (please us) but only if *visa* (they are seen)—and seen without being suffered. The painter who was certainly the greatest exponent of the experience of the sublime was Caspar David Friedrich, and when representing it he almost always placed human beings in the foreground, gazing upon a natural spectacle they were struck by as by the sublime.

The human figures are seen from behind and, by a sort of theatrical mise-en-scène, if the sublime is the stage, then they are on the proscenium, inside the show—for us in the audience—but also representing someone who is outside the show, so that we are obliged to detach ourselves from the spectacle by looking at it through them, putting ourselves in their place, seeing what they see, and—as they do—feeling like a negligible element in the great spectacle of nature, but still one who is able to flee the natural power looming large over us and capable of destroying us.

I believe that, across centuries, the experience of beauty has always been similar to the way we feel, as if seen from the back, when we are in the presence of something we are not a part of and do not wish to become a part of at any cost. In that distance lies the slender thread that separates the experience of beauty from other forms of passion.

[La Milanesiana, 2005]

3. Ugliness

Whereas in almost every century philosophers and artists have written down their ideas on beauty, important texts on the concept of ugliness amount to only a handful, one being Karl Rosenkrantz's 1853 *Aesthetic of Ugliness*. Ugliness, however, has always been present as the foil to beauty—Beauty and the Beast has taken many forms. This is to say, once you set a criterion for beauty, a corresponding criterion for ugliness always seems to present itself pretty much automatically: "Only beauty orders symmetry," Iamblichus tells us in *Life of Pythagoras*, and "conversely, ugliness disorders symmetry." Thomas Aquinas teaches that three qualities are required for beauty—first among them wholeness or perfection—so that incomplete things, precisely because they are incomplete, "are ugly." William of Auvergne adds: "We would call a man with three eyes or one eye ugly."

Like beauty, therefore, ugliness is a relative concept.

Ugliness was defined very well by Marx in his *Economic and Philosophic Manuscripts* of 1844 as something that was only meaningful in the absence of money or, as we might understand his words, of power. Marx wrote:

> I *am* ugly, but I can buy for myself the *most beautiful* of women. Therefore I am not ugly, for the effect of *ugliness*—its deterrent power—is nullified by money. I, according to my individual characteristics, am *lame*, but money furnishes me with twenty-four feet. Therefore I am not lame. I am bad, dishonest, unscrupulous, stupid; but money is honored, and hence its possessor.... I am *brainless,* but money is the *real brain* of all things and how then should its possessor be brainless? Besides, he can buy clever people for himself, and is he who has power over the clever not more clever than the clever?

As for this last point, it is not always true—many people with money have bought only stupid people—but that's another story. So, over the centuries, there have been many texts on the relativity of ugliness, and of beauty. In the thirteenth century, Jacques de Vitry wrote: "Probably the cyclopes, who have only one eye, marvel at those who have two, as we . . . judge the black Ethiopians ugly, but among them the blackest is considered the most beautiful." A few centuries later, Voltaire wrote: "Ask a toad what beauty is . . . he will reply that it is his toad wife, with her big round eyes protruding from her little head, her broad, flat throat, her brown back. . . . Question the devil: he'll tell you that beauty is a pair of horns, four claws, and a tail." When Darwin wrote that feelings of contempt and repulsion were expressed in identical ways in most parts of the world—"Extreme disgust is expressed by movements round the mouth identical with those preparatory to the act of vomiting"—he added that, in Tierra del Fuego, a native reached out to feel the "cold preserved meat which I was eating at our bivouac, and plainly showed utter disgust at its softness; whilst I felt utter disgust at my food being touched by a naked savage, though his hands did not appear dirty."

Are there universal ways in which people react to beauty? No, because beauty is detachment, absence of passion. Ugliness, by contrast, is passion. Let's try to understand this point, in light of others' earlier observations that there cannot be an aesthetic judgment of ugliness. In other words, an aesthetic judgment implies detachment. I can consider a thing to be beautiful even without feeling I must possess it. I silence my passions. It seems, however, that ugliness does imply a passion—namely, disgust or repulsion. So how can there be an aesthetic judgment of ugliness if there is no possibility of detachment?

Probably there is ugliness in art and ugliness in life. There is a judgment of ugliness as a non-correspondence to the ideal of beauty, for example, when we say that a painting of a vase of flowers is ugly. Who painted it? Hitler. We are talking about a work by the young Hitler. While instead there is a passionate reaction to what we consider to be unpleasant, repellent, horrible, disgusting, grotesque, horrendous, revolting, repugnant, frightening, abject, monstrous, horrid, hair-raising, foul, terrible, terrifying, nightmarish, ungainly, deformed, disfigured, simian, bestial . . . (in the thesaurus there are more synonyms for ugly than for beautiful).

Contrary to Plato, who said that the representation of ugliness should be avoided, from Aristotle onwards it has been admitted in all periods that even the ugliness in life can be beautifully portrayed, and that it actually serves to make beauty stand out or to support a certain moral theory. And, as Saint Bonaventure said, "*imago diabolo est pulchra, si bene repraesentat foeditatem diaboli*"—the image of the devil is beautiful if it is a good representation of ugliness.

And so, art has given of its best in representing the ugliness of the devil. But the competition to portray ugliness well makes us suspect that, in reality, some have, however covertly, taken true pleasure in the horrendous, and not only in the various visions of hell. You cannot tell me that some hells were conceived only to terrify the faithful: they were also conceived to give us a hell of a kick. If we consider the various *Triumphs of Death*, with the beauty of the skeleton, or Mel Gibson's film *The Passion of Christ*, we can see the horrifying as a source of pleasure. Friedrich Schiller wrote in his 1792 essay "On the Tragic Art":

> It is a phenomenon common to all men, that sad, frightful things, even the horrible, exercise over us an irresistible seduction, and that in the presence of a scene of desolation and of terror we feel at once repelled and attracted by two equal forces. . . . Any ghost story, however embellished by romantic circumstances, is greedily devoured by us, and the more readily in proportion as the story is calculated to make our hair stand on end. . . . See what a crowd accompanies a criminal to the scene of his punishment!

Consider all the countless descriptions of executions—for which there was no real call other than the enjoyment of describing an execution, because otherwise it would have sufficed to say "the guilty man was put to death." See the *Annals* of Niketas Choniates for this description of the torments inflicted upon Andronikos, who was deposed as basileus of Byzantium at the beginning of the thirteenth century:

> Bound in this fashion he was paraded before Emperor Isaakios. He was slapped in the face, kicked on the buttocks, his

beard was torn out, his teeth pulled out, his head shorn of hair; he was made the common sport of all those who gathered; he was even battered by women who struck him in the mouth with theirs fists, especially by all those whose husbands were put to death or blinded by Andronikos. Afterwards, his right hand cut off by an ax, he was cast again in the same prison without food and drink, tended by no one.

Several days later, one of his eyes was gouged out, and, seated upon a mangy camel, he was paraded through the agora . . . . Some struck him on the head with clubs, others befouled his nostrils with cow-dung, and still others, using sponges, poured excretions from the bellies of oxen and men over his eyes. . . . There were those who pierced his ribs with spits.

But not even after having hung him up by his feet did the idiotic mob leave the martyred Andronikos or spare his flesh. Having torn off his shirt, they butchered his genital organs. One villain sank a long sword into his guts through his mouth, others used both hands to hold their swords aloft, and bring them down at his backside, competing over who could make the deepest cut and boasting over the best-dealt blows.

Some centuries later, in the early 1950s, Mickey Spillane, the poet of McCarthyism and master of the hard-boiled novel, tells us how private eye Mike Hammer kills communist spies in *One Lonely Night*:

They heard my scream and the awful roar of the gun and the slugs tearing into bone and guts and it was the last they heard. They went down as they tried to run and felt their insides tear out and spray against the walls.

I saw the general's head splinter into shiny wet fragments and splatter over the floor. The guy from the subway tried to stop the bullets with his hands and dissolved into a nightmare of blue holes.

There was only the guy in the pork-pie hat who made a crazy try for a gun in his pocket. I aimed the tommy gun for the first time and took his arm off at the shoulder. It dropped on the floor next to him and I let him have a good look at it. He couldn't believe it happened. I proved it by shooting him in the belly. They were all so damned clever!

They were all so damned dead!

But let's take a step back. The Greeks, by identifying beauty with goodness—*kalòs kai agathòs*—identified physical ugliness with moral ugliness. In the *Iliad*, Thersites, "the ugliest man who had come to Ilium, twisted, lame in one foot, his shoulders curved over his chest, his pointed head covered with wispy hair," was bad. So were the sirens, who were disgusting, birdlike creatures and nothing like the sirens portrayed later by the European Decadents, who cast them as beautiful women. The harpies, who were equally ugly, were bad—and they continued to be so in Dante's forest of the suicides. The Minotaur was hideous, too, as were the Medusa, the Gorgon, and the cyclops Polyphemus.

But, after Plato's time, Greek culture found itself faced with a problem: how was it that Socrates, who had such a great soul, was so ugly? And why was Aesop an eyesore? According to *The Aesop Romance* of the Hellenic period, the fabulist was "a slave . . . of loathsome aspect, worthless as a servant, potbellied, misshapen of head, snub-nosed, swarthy, dwarfish, bandy-legged, short-armed, squint-eyed, liver-lipped—a portentous monstrosity." What's more, "he was dumb and could not talk." A good thing he could write well.

For Christianity, apparently, everything is beautiful; in fact, Christian cosmology and theology expatiates on the beauty of the universe, so that even monsters and ugliness fall within the cosmic order, acting like chiaroscuro in a painting to make the light stand out. Countless pages have been written about this, by Saint Augustine above all. But it was Hegel who pointed out that it was only with Christianity that ugliness came into the history of art, because "Christ scourged, with the crown of thorns, carrying his cross to the place of execution, nailed to the cross, passing away in the agony of a torturing and slow death—this cannot be portrayed in the forms of Greek beauty." Christ can only appear ugly because he is suffering. And likewise, according to Hegel, "the enemies are presented to us as inwardly evil because they place themselves in opposition to God, condemn him, mock him, torture him, crucify him, and the idea of inner evil and enmity to God brings with it on the external side, ugliness, crudity, barbarity, rage, and distortion of their outward appearance." Nietzsche, extreme as usual, offered his own view: "The Christian resolution to find the world ugly and bad has made the world ugly and bad."

Above all, in this ugly world, the penitential humility of the body takes on a particular value. In case you thought this was limited to medieval penances, here is a seventeenth-century text in which Father Segneri reports on the penances and painful self-inflicted torments of Saint Ignatius of Loyola:

> wearing a garment of sackcloth over a rough hair-shirt, binding around his loins a girdle composed of prickly nettles, sharp thorns, or points of iron; fasting on bread and water every

day, except Sundays, and then allowing himself no other indulgence than a dish of bitter herbs mingled with earth or ashes; passing sometimes whole days, three, six, or even eight at a time, without partaking of any food at all; scourging himself five times a day, and always to blood; cruelly beating his bare breast with a heavy stone . . . . Seven hours daily he spent in profound contemplation; his tears were unceasing, his mortifications continuous.

This was the unbroken tenor of the life he led in the cave of Manresa, which he did not moderate despite the tedious and painful infirmities that soon resulted—the "languors, swoons, paroxysms of pain, attacks of devility, and even dangerous fevers" that would eventually prove fatal.

Of course, the Middle Ages abounded with monsters, but it is our sensibility that leads us to see medieval monsters, as I noted regarding beauty, as ugly. They are strange, made with only one foot and with a mouth on their chest, well outside the norm. They are *portenta*, but were created that way by God to be the vehicle of supernatural meanings. Every monster comes with its own spiritual meaning. In this sense, medieval people did not see them as ugly—if anything, they saw them as interesting, fabled creatures. They saw them the way our children now see dinosaurs, which they know by heart so well that they can tell the difference between a tyrannosaurus and a stegosaurus with ease. They saw them as traveling companions. Even the dragons of the Middle Ages were viewed with this fond curiosity, because they were faithful emblems. They had a place on Noah's ark, albeit with a deck to themselves—but still, together with animals who were not monstrous, all saved by Noah himself.

Scientific interest in real teratology made headway between the sixteenth and seventeenth century, when people began to get interested in curious or monstrous births and freaks of nature; collectors sought their skeletons or evidence inscribed on them, and even their bodies preserved in alcohol.

It was in this climate that physiognomy had caught on. This was a field of study in which, through analogies between the human and the animal face, the outcome being almost always ugliness (except for a few cases such as the lion man and a few others), people tried to understand the character of an individual through analogies with the animal world. But within a few centuries, from physiognomy we come to Cesare Lombroso, the anthropologist behind *L'Uomo Delinquente* (The Criminal Man), in which we find the following passage:

Who can know to what point scrofula, arrested development, and rickets may have influenced the cause or the modification of criminal tendencies? We have found 11 hunchbacks out of 832 criminals, almost all thieves or rapists. Virgilio found 3 rickets sufferers and 1 with arrested development of the skeleton out of 266 convicts examined by him, and 6 stutterers, 1 with a hare lip, 5 with strabismus, 45 with scrofula, and 24 with caries. According to him, 143 out of 266 of them carried traces of degenerative physical conditions. Vidocq observed that all the great murderers he had chanced to deal with were bowlegged. . . . In all criminals, especially thieves and murderers, the development of the genitals is extremely precocious and especially in female thieves, in whom we found a tendency to prostitution as early as six to eight years.

But long before Lombroso, the physiognomy of the enemy—be he mystical or political or religious—was developed over the centuries. In some Protestant cartoons, for example, the Pope was portrayed as the Antichrist. And in various texts of the early centuries—I will quote the *Testamentum Domini*, an apocryphal "Testimony of Our Lord" of the fourth to fifth century—the Antichrist has striking features: "his head as a fiery flame, his right eye shot with blood, his left blue-black, and he hath two pupils. His eyelashes are white and his lower lip is large; but his right thigh slender, his feet broad, his great toe is bruised and flat. This is the sickle of desolation." For Hildegard of Bingen (in the twelfth century) the son of perdition had "a black and monstrous head. It had fiery eyes, and ears like an ass's, and nostrils and mouth like a lion's; it opened wide its jowls and terribly clashed its horrible iron-colored teeth." Racial enemies were also ugly, like the Saracens in Sicilian puppet theatre, and the poor were ugly, too. And out of them all, even though the sculptures have provided nothing truly satisfying, I can offer you the portrait of Franti, from the 1886 children's novel *Cuore* (Heart) by Edmondo De Amicis: "I detest that fellow. He is wicked. . . . There is something beneath that low forehead, in those turbid eyes, which he keeps nearly concealed under the visor of his small cap of waxed cloth . . . his paper, books, and copy-books are all crushed, torn, dirty, his ruler is jagged, his pens gnawed, his nails bitten, his clothes covered with stains and rents which he has got in his brawls."

Finally there is the racial enemy. Think of the black Americans as portrayed by fascist propaganda during World War II. Here is the description of the negro from the *Encyclopedia Britannica* of 1798:

Round cheeks, high cheekbones, a forehead somewhat elevated, a short, broad, flat nose, thick lips, small ears, ugliness, and irregularity of shape characterize their external appearance. . . . Vices the most notorious seem to be the portion of this unhappy race: idleness, treachery, revenge, cruelty, impudence, stealing, lying, profanity, debauchery, nastiness and intemperance are said to have extinguished the principles of natural law, and to have reproofs of conscience.

And, naturally, in a later, presumably more mature society, here is the Jew:

Those spying, mendaciously pale eyes . . . that edgy smile . . . those chops so reminiscent: of a hyena . . . And then all of a sudden there's that heavy, leaden, moronic look . . . the negro blood flowing within. The corners of the nose and mouth forever twitching anxiously, twisted, furrowed, defensive, and then erupting in hatred and disgust. For you! For you, the abject, accursed animal of the enemy race, to be destroyed. Their noses, the "toucan's beak" of the swindler, of the traitorous, of the treacherous . . . for all the sleazy schemes, all the betrayals, the nose that hangs down over the mouth, their hideous slots, that rotten banana, their croissant, the foul smirk of the kike, the curving snout that sucks: the Vampire. . . .

Cursed damned souls! Drop dead then, you inconceivable animal!

Whose description is this? Hitler's? No, this is the novelist Louis-Ferdinand Céline in his 1937 pamphlet *Bagatelles pour un massacre*. Then comes another text, which advises that Jews cannot be either actors or musicians:

We can conceive no representation of an antique or modern stage-character by a Jew, be it as hero or lover, without feeling instinctively the incongruity of such a notion. . . .

By far more weighty, nay, of quite decisive weight for our inquiry, is the effect the Jew produces on us through his *speech*. . . .

The first thing that strikes our ear as quite outlandish and un-pleasant, in the Jew's production of the voice-sounds, is a creaking, squeaking, buzzing snuffle. . . . How exceptionally weighty is this circumstance, particularly for explaining the impression made on us by the music-works of modern Jews. . . .

. . . and on any natural hypothesis, we might hold the Jew adapted for every sphere of art, excepting that whose basis lies in Song.

Who's this? Céline again? No, it's Richard Wagner in his *Judaism in Music* (1850). On the other hand, ugliness is deep rooted, it is in the blood. Consider this:

Our racism must be that of flesh and muscle . . . otherwise we'll end up playing the game of the half-breeds and the Jews, of the Jews who, as they have been able to do in too many cases, change their name and merge with us, so they can— even more easily and without even the need for costly and laborious procedures—feign a change of heart. . . . There is only one proof with which it is possible to halt interbreeding and Judaism: the proof of blood.

Who's this? Still Wagner? No, it's Giorgio Almirante [founder and leader of Italy's major postwar neofascist party], speaking out against the little lost sheep of ideological pseudo-racism.

At a certain point in the course of history—leaving aside ugliness in the comic and the obscene, which runs through all periods, the rustic epics and so on—mannerism marks a move toward a greater attention to more interesting things, and texts begin to appear that reveal understanding and sympathy for ugliness. Just think of Caliban in Shakespeare's *The Tempest*. Then, too, there is praise for fine silver hair in the poetry of Joachim du Bellay, praise for flaccid breasts in Marot, praise for lame women in Montaigne, and the exploration of old age in Leonardesque caricature, which at a certain point almost makes us think of Michelangelo, who describes himself as an old man, saying: "spent, faded eyes, teeth like the keys of an instrument. . . . My face is a fright."

Alongside understanding through compassion, we find an engrossment in the decomposition of once beautiful bodies, which has nothing to do with the educational benefit that medieval representations of hell and its torments intended to provide. This is corruption for corruption's sake, without moral teachings. The German lyric poet, Andreas Gryphius, wrote in the seventeenth century "On the Skeleton of Filosette Exhumed":

Horrid sight! Where is the golden hair,
The snowy brow, the splendor of the cheeks,
Her cheeks suffused with blood and lilies?
Her pinkish red mouth, and where are her teeth?

Where did the stars end, where are the eyes
With which love plays? Now black serpents

Coil around the gaping mouth, the nose
Once whiter than ivory is now gone.

Who with sound heart and without horror
Observes the desert of the ears, the caverns of the eyes,
Who may not shudder at this brow?

Also in the seventeenth century we find the ugliness of Cyrano de Bergerac, whom Edmond Rostand would later give to us not with a long nose but one like a beak. Moreover, we know the actual Cyrano de Bergerac was not a generous man, because he had exploited his father; and he did not love Roxane because he was homosexual and a syphilitic. This takes nothing away from the fact that he was a poet. But this is not the Cyrano of the tradition, who confides in his friend Le Bret:

Look me in the face, and tell me what hope
This protuberance of mine might permit me!
I don't fool myself, not me. At times I, too, chance
To soften on a serene night
And, if I enter some garden, breathing in May
With my poor wretch of a nose, beneath a silvery beam
I see some woman strolling arm in arm
With a gallant, and my heart leaps in my breast,
And I think, alas, that I too would like
To stroll with a woman in the moonlight.
And I get carried away, and forget myself . . .
When suddenly I see the shadow of my profile on the wall!

As time went by, there arose the decadent sense of the beauty of illness, from Violetta Valéry, who dies of consumption, to the various dying Ophelias, with poetic pieces such as Barbey d'Aurevilly's description of Léa. Then we come to the fellow who was made ugly by wickedness and bad by ugliness. Hear the lament of the monster in Mary Shelley's *Frankenstein*: "Believe me, Frankenstein, I was benevolent; my soul glowed with love and humanity; but am I not alone, miserably alone? You, my creator, abhor me; what hope can I gather from your fellow creatures. . . . They spurn and hate me."

The moment in which we become truly aware of the centrality of ugliness to the history of art comes with the beginning of the pre-Romantic sensibility of the sublime, in which the sublime is the grandeur of the horrendous, the storm and ruins. The one who perhaps expressed best this Romantic sentiment was Victor Hugo in his preface to *Cromwell* (1827): "Man, withdrawing within himself in presence of these imposing vicissitudes, began to take pity upon mankind, to reflect upon the bitter disillusionments of life. . . . Until then, the purely epic muse of the ancients had studied nature in only a single aspect, casting aside without pity almost everything in art which, in the world subjected to its imitation, had no relation to a certain type of beauty."

Even more significant, regarding the representation of ugliness, is Hugo's *The Man who Laughs* (1869):

Nature had been prodigal of her kindness to Gwynplaine. She had bestowed on him a mouth opening to his ears, ears folding over to his eyes, a shapeless nose to support the spectacles of the grimace maker, and a face that no one could look upon without laughing.

We have just said that nature had loaded Gwynplaine with her gifts. But was it nature? Had she not been assisted? . . .

According to all appearance, industrious manipulators of children had worked upon his face. It seemed evident that a mysterious and probably occult science . . . had chiselled his flesh . . . skilled in obtusions and ligatures, had enlarged the mouth, cut away the lips, laid bare the gums, distended the ears, cut the cartilages, displaced the eyelids and the cheeks, enlarged the zygomatic muscle, pressed the scars and cicatrices to a level, turned back the skin over the lesions whilst the face was thus stretched, from all which resulted that powerful and profound piece of sculpture, the mask, Gwynplaine.

It seems like the description of many gentlemen today. But precisely because he is so ugly, Gwynplaine triggers the erotic passion of such a corrupt and decadent woman as Lady Josiana—who, when she comes to know that, in reality, Gwynplaine is Lord Clancharlie, wants him to be her lover:

I love you not only because you are deformed, but because you are low. . . . A lover humiliated, cuffed, grotesque, hideous, exposed to jeers . . . has an extraordinary savor. Tis biting into the forbidden fruit of the abyss. An ignominious lover is exquisite. What tempts me is to have between my teeth the apple, not of paradise but of hell. I have that hunger and that thirst. I am that Eve—the Eve of the gulf. . . .

Gwynplaine, I am the throne, you are the stool. Let us place ourselves on a level. . . . You are not ugly, you are deformed. The ugly is petty, the deformed is grand. The ugly is the devil's grimace behind the beautiful. The deformed is the opposite of the sublime. . . . You are Titan . . . I love you!

From the eighteenth century onward, there were the ugly and the damned, and only my natural modesty obliges me to edit out much of the description offered by the Marquis de Sade of his character Monsieur de Courval—the *Président* de Courval—in *The 120 Days of Sodom*:

> worn by debauchery to a singular degree, he offered the eye not much more than a skeleton. He was tall, he was dry, thin, had two blue lusterless eyes, a livid and unwholesome mouth, a prominent chin, a long nose. Hairy as a satyr, flat-backed, with slack, drooping buttocks that rather resembled a pair of dirty rags flapping upon his upper thighs; the skin of those buttocks was, thanks to whipstrokes, so deadened and toughened that you could seize up a handful and knead it without his feeling a thing.

As far as the rest of his person is concerned, it was "just as filthy." He was "a figure whose rather malodorous vicinity might not have succeeded in pleasing everyone."

I cannot show you images of Bond villains because they have been prettified in the films, but in Ian Fleming's novels the descriptions are far more precise: "It was as if Goldfinger had been put together with bits of other people's bodies." That is not how it is in the movies. In print, Rosa Klebb "looked like the oldest and ugliest whore in the world." And as for Doctor No:

> The head also was elongated and tapered from a round, completely bald skull down to a sharp chin so that the impression was of a reversed raindrop—or rather oildrop, for the skin was of a deep almost translucent yellow. . . .

There was something Dali-esque about the eyebrows, which were fine and black and sharply upswept as if they had been painted on as makeup for a conjurer. Below them, slanting jet black eyes stared out of the skull. They were without eyelashes. They looked like the mouths of two small revolvers, direct and unblinking and totally devoid of expression.

Fleming goes on to write that Doctor No stepped closer and then stopped. "Forgive me for not shaking hands with you," he said in a deep, flat, and even voice. "I am unable to." As his sleeves slowly parted and opened, he explained: "I have no hands." And last, consider Mr. Big:

It was a great football of a head, twice the normal size and very nearly round. The skin was grey-black, taut and shining like the face of a week-old corpse in the river. It was hairless, except for some grey-brown fluff above the ears. There were no eyebrows and no eyelashes and the eyes were extraordinarily far apart so that one could not focus on them both, but only on one at a time.

From the seventeenth century at least, and then with the first fabulists of the eighteenth and nineteenth century, children's early years were full of nightmares, from the wolf in *Little Red Riding Hood* and the terrifying Mangiafuoco in *Pinocchio*, to uncanny, mysterious woods. And the idea of the uncanny then led naturally in adult literature, so far still for children, to vampires, golems, and ghosts.

But with the advent of steam power and mechanization, our culture began to dwell on the ugliness of modern cities. The first and most famous text comes from Dickens (*Hard Times*, 1854):

> Coketown was a triumph of fact. . . . It was a town of red brick, or of brick that would have been red if the smoke and ashes had allowed it; but as matters stood, it was a town of unnatural red and black like the painted face of a savage. It was a town of machinery and tall chimneys, out of which interminable serpents of smoke trailed themselves for ever and ever, and never got uncoiled.

There is an impressive abundance of descriptions portraying the ugliness of the industrialized world, starting with Dickens and extending to Don DeLillo and writers since. And it was in this very period, as a reaction to industrial ugliness, and by way of an escape into pure aestheticism, that a religion of beauty arose that was also a religion of the horrendous. Here is how Baudelaire begins his 1857 poem *The Carcass*:

> Remember that object we saw, dear soul,
> In the sweetness of a summer morn:
> At a bend of the path a loathsome carrion
> On a bed with pebbles strewn,
>
> With legs raised like a lustful woman,
> Burning and sweating poisons,
> It spread open, nonchalant and scornful,
> Its belly, ripe with exhalations.
>
> The sun shone onto the rotting heap,
> As if to bring it to the boil,

And tender a hundredfold to vast Nature
All that together she had joined.

And in Italy, "The Song of Hate" (1877) by Olindo Guerrini:

When you sleep forgotten
Beneath the rich soil
And the cross of God is planted
Upright over your coffin

When your rotting cheeks run
Into your loose teeth
And in your stinking, empty eye sockets
Worms are writhing

For you the sleep that for others is peace
Will be a new torment
And remorse will come cold and tenacious
To bite at your brain.

A keen and atrocious remorse
Will come to your grave
Despite God, and his cross,
To gnaw your bones.

. . . .
Oh, with what joy will I sink my claws
Into your shameless belly!

Squatting on your stinking belly,
I will sit for eternity.

Specter of vendetta and sin,
Terror from hell.

Praise for mourning shows up in the works of the avant-garde, where it is not important to compare, say, the Futurists with Picasso or the Surrealists with the practitioners of Arte Informale. A decision to go against classicism was made. This begins with the *Songs of Maldoror*, by Lautréamont (1868):

> I am filthy. I am riddled with lice. Hogs, when they look at me, vomit. My skin is encrusted with the scabs and scales of leprosy, and covered with yellowish pus. I know neither the water of rivers nor the dew of clouds. An enormous mushroom with umbelliferous stalks is growing on my nape, as on a dunghill.

Then, too, there is *The Technical Manifesto of Futurist Literature* (1912):

> We make use, instead, of every ugly sound, every expressive cry from the violent life that surrounds us. We bravely create the "ugly" in literature. . . . Each day we must spit on the *Altar of Art*.

And Aldo Palazzeschi in his futuristic 1913 manifesto *Il contro-dolore*:

> We have to teach our children to laugh, to laugh the most un-restrained, insolent laughter. . . . We will supply them with educational toys, humpbacked, blind, gangrenous, crippled, consumptive, syphilitic puppets, that mechanically cry, shout,

complain, are afflicted with epilepsy, plague, cholera, hemor-
rhaging, hemorrhoids, the clap, insanity, puppets that faint, emit
a death rattle, and die.... Consider the happiness you'll feel on
seeing dozens of little hunchbacks, dwarfs, cross-eyed, and lame
children grow up around you, the divine explorers of joy....
We futurists want to cure the Latin races, especially our own, of
conscious pain, conformist syphilis aggravated by chronic ro-
manticism, and of the monstrous susceptibility and piteous
sentimentalism that depress every Italian.... Teach children
the maximum variety of jeers, grimaces, groans, lamentations
and shrieks, substitute the use of perfumes with that of stinks.

Of course, the massified world could only oppose this provocation of the part on the avant-garde with kitsch—that is to say, the
caricature of art. And so we have fabulous kitsch, sacred kitsch, or
a fusion of kitsch and avant-garde, as in the fascist period.

Kitsch can be different things. Kitsch could be said to be an absence of taste: garden gnomes, glass snow globes with the Madonna of Oropa, but also good things in terrible taste as in Guido
Gozzano's "Grandmother Speranza's Friend" of 1911:

Poll parrot stuffed and the bust of Napoleon, of Alfieri,
the flowery moldings (the very good things in terrible taste),

the dark fireplace, the collection of boxes without any candy,
the clusters of marble fruit standing under the bell jars' protection,

the odd toy, the coconuts there, the box made of seashells, the
warning of *Pray* or *Remember* adorning the keepsakes that lie
everywhere,

the albums with painted archaic wildflowers, an engraving or
two, the pale watercolors, the view of Venice done all in mosaic,

the miniatures there in profusion, a painting or two by
d'Azeglio, daguerreotypes (just a bit yellow) with figures in
dreamy confusion,

. . . .

The red damasked chairs, in the corner the cuckoo clock . . .

But there is also kitsch as the search for effect. In other words, if
I portray a woman, that woman must make me feel like bedding
her. The essence of kitsch consists in exchanging the ethical category with that of aesthetics.

As Hermann Broch explains, "kitsch wants to produce not the
'good' but the 'beautiful.' And if this means . . . describ[ing] the
world not as it really is but as it is hoped and feared to be . . . still
one must concede that no art can work without some effect."

In show business, effect is an absolutely essential component, an
aesthetic component, while there is one entire artistic genre, a specific bourgeois genre—namely, opera—in which that effect represents a fundamental element of construction.

But kitsch can be something that feigns the condition of art
without actually attaining it. And if the term *kitsch* has a meaning
it is not because it designates solely an art that aims to engender
effects, because in many cases great art has also set itself this goal.
In and of itself, kitsch is not a formally imbalanced work, because
in that case it would merely be an ugly work. Nor does it characterize a work that uses stylistic features that have appeared in another context, because this can happen without lapsing into bad
taste. In order to justify its function as a stimulator of effects, kitsch
tries to pass itself off as art, but by doing little more than adopting

and making a great show of the "look" of other works. In my opinion, a genuine model of kitsch is Giovanni Boldini, who constructed his portraits from the waist up according to the best rules of the creation of effect. The head and shoulders—in other words, the uncovered parts—obey all the canons of a refined naturalism. The lips of his women are full and moist, their flesh calls up tactile sensations, their gaze is sweet, provocative, sexy, dreamy. But as soon as he turns to painting clothing, Boldini abandons this "gastronomic" technique, outlines are no longer precise, fabrics dissolve in bright brush strokes, things become clots of color, objects melt in explosions of light. The lower part of Boldini's paintings evoke an Impressionist culture; Boldini is now clearly working within the avant-garde, quoting from the repertoire of contemporary painting. In the upper part he is seeking the *effect*. His women are stylemic sirens. The face must satisfy the person commissioning the work, as far as the artist's approach to the woman goes. But the work must be satisfying in terms of the painter's approach to art.

While kitsch is so ambiguous, we also discover that what was kitsch in the past can become art in the present. Susan Sontag was reflecting on this when she worked out her theory of camp. Camp is not measured by the beauty of something but by its degree of artifice and stylization. The best example of this is Art Nouveau, insofar as it transforms light fixtures into flowering plants, living rooms into grottoes and vice versa, and cast-iron bars into orchid stems, as in Hector Guimard's Paris Metro entrances. The camp canon includes some of the most disparate objects, from Tiffany lamps to Beardsley, from *Swan Lake* and the works of Bellini to Visconti's *Salomé*, from certain fin-de-siècle postcards to *King Kong*, down to old Flash Gordon comics, women's clothing of the 1920s, ostrich boas, and dresses with fringes and beads. The thing that camp taste cares for is "instant character," the thing that really does not excite it is character development. This is why opera and ballet are held to be inexhaustible reserves of camp: because neither of these forms can do complete justice to human nature. Where there is character development, the element of camp diminishes. Among operas, for example, *La Traviata*, which has some small degree of character development, is less camp than *Il Trovatore*, which has none at all. When something is merely ugly, rather than camp, it is not because its ambitions are too mediocre. The artist has not attempted to do anything that is truly bizarre. "It's too much, it's too fantastic, it's unbelievable." This is an expression typical of camp enthusiasm. There is an element of camp in the series of great Italian films based on the heroic character Maciste, and architect Antoni Gaudí's Sagrada Família in Barcelona is also camp, one man's ambition to do alone something that would require the efforts of generations in order to be realized. Things are camp not when they become old, but when we are less involved in them, and we can enjoy watching the attempt fail instead of making use of the results. Camp taste rejects the distinction between beauty and ugliness typical of normal aesthetic judgment; it does not turn things on their head; it does not maintain that beauty is ugly or vice-versa; it restricts itself to offering art and life a different and complementary set of criteria for judgment. Just think of all the important works of art of the twentieth century, whose aim was not to create harmony, but to stretch the medium to the limit so as to tackle ever more violent and irresolvable themes. Camp maintains that good taste is not merely good taste. Actually, there is a sort of good taste in bad taste. Camp is beautiful because it is awful.

At this point, many ideas disappear from art, albeit not from life, because we do not know whether fascinating characters from outer space are ugly or beautiful, or whether the characters of Frank Frazetta

are ugly or frightening. We do not know whether the "living dead"—
to pay tribute to filmmaker George Romero—are merely horrible or,
as he suggests, the bearers of a political message. Is splatter ugly or
beautiful? Was Piero Manzoni's *Artist's Shit* (1961) meant to be beautiful? On the internet you can find a series of "uglifications" of art
masterpieces, one, we might say, more beautiful than the next. There
is ugliness in art, too, but see how difficult it is to establish whether
foul is fair or fair is foul, as the witches in *Macbeth* put it.

And in life? In life, the models would seem to be clear. The mass
media, cinema, and television tell us who is beautiful and who is
ugly, but then on the street we meet different, not beautiful, people
and sometimes some of us marry them, or sleep with them—which
some feminist authors tell us is one way to defy gender and sexual
biases.

There is a short story which perhaps you will know, but it is
worth highlighting its fundamental point. Here is Fredric Brown's
"Sentry":

He was wet and muddy and hungry and cold, and he was fifty
thousand light-years from home.

A strange blue sun gave light and the gravity, twice what he
was used to, made every movement difficult. . . .

And now it was sacred ground because the aliens were there
too. *The* aliens, the only other intelligent race in the Galaxy . . .
cruel, hideous and repulsive monsters. . . .

He was wet and muddy and hungry and cold, and the day was
raw with a high wind that hurt his eyes. But the aliens were
trying to infiltrate and every sentry post was vital.

He stayed alert, gun ready. Fifty thousand light-years from home, fighting on a strange world and wondering if he'd ever live to see home again.

And then he saw one of them crawling toward him. He drew a bead and fired. The alien made that strange horrible sound they all make, then lay still.

He shuddered at the sound and sight of the alien lying there. One ought to be able to get used to them after a while, but he'd never been able to. Such repulsive creatures they were, with only two arms and two legs, ghastly white skins and no scales.

Brown's sensibility brings us back to the initial theme of the relativity of ugliness. Perhaps all of us will appear horrible to the future colonizers of this planet.

But since our history of ugliness has taught us that the ugly should also be understood and justified, let me leave you with the portrait by Quentin Metsys of the *Donna Grottesca*, and as you look at it, an excerpt from a wonderful seventeenth-century text, *The Anatomy of Melancholy* by Robert Burton:

> Love is blind, as they say. . . . Every lover admires his mistress, though she be very deformed of herself, ill-favored, wrinkled, pimpled, pale, red, yellow, tanned, tallow-faced, have a swollen Juggler's platter-face, or a thin, lean, chitty-face, have clouds in her face, be crooked, dry, bald, goggle-eyed, bleary-eyed, or with staring eyes, she looks like a squis'd cat, hold her head still awry, heavy, dull, hollow-eyed, black or yellow about the eyes, or squint-eyed, sparrow-mouthed, Persian hook-nosed,

have a sharp Fox nose, a red nose, China flat great nose, snub-nose with wide nostrils, a nose like a promontory, gubber-tushed, rotten teeth, black, uneven, brown teeth, beetle-browed, a Witch's beard, her breath stink all over the room, her nose drop winter and summer, with a Bavarian poke under her chin, a sharp chin, lave eared, with a long crane's neck, which stands awry too, with hanging breasts, "her dugs like two double jugs," or else no dugs, in the other extreme . . . a vast virago, or an ugly Tit, a slug, a fat fustilugs, a truss, a long lean rawbone, a skeleton, a sneaker . . . and to thy judgment looks like a merd in a lanthorn, whom thou couldest not fancy for a world, but hatest, loathest, and wouldest have spit in her face, or blow thy nose in her bosom, the very antidote of love to another man, a dowdy, a slut, a scold, a nasty, rank, rammy, filthy, beastly quean, dishonest peradventure, ob-scene, base, beggarly, rude, foolish, untaught, peevish . . . if he love her once, he admires her for all this, he takes no no-tice of any such errors, or imperfections of body or mind . . . . he had rather have her than any woman in the world.

[La Milanesiana, 2006]

4. The Absolute and the Relative

I want you to think for a moment about the image of Magritte's *Absolute Knowledge*, as a sort of morale booster. You must be prepared for anything in this next hour, because a serious lecture on the concepts of the absolute and the relative would have to last at least two thousand five hundred years—just as long as they have been debated in reality. I have long asked myself what the term "absolute" means; it is the most elementary question a philosopher should pose.

I went to look for images by artists that refer to the absolute, and—as well as the fine Magritte, which however does not tell me a lot in a philosophical sense—I found others: *Painting the Absolute, Quéte d'absolu, In Search of the Absolute,* and *Marcheur d'absolu,* not to mention advertisements using the term, with their images of Absolu by Valentino, Absolut vodka, and Absolu mincemeat. It would seem that the absolute is a big seller.

Moreover, the notion of the absolute brought to mind one of its opposites—namely, the notion of the relative. This has become a rather fashionable term since prominent churchmen and even secular thinkers launched a campaign against so-called "relativism"—which has in turn become a disparaging term used for almost terroristic purposes, rather like the way Silvio Berlusconi uses the word "communism." I set myself the task, therefore, not to clarify your ideas but to muddle them up, by trying to show how ambiguous these terms are—according to the circumstances and context, they mean very different things among themselves—and to suggest that they should not be used like baseball bats.

According to dictionaries of philosophy, the absolute is all that is *ab solutus*, free of all bonds or limits. It does not depend on something else, but holds within itself its own reason, cause, and explanation. This is something, therefore, very close to God, whose own self-definition, "I am who I am," cast everything else as *contingent*. That is to say, none of the rest has its own cause within itself and, although by some accident it came to exist, it could just as well not exist, or could no longer exist tomorrow—and this is the case for the solar system and for all of us.

As we are contingent beings, and therefore destined to die, we have a desperate desire to be anchored to something that does not perish—something absolute. But this absolute can be *transcendent*, like the biblical divinity, or *immanent*—to invoke the theory of a Spinoza or Giordano Bruno. According to idealist philosophers (F. W. J. von Schelling, for example), we too become part of the absolute because the absolute is the indissoluble unity of the subject that knows and that which was once considered to be extraneous to the subject—for example, nature or the world. In the absolute, we identify with God and are part of something that is not yet fully complete: process, development, infinite growth, and infinite self-definition. But if that is how things stand, we could never either define or know the absolute because we are part of it; trying to conceive of it would be like Baron Münchausen dragging himself out of a swamp by his own hair.

So the alternative is to think of the absolute as something we are not and that lies elsewhere, not dependent on us—like Aristotle's God, who thinks of himself thinking and who, as Joyce wrote in *A Portrait of the Artist as a Young Man*, "remains within or behind or beyond or above his handiwork, invisible, refined out of existence, indifferent, paring his fingernails." As a matter of fact, in the fifteenth-century work *De docta ignorantia*, Nicholas of Cusa had already said: *Deus est absolutus.*

But in Nicholas's view, insofar as God is absolute, God can never be reached. The relationship between our awareness and God is the same as the one between an inscribed polygon and the circumference within which it is inscribed: as the sides of the polygon gradually multiply, we get closer and closer to the circumference, but the polygon and the circumference will *never* be equal. Nicholas said that God is like a circle whose center is everywhere and whose circumference is nowhere.

Is it possible to *conceive of* a circle whose center is everywhere and whose circumference is nowhere? Evidently not. Yet we can *describe* it, and that is what I am doing right now, and you all understand that I am talking about something that has to do with geometry, except that it is geometrically impossible and unimaginable. So there is a difference between being able to conceive something or not and being able to describe it and attribute some meaning to it.

What does it mean to use a word and give it a meaning? It means a lot of things.

A. Having instructions for recognizing an object, situation, or event. For example, part of the meaning of words such as *dog* or *stumble* is made up of a series of descriptions, also in the form of images, for recognizing a dog and telling one from a cat, and for telling the difference between *stumble* and *jump*.

B. Having a definition and / or a classification. I have the definition and classification of dog but also of events or situations such as *voluntary manslaughter*, which by definition I can distinguish from *involuntary manslaughter*.

C. Knowing the so-called "factual" or "encyclopedic" properties of a given entity: for example, I know that dogs are faithful, good for hunting or for guarding the home, and that according to the law involuntary manslaughter will lead to a determined sentence, and so on.

D. Possibly having instructions explaining how to produce the object or the corresponding event. I know the meaning of the word *vase* because even though I am not a potter I know how a vase should be produced—and it is the same with terms such as *decapitation* or *sulfuric acid*. Instead, for a term such as *brain* I know meanings A and B, some of the properties C, but I do not know how to produce one.

A splendid case in which I know the properties A, B, C, and D was provided by C. S. Peirce, who defined lithium this way:

If you look into a textbook of chemistry for a definition of *lithium* you may be told that it is that element whose atomic weight is 7 very nearly. But if the author has a more logical mind he will tell you that if you search among minerals that are vitreous, translucent, grey or white, very hard, brittle, and insoluble, for one which imparts a crimson tinge to an unluminous flame, this mineral being triturated with lime or witherite rats-bane, and then fused, can be partly dissolved in muriatic acid; and if this solution be evaporated, and the residue be extracted with sulfuric acid, and duly purified, it can be converted by ordinary methods into a chloride, which being obtained in the solid state, fused, and electrolyzed with half a dozen powerful cells, will yield a globule of a pinkish silvery metal that will float on gasoline; and the material of *that* is a specimen of lithium. The peculiarity of this definition—or rather this precept which is more serviceable than a definition—is that it tells you what the word *lithium* denotes, by prescribing what you are to *do* in order to gain a perceptual acquaintance with the object of the word.

This is a fine example of a complete and satisfactory representation of the meaning of a term. But other expressions instead have fuzzy, imprecise meanings—and diminishing degrees of clarity. For example, even the expression *the highest even number* has a meaning; we immediately know that it would have to have the property of being divisible by two (and so we would be able to distinguish it from the highest odd number) and we even possess a vague instrument for producing it, in the sense that we can imagine counting higher and higher numbers, separating the odd ones from the even ones. It's just that we realize we will never manage to do that—in the way that in a dream we sometimes have a sense that we can grasp something but are not quite able to do so. An expression such as *a circle whose center is everywhere and whose circumference is nowhere* instead suggests no rule for the production of a corresponding object; not only does it not support any definition, it also defies all our efforts to imagine it, apart from making our head spin. All things considered, the definition of a term such as *absolute* is tautological—something that is not contingent is absolute, but something that is not absolute is contingent—but it does not suggest descriptions, definitions, and classifications. We cannot think of instructions for the production of a corresponding thing. We know none of its properties, except to suppose that it has them all—and that it is probably the *id cuius nihil maius cogitari possit* (something compared to which nothing greater can be thought) that Saint Anselm of Canterbury talked about. (And this, by the way, reminds me of a comment attributed to Arthur Rubinstein: "Do I believe in God? No, I believe in something much greater.") The best we can manage to imagine in trying to conceive of God is the reduction of the world's variety into what Hegel ridiculed as a "night in which all cows are black."

It is certainly possible not only to name but also to represent visually those things that we cannot conceive. But these images do not *represent* the inconceivable: they simply invite us to try to imagine something inconceivable, and then frustrate our expectations. What we feel in trying to understand them is precisely the sense of powerlessness expressed by Dante in the last canto of the *Paradiso* (XXXIII, 82–86) where he would like to tell us what he saw when he was able to look upon the divinity, but all he can manage to say is that he cannot put it into words, and he falls back on the intriguing metaphor of a book with an infinite number of pages:

> O grace abounding, by which I have dared
> To fix my eyes through the eternal Light
> So deeply that my sight was spent in it!
>
> Within its depths I saw gathered together,
> Bound by love into a single volume,
> Leaves that lie scattered through the universe.
>
> Substance and accidents and their relations
> I saw as though they fused in such a way
> That what I say is but a gleam of light.

The universal pattern of this knot
I believe I saw, because in telling this,
I feel my gladness growing ever larger.

One moment made more slip my memory than
Twenty-five centuries reft from the adventure
That awed Neptune with the shadow of the Argo.

Nor is this any different from the feeling of impotence expressed by Giacomo Leopardi when he describes the infinite ("thus my mind sinks into this immensity / and sweet it is to founder in this sea"). This is reminiscent of a Romantic painter such as Caspar David Friedrich when he tried to express the sublime, which was the earthly thing best able to call up the experience of the absolute.

In times long gone by Pseudo-Dionysius the Areopagite wrote that, since the divine One is so far from us as not to be either understood or reached, we must perforce talk about it through metaphors and allusions, but especially, owing to the poverty of our language, through negative symbols and dissimilar expressions: "The lowest images are also used, such as fragrant ointment, or the cornerstone, and they even give It the forms of wild animals and liken It to the lion and panther, or name It a leopard, or a raging bear bereaved of its young" (Pseudo-Dionysius the Areopagite, *The Celestial Hierarchy,* book II).

Some naive philosophers have suggested that poets alone can tell us what being and the absolute may be, but all they are really expressing is the *indefinite*. This was the poetics of Stéphane Mallarmé, who spent a lifetime trying to provide an "orphic explanation of the world." "I say a flower, and beyond the oblivion whence my voice relegates all shapes, insofar as it is something other than any known calyx, there arises musically a pleasant idea, the absence of all bouquets and fragrance." In point of fact this statement is untranslatable; all it tells us is that a word is selected, detached from the white space surrounding it, and from it the totality of the unsaid must spring, but in the form of an absence. "To nominate an object is to suppress three-quarters of the power of poetry, which is all about working things out gradually: to suggest, that is the dream." Mallarmé spent all his life in the quest for this dream, but it never came true. Dante had taken this problem for granted right from the start, understanding as he did that it would take the pride of Lucifer to claim to express the infinite in finite terms, and he avoided this problem of poetry by making the poetry of the problem, not the poetry of the unsayable but the poetry of the impossibility of saying it.

We should consider the fact that Dante (like Pseudo-Dionysius and Nicholas of Cusa) was a believer. Is it possible to believe in an absolute and state that it is unthinkable and undefinable? Of course, by accepting the substitution of the impossible thought of the absolute with the *feeling* of the absolute and hence of faith, since "faith is the substance of things that are hoped for and the evidence of things that are not seen." During a conference, Elie Wiesel quoted Kafka's observation that it is possible to talk *with* God but not *about* God. While for philosophers the absolute is a night in which all cows are black, for the mystic who, like Saint John of the Cross (sixteenth century), saw it as *noche oscura* ("Oh night that guided me / oh night more lovely than the dawn"), it is the source of ineffable emotions. Saint John of the Cross expresses his mystical experience through poetry: faced with the indescribable nature of the absolute, we might find comfort in the fact that this unsatisfied tension may resolve itself materially in a finished form. And this allowed Keats in his "Ode on a Grecian Urn" (1819) to see beauty as a substitute for the experience of the absolute:

"Beauty is truth, truth beauty: that is all ye know on earth and all ye need to know."

This is fine for those who have decided to practice an aesthetic religion. But Saint John of the Cross would have told us that it was only his mystical experience of the absolute that guaranteed him the sole possible truth. This has led many persons of faith to maintain that philosophical systems that reject any possibility of knowing the absolute automatically reject all criteria of truth or, by not accepting an absolute criterion of truth, they reject the possibility of any experience of the absolute. But it is one thing to say that a philosophical system does not accept any possibility of knowing the absolute and another to say that it rejects all criteria of truth—even for matters concerning the contingent world. Are truth and the experience of the absolute so inseparable?

The belief that some things are true is of fundamental importance for the survival of humankind. If we did not think that the things other people tell us can be either true or false, society would be impossible. We could not even rule out the idea that a box with "aspirin" written on it might contain strychnine instead.

A specular theory of truth is *adaequatio rei et intellectus* (the adequation of the intellect and the thing), as if our mind were a mirror that, when working properly and not a distorting one or misted over, must faithfully *reflect things as they are*. This is the theory put forward by Thomas Aquinas, for example, but also by Lenin in his *Materialism and Empirio-Criticism* (1909). And since Aquinas could not have been a Leninist, it follows that when it came to philosophy, Lenin was a Neo-Thomist. But, with the exception of ecstatic states, *we are obliged to speak* and to say what our intellect reflects. Hence we define as true (or false) not things but the assertions we make about how things are. According to Alfred Tarski's famous definition, the statement "snow is white" is only true if the snow *is* white. Now, if we forget the whiteness of snow for a moment, because the way things are going it has become a highly debatable subject, we might consider another example: the statement "it's raining" (between quote marks) is true only if outside it is actually raining (without quote marks).

The first part of the definition (the one between quote marks) is a verbal statement and represents nothing other than itself, but the second part ought to express how things actually are. But what ought to be a state of things is once more expressed in words. To avoid this linguistic mediation we should say that "it's raining" (between quote marks) is true if "that thing there" (while pointing to the falling rain without saying a word). But, while we can make this indexical appeal to the senses with the rain, it would be harder to do the same thing with the statement "the Earth revolves around the sun" (because if anything our senses would tell us the exact opposite).

To establish whether the statement corresponds to a state of things, we first need to interpret the term *to rain* and stipulate a definition for it. We need to establish that in order to state that it is raining it is not enough to notice drops of water falling from above, because it may be that someone is watering flowers on a balcony; second, the consistency of the drops must be of a certain size, otherwise we would talk of dew or frost; third, the sensation must be constant (otherwise we would say that it tried to rain but stopped right away), and so on. This having been established, we must move on to an empirical test, which in the case of rain is available to all (you just hold out your hand and trust in your senses).

But in the case of the statement "the Earth revolves around the sun," the verification procedure is more complex. What is the meaning of the word *true* in each of the following statements?

1. I have a bellyache.
2. Last night I dreamed that Padre Pio appeared to me.
3. It will definitely rain tomorrow.
4. The world will end in 2536.
5. There is life after death.

Statements 1 and 2 express subjective facts, but a bellyache is an evident feeling that cannot be suppressed whereas, in recalling a dream of the night before, I might not be sure of the accuracy of my recollections. In addition, the two statements cannot be immediately verified by others. Of course, a doctor who wants to know if I really have colitis or if I am a hypochondriac would have the means to check that out. But if I told a psychoanalyst I had dreamed about Padre Pio, she would have more of a problem, because I could easily be lying.

Statements 3, 4, and 5 are not immediately verifiable. But the chance of rain tomorrow can be verified tomorrow, whereas the idea of the world ending in 2536 would pose us a few problems (and that is why we make a distinction between the credibility of a met office forecaster and that of a prophet). The difference between 4 and 5 is that 4 will become true or false at least in 2536, whereas 5 can never be empirically verified.

6. Every right angle necessarily has 90 degrees.
7. Water always boils at 100 degrees.
8. Apples are angiosperms.
9. Napoleon died on May 5, 1821.
10. If you follow the path of the sun you will come to the coast.
11. Jesus is the son of God.

12. The correct interpretation of Holy Writ is determined by the teachings of the Church.

13. Embryos are already human beings and have a soul.

Some of these statements are true or false in relation to rules we have established. A right angle only has 90 degrees within the ambit of a system of Euclidean postulates. That water boils at 100 degrees is true not only if we accept a physical law worked out through inductive generalization but also on the basis of the definition of degrees centigrade. An apple is an angiosperm only on the basis of some rules of botanical classification.

Some others require us to trust in matters checked out by others before our time: we believe it to be true that Napoleon died on May 5, 1821, because we accept what the history books tell us, but we must always recognize the possibility that some hitherto unknown document might be discovered tomorrow in the archives of the British admiralty that says he died on another date. Sometimes for utilitarian reasons we take as true an idea that we know is false: for example, to find our way in the desert, we behave as if it were true that the sun moves from east to west.

As for statements concerning religion, I don't think they admit of no resolution. If we accept the Gospels as historically accurate testimony, the proof of Christ's divinity ought to convince even a Protestant. But this is not the case with the teachings of the Catholic Church. The statement regarding the soul of the embryo depends solely on establishing the meanings of terms such as *life*, *human*, and *soul*. Thomas Aquinas, for example, held that embryos had only a sensitive soul, like the animals, and therefore as they are not yet human beings with a rational soul they will not take part in the resurrection of the flesh. Today he would be accused of heresy, but in that most civilized age they made him a saint.

It is therefore a matter of deciding each time which criteria of truth we are using.

Our sense of tolerance is based on this very recognition of the different degrees of verifiability or acceptability of a truth. I can have the scientific and didactic duty to fail a student who maintains that water boils at 90 degrees like the right angle—this was apparently suggested in an exam—but a Christian would also have to accept that for some people there is no other god than Allah and that Mohammed is his prophet (and Christians expect Muslims to return the compliment).

Instead in the light of some recent polemics it seems that this distinction between different criteria of truth, typical of modern thought and especially of logical-scientific thinking, gives rise to a relativism understood as the historical malady of contemporary culture, which rejects any idea of truth. But what do anti-relativists mean by relativism?

Some encyclopedias of philosophy tell us that there is a *cognitive* relativism, according to which objects can be known solely under conditions determined by human faculties. But in this sense, Kant, too, would have been a relativist as he never denied that it was possible to state laws of universal value—and, moreover, he believed in God, albeit only on moral grounds.

In another encyclopedia of philosophy I find that relativism means "every concept that does not admit of absolute principles in the field of knowledge and action." But rejecting absolute principles in the field of knowledge or in the field of action is not the same thing. Some people are prepared to maintain that "pedophilia is a bad thing" is a truth relative only to a particular system of values, since in certain cultures it was or is allowed or tolerated, while claiming nonetheless that Pythagoras's theorem must be valid for all times and in all cultures.

No one could seriously label Einstein's theory of relativity as an example of relativism. To say that any measurement of motion depends on how fast or slow the observer is moving is considered to be a valid principle for every human being in every time and in every place.

Relativism as a philosophical doctrine of that name arose together with nineteenth-century positivism, which held that the absolute was unknowable and that at best it could be understood as the constantly fluid limit of ongoing scientific research. But no positivist has ever claimed that objectively verifiable scientific truths valid for everyone cannot be attained.

One philosophical position that, after a hasty reading of the textbooks, could be defined as relativistic is so-called *holism*, according to which all statements are true or false (and acquire a meaning) only within an organic system of assumptions, a given conceptual scheme or, as others have said, within a given scientific paradigm.

A holist maintains (rightly) that the notion of space has a different meaning in the Aristotelian and Newtonian systems, thus making them incommensurable, and that one scientific system is as good as another to the extent to which it successfully explains a set of phenomena. But holists are the first to tell us that some systems *fail to explain* a set of phenomena and that in the long term some systems prevail simply because they explain things better than others. So, in their apparent tolerance, holists are faced with *something* they have to explain and, even when they do not say so, they stick to what I would define as a minimal realism, according to which *things must exist or behave in a certain way*. Perhaps we will never know how this is, but if we do not believe that it exists, our research would make no sense, nor would it make any sense to keep on trying out new systems for explaining the world.

Holists are usually said to be *pragmatists*, but in this case, too, we should not read the philosophy textbooks in haste: the true pragmatist, as Charles Sanders Peirce was, did not say that ideas are true only if they show themselves to be effective, but that they show their effectiveness when they are true. And when he supported fallibilism—namely, the possibility that all our knowledge can always be questioned—at the same time he maintained that through the constant correction of knowledge the human community continues to carry "the torch of truth."

What makes people suspect that these theories are relativistic is the fact that the various systems are mutually *incommensurable*. The Ptolemaic system is certainly incommensurable with the Copernican one, and only in the former do the notions of epicycle and deferent take on a precise meaning. But the fact that the two systems are incommensurable does not mean they are not *comparable*, and it is precisely by comparing them that we understand the nature of the celestial phenomena that Ptolemy explained with the notions of epicycle and deferent, and we realize that they were the same phenomena that the Copernicans wanted to explain in accordance with a different conceptual scheme.

Philosophical holism is similar to linguistic holism, according to which the semantic and syntactical structure of a given language imposes a determined world view of which the speaker of that language is, so to speak, a prisoner. Benjamin Lee Whorf (1897–1941) pointed out, for example, that western languages tend to analyze many events as objects, and an expression such as "three days" is grammatically equivalent to "three apples," whereas some native American languages are oriented toward the *process* and see events where we see things—with the result that the Hopi language would be better equipped than English to define certain phenomena studied by modern physicists. Whorf also pointed out that, instead of the word *snow*, the Eskimos apparently have four different terms according to the consistency of the snow itself and so they would see several different *things* whereas we see only one. Leaving aside that this idea has been challenged, even a western skier can tell the difference between different kinds of snow with different consistencies, and were an Eskimo to come into contact with us he would understand perfectly well that when we say *snow* for the presumed four things that he calls by different names, we are behaving just like the Frenchman who uses *glace* to describe ice, ice lollies, ice cream, mirrors, and window glass, yet in the morning is not such a prisoner of his own language as to shave while looking at himself in an ice cream.

Finally, apart from the fact that not all contemporary thinkers accept the holistic perspective, it is nonetheless in line with all those theories of knowledge according to which reality can be seen from different perspectives and each perspective matches one aspect of it, even if it does not exhaust its unfathomable richness. There is nothing relativistic in maintaining that reality is always defined from a particular (which does not mean subjective and individual) point of view. Nor does asserting that we see it always and only *in accordance with a certain description* exempt us from believing and hoping that what we are seeing is always *the same thing*.

Alongside cognitive relativism, the encyclopedias list *cultural relativism*. That different cultures have not only different languages and mythologies but different moral concepts (all reasonable in their context) was understood, first by Montaigne and then by Locke, when Europe came more critically into contact with other cultures. That primitive tribes in New Guinea still think cannibalism is legitimate and commendable while we in the West do not strikes me as an indisputable observation, as it is equally indisputable that in certain countries adulterers are censured in ways that differ from ours. But, firstly, recognizing the variety of cultures does not mean denying that there are some more universal behaviors (for example, a mother's love for her children, or the fact that we use the same facial expressions to express disgust or merriment), and secondly, such recognition does not automatically imply moral relativism—that is, the notion that since no ethical values are the same for all cultures we can freely modify our behavior to suit our desires or interests. Recognizing that an *other* culture is different, and that its diversity must be respected, does not mean abdicating our own cultural identity.

So how did the specter of relativism come to be constructed as a uniform ideology, a blight on contemporary culture?

There is a secular critique of relativism, the main thrust of which addresses the excesses of cultural relativism. Marcello Pera, who presents his ideas in a book written with Joseph Ratzinger, *Senza radici* (2004), is well aware that there are differences between cultures but he maintains that some values of western culture (such as democracy, the separation of church and state, and liberalism) have proved superior to the values of other cultures. Western civilization has good reason to believe it is more advanced than others with regard to these topics but, in maintaining that this superiority ought to be universally evident, Pera uses a questionable argument. He says: "If members of culture B freely show that they prefer culture A and not vice-versa—if, for example, the flow of migration runs from Islamic countries to the West and not vice-versa—then there is reason to believe that A is better than B." The argument is weak because in the nineteenth century the Irish did not emigrate en masse to the United States because they preferred that Protestant country to their beloved Catholic Ireland, but because at home they were dying of starvation on account of the potato blight. Pera's rejection of cultural relativism is dictated by a concern that tolerance for other cultures may degenerate into submissiveness and that the pressure of immigration will lead to the West's acquiescing to the demands of foreign cultures. Pera's problem is not the defense of the absolute, but the defense of the West.

In his *Contro il relativismo* (2005), Giovanni Jervis gives us a relativist who is a strange hybrid made up of a late Romantic, a postmodern thinker with Nietzschean roots, and a disciple of New Age thinking, whose relativism, handily for Jervis's purposes, looks anti-scientific and irrational. Jervis sees a reactionary streak in cultural relativism: asserting that all forms of society should be respected and justified, even idealized, encourages the segregation of peoples. What's more, those cultural anthropologists who, rather than attempting to identify the biological characteristics and behavioral constants of populations, have emphasized diversity owed solely to culture—by attaching too much importance to cultural factors and by ignoring biological factors—have again indirectly supported the primacy of spirit over matter, and by so doing they have proved sympathetic to the views of religious thinkers.

This statement should definitely bewilder those believers whose twofold fear is (1) that cultural relativism necessarily leads to moral relativism—as if recognizing the right of Papuan natives to drive spikes through their noses means that people in Ireland have the right to abuse seven-year-old children; and (2) that maintaining there are various ways of ascertaining the truth of a proposition casts doubt on the possibility of recognizing an absolute truth. Clearly this is not true and it has been proved that there are some people who believe that the Virgin Mary really did appear at Lourdes, but at the same time hold that the New Zealand cormorant is a *Phalacrocorax carbo* only by classificatory convention.

With regard to cultural relativism, in some doctrinal notes on the Congregation for the Doctrine of the Faith (2002), Joseph Ratzinger, still a cardinal at the time—I choose to challenge cardinals but not popes, given that you never know these days—saw a close relationship between cultural relativism and ethical relativism:

> Cultural relativism . . . shows clear signs of its presence in the theorization and defense of ethical pluralism that sanctions the decadence and dissolution of reason and the principles of the natural moral law. Following this trend it is not unusual, unfortunately, to come across public statements claiming that this ethical pluralism is a condition for democracy.

Pope John Paul II, in his encyclical *Fides et ratio* (September 14, 1998), said:

> Forgetting to orient its investigation of being, modern philosophy has concentrated on human knowledge. Instead of working on man's capacity to know the truth, it has preferred to highlight the limitations and conditioning of that capacity. This has given rise to various forms of agnosticism and relativism, which have led philosophical research to lose itself in the shifting sands of a pervasive skepticism.

And Ratzinger, in a homily of 2003, said: "A dictatorship of relativism is being established, whereby nothing is recognized as definitive and whose sole measure is one's own ego and desires. We, however, have another measure: the Son of God, the true man."

Here two notions of truth are in opposition, one as the semantic property of statements and the other as the property of divinity. This is due to the fact that both notions of truth appear in Holy

Writ (at least according to the translations through which we know it). Sometimes truth refers to the correspondence between something that is *said* and the way in which things *are* ("verily, verily I say unto you," in the sense of "what I'm saying is true") and sometimes instead the truth is an intrinsic quality of divinity ("I am the way, the truth, and the life"). This has led many Fathers of the Church to positions that Ratzinger would call relativistic today, since they said that the important thing was not to worry whether a given statement on the world corresponded to the way things were, as long as attention was paid to the only truth worthy of this name, the message of salvation. Saint Augustine, faced with the dispute as to whether the Earth was round or flat, seemed inclined to think it was round, but pointed out that since such knowledge does not serve to save the soul, one theory is practically as good as another.

It is hard to find a definition of truth among Cardinal Ratzinger's many writings that is other than the truth as revealed and embodied in Christ. But, if the truth of faith is truth revealed, why contrast it with the truth of scientists and philosophers, which is a concept of a different sort and one with different ends? It would suffice to follow Thomas Aquinas who, in his *De aeternitate mundi*, knowing full well that supporting Averroës's theory of the eternity of the world was a terrible heresy, accepted through faith that the world was created, but from a cosmological point of view admitted that it was not possible to rationally demonstrate either that it was created or that it was eternal. For Ratzinger, instead, as reported in his *Il monoteismo* (2002), the essence of all philosophical and modern scientific thinking is that:

> the truth as such—so it is thought—cannot be known, and
> we can go forward little by little only with the small steps of

ON THE SHOULDERS OF GIANTS

verification and falsification. The tendency to replace the concept of truth with that of consensus is strengthened. But this means that man becomes separated from the truth and hence also from the distinction between good and evil, submitting completely to the principle of the majority. . . . Man plans and "assembles" the world without preestablished criteria and thus necessarily goes beyond the concept of human dignity, so that even human rights become problematic. In such a conception of reason and rationality there is absolutely no space for the concept of God.

This extrapolation, which moves from a prudent concept of scientific truth as an object of continuous verification and correction to a declaration of the destruction of all human dignity, is untenable; that is to say, it is a position that cannot be defended without identifying all modern thought with the notion that *there are no facts but only interpretations*, the next step being to claim that existence is devoid of any foundation, that therefore God is dead, and finally that, if God does not exist, then everything is possible.

Neither Ratzinger nor the anti-relativists in general are visionaries or conspiracy theorists. The simple fact is that those anti-relativists I would define as moderates or critics identify their enemy *solely* with that specific form of extreme relativism according to which there are no facts but only interpretations, while the anti-relativists I define as radicals extend the claim that there are no facts but only interpretations to include all of modern thought, making an error that—at least in the university of my day—would have caused them to fail their history of philosophy exam.

The idea that there are no facts but only interpretations begins with Nietzsche who explained it very clearly in *On Truth and Lies in an Extra-Moral Sense* (1896). Since nature has thrown away the key, the intellect plays on conceptual fictions it calls truth. We think we talk about trees, colors, snow, and flowers, but these are metaphors that do not correspond to the original entities. Faced with the multiplicity of individual leaves there is no one primordial "leaf," an "original form according to which all leaves are supposedly woven, sketched, circled off, colored, curled, or painted—but by awkward hands." Birds and insects perceive the world in ways different than ours, and it makes no sense to say which of those perceptions is the most correct, because that would require a criterion of "right perception" which does not exist. Nature "knows no forms and concepts, and hence not even species, but only an x that is inaccessible and indefinable for us." Truth, then, becomes "a mobile army of metaphors, metonymies, anthropomorphisms," of poetic inventions subsequently hardened into knowledge—illusions whose illusory nature has been forgotten, But Nietzsche avoids considering two phenomena. One is that, by falling into line with the constrictions of this dubious knowledge of ours, we manage in some way to deal with nature: if someone has been bitten by a dog, a doctor knows which kind of injection to give, even though she has no knowledge of the particular dog that bit the patient. The other is that, every so often, nature obliges us to recognize that our knowledge is illusory and to choose an alternative form (which is, moreover, the problem of the revolution of cognitive paradigms). Nietzsche saw the presence of natural constrictions that struck him as "terrible powers" which constantly press upon us, challenging our "scientific" truths. But he refused to conceptualize them, seeing that it was to defy them that we constructed conceptual armor to defend ourselves with. Change is possible, not as a restructuring, but as a permanent poetic revolution: "if we had, each taken singly, a varying sensory perception, we could see now like a bird, now like a worm, now like a plant; or if one of us saw the same stimulus as red, another as blue, while a third heard it even as a sound, then no one would speak of such a regularity of nature."

So, he says, art (and with it, myth) "constantly confuses the categories and cells of the concepts by presenting new transferences, metaphors, and metonyms; constantly showing the desire to shape the existing world of the wideawake person to be variegatedly irregular and disinterestedly incoherent, exciting, and eternally new, as is the world of dreams."

If these are the premises, the first possibility would be to take refuge in dreams as an escape from reality. But Nietzsche himself admits that this dominion of art over life would be deceptive, albeit supremely enjoyable. Or—and this is the real lesson that posterity has learned from Nietzsche—art can say what it says because it is Being itself that accepts any definition, because it has no foundation. For Nietzsche, this fading away of Being coincided with the death of God. And this allowed some believers to draw a false Dostoyevskian conclusion from this death foretold: if God does not exist or exists no longer, then all things are permitted. But if there is no heaven or hell, it is the nonbeliever who realizes that if we are to save ourselves here on earth then we must establish good will, understanding, and moral law. In 2006, Eugenio Lecaldano published his book *Un'etica senza Dio*, an ethics without God, which draws on a wealth of anthological documentation to argue that only by putting God to one side can we truly lead a moral life. I certainly do not want to establish here whether Lecaldano and the other authors he cites are right. I merely wish to point out that there are some who hold that the absence of God does not eliminate the ethical problem—and this was quite clear to Cardinal Carlo Maria Martini when he founded a "nonbelievers teaching chair" in Milan. The fact that Martini did not go on to become Pope may cast doubt on the divine inspiration of the conclave, but I am not competent to judge such matters. I just remember that Elie Wiesel used to say that those who believe that all things are permitted are not those who believe that God is dead, but those who think *they* are God (a shortcoming of all dictators great and small).

The idea that there are no facts but only interpretations is by no means shared by all contemporary thinkers, most of whom put the following objections to Nietzsche and his followers: First, if there were no facts but only interpretations, then what would an interpretation be an interpretation of? And second, even if interpretations interpreted one another, there still ought to be some initial object or event that triggered our interpretation. Third, even if the entity were indefinable, we would have to specify *who* is talking about it metaphorically, and the problem of saying something true would shift from the object to the subject of knowledge. God might be dead, but not Nietzsche. On what basis do we justify Nietzsche's presence? By saying he is merely a metaphor? But if he is, *who* is saying so? And not just that. Even though we often use metaphors to describe reality, in order to formulate them we would need words with a literal meaning that denote things we know through experience: I cannot call the thing that holds up the table a "leg" if I do not have a non-metaphorical notion of the human leg, knowing its form and function. And finally, fourth, in asserting that there is no longer an intersubjective criterion for verification, we forget that *every so often* certain things outside of us (which Nietzsche called the terrible powers) oppose our attempts to express that criterion even metaphorically; in other words, if you treat an inflammation with, say, phlogiston theory you cannot heal it, whereas by administering antibiotics you can. And therefore one medical theory is better than another.

So perhaps there is no absolute, or if it does exist it will be neither conceivable nor attainable, but there are natural forces that back up or challenge our interpretations. If I interpret a trompe l'oeil painting of an open door as a real door and march straight on to go through it, the fact that is the impenetrable wall will considerably weaken my interpretation.

There must be a way in which things are or go—and the proof of this is not just that all men are mortal but also that, if I try to walk through a wall, I am going to break my nose. Death and that wall are the only forms of the absolute that we cannot doubt.

The evidence of that wall, which tells us "no" when we wish to interpret it as if it was not there, is arguably a very modest criterion of truth for the guardians of the absolute, but as Keats put it, "that is all ye know on earth, and all ye need to know."

Perhaps there is more to say on the absolute, but for the time being nothing comes to mind.

[La Milanesiana, 2007]

5. Beautiful Flame

When they asked me to talk about one of the four elements, I chose fire.

Why? Because although fire is fundamental to all our lives, of all the elements it is the one most likely to be forgotten about. We breathe air unceasingly, we use water every day, we constantly tread the earth, but our experience of fire runs the risk of diminishing more and more. Fire's former functions have gradually been taken over by invisible forms of energy; we no longer associate the idea of light with that of a flame and our experience of fire is limited to gas (which we barely notice), and matches and lighters (but only for those who still smoke), and candle flames (but only for churchgoers).

For the privileged few, this leaves the hearth, and that is where I would like to begin. Back in the Seventies I bought a house in the country with a fine fireplace. For my children, then aged ten and twelve, the experience of fire—the burning logs, the flames—was an absolutely new phenomenon. And I noticed that when the fire was lit they were no longer interested in the television. The flames were more beautiful and more varied than any program, told countless stories, changed constantly, and did not follow set routines like TV shows. Among recent philosophers, the person who perhaps reflected most on the poetry, mythology, psychology, and psychoanalysis of fire was Gaston Bachelard. Given the focus of his research on the archetypal figures that have populated the human imagination since the dawn of time, he could hardly fail to come across fire.

The heat of fire evokes the heat of the sun, in its turn seen as a ball of fire. Fire is hypnotic and is therefore a prime subject and mainspring of the imagination. Fire is a reminder of the first universal prohibition (do not touch it), thus becoming the epiphany of the law. Fire is the first creature that, if it is to be born and grow, must devour the two pieces of wood that generated it. And this birth of fire has a strong sexual valence, because the seed of the flame issues from rubbing—and if we wish to take this psychoanalytic interpretation even further, we could recall Freud's view that "the control of fire could be gained only after man had renounced the homosexually tinged pleasure of extinguishing it with urine." Mastery of it meant foregoing our biological drives.

Fire serves as a metaphor for many drives, from burning rages to flames of amorous infatuation; fire is metaphorically present in every discourse on the passions, just as it is always metaphorically linked with life through the color it shares with blood. Fire as energy accomplishes the maceration of nutritional matter we call digestion, and like the feeding process it must be continuously fueled.

Fire is the immediate instrument of all transformation and is called for when something needs to be changed. To keep a fire from going out, it must be cared for like a newborn child. The contradictions of our life instantly emerge in fire: it is an element that gives life and also one that gives death, destruction, and suffering. It is a symbol of purity and purification but also produces filth, leaving ashes as its excrement.

Fire can be a light so dazzlingly bright that you cannot look at it directly, any more than you can look at the sun. But when properly tamed, as when it becomes candlelight, it regales us with a play of light and shade, nocturnal vigils in the course of which a solitary flame induces our fancy to wander, with its gleaming rays that fade away in the darkness, and at the same time the candle hints at a source of life and a sun that is dying. Fire is born from matter and is transformed into an ever lighter and airier substance, from the red or bluish flame at its base to the white flame at its tip, until it fades away in smoke. In this sense, fire is ascensional in nature, it reminds us of transcendence, and yet, perhaps because we have learned that it lives in the heart of the earth from where it spews out only when volcanos erupt, it is a symbol of infernal depths. It is life but it is also the experience of life's quenching and constant fragility.

And, to sum things up with Gaston Bachelard, I would like to quote from his *Psychoanalysis of Fire*:

> From the notched teeth of the chimney hook there hung the black cauldron. The three-legged cooking pot projected over the hot embers. Puffing up her cheeks to blow into the steel tube, my grandmother would rekindle the sleeping flames. Everything would be cooking at the same time: the potatoes for the pigs, the choice potatoes for the family. For me there would be a fresh egg cooking under the ashes. The intensity of a fire cannot be measured by the egg timer; the egg was done when a drop of water, often a drop of saliva, would evaporate on the shell. Recently I was very much surprised to read that

Denis Papin used the same procedure as my grandmother in tending his cooking pot. Before getting my egg I was condemned to eat a soup of bread and butter boiled to a pulp. . . . But on days when I was on my good behavior, they would bring out the waffle iron. Rectangular in form, it would crush down the fire of thorns burning red as the spikes of sword lilies. And soon the gaufre or waffle would be pressed against my pinafore, warmer to the fingers than to the lips. Yes, then indeed I was eating fire, eating its gold, its odor and even its crackling while the burning gaufre was crunching under my teeth. And it is always like that, through a kind of extra pleasure—like dessert—that fire shows itself a friend of man.

Fire is therefore too many things and—as well as being a physical phenomenon—it becomes a symbol, and like all symbols it is ambiguous, polysemic, and evokes different meanings according to the situation. So I will not attempt a psychoanalysis of fire here, but a rough and ready semiotics, trying to seek out the various meanings it has acquired for all of us who warm ourselves with it and sometimes die from it.

Fire as a Divine Element

Since our first experience of fire is indirect, through sunlight, and direct, through lightning bolts and uncontrollable blazes, fire clearly had to be associated with divinity from the beginning, and in all primitive religions we find some kind of fire cult, from the greeting extended to the rising sun to tending the sacred fire that must never go out in the penetralia of the temple.

In the Bible fire is always the epiphanic image of the divinity: Elijah was carried off on a chariot of fire, and the just will rejoice amid the splendor of fire (Judges 5:31: So perish all thine enemies, O Lord, but let them that love him be as the sun when he goeth forth in all his might; *Daniel* 12:3: And they that be wise shall shine as the brightness of the firmament; and they that turn many to righteousness as the stars for ever and ever; *Wisdom* 3:7: In the time of their visitation they will shine forth, and will run like sparks among the stubble). The Fathers of the Church refer to Christ as *lampas, lucifer, lumen, lux, oriens, sol iustitiae, sol novus, and stella.*

The first, philosophers thought of fire as a cosmic principle. According to Aristotle, Heraclitus thought that fire was the *archè*, the origin of all things, and in some fragments it seems that Heraclitus actually supported this idea. He is believed to have said that in all eras the universe is renewed through fire, that there is a reciprocal exchange of all things with fire and vice-versa, like goods for gold and gold for goods. According to Diogenes Laertius, he also claimed that all things are formed from fire and return to fire— that all things are, by condensation or rarefaction, mutations of fire (which on condensing becomes moisture, which on consolidating becomes earth, which in its turn liquefies into water, allowing the water to produce luminous evaporation that fuels new fire). But, alas, it is well known that Heraclitus was obscure by definition, and that the lord whose oracle is in Delphi neither reveals nor conceals, but shows things through signs. Many believe that the references to fire were merely metaphors to express the extreme mutability of all things. In other words, *panta rhei*, everything flows, and not only (I might add) can we never step in the same river twice, we can never be burned twice by the same flame.

Perhaps the finest identification of fire with the divine is found in the works of Plotinus. Fire is the manifestation of divinity precisely because, paradoxically, the One from which all things emanate and of which nothing can be said does not move or consume itself in the act of creation. And it is possible to conceive of this "First" only as if it were an irradiation that spreads out from itself, like the brilliant light that encircles the sun and irradiates it in an ever-changing way, while the sun remains exactly as it was, without consuming itself (*Fifth Ennead*, tractate 1, section 6).

And if things are born from an irradiation, nothing on earth can be more beautiful than the very image of divine irradiation: fire. The beauty of a color, which is a simple thing, springs from a form that conquers the darkness of matter and from the presence in the color of an incorporeal light, which is its formal reason. This is why fire is more beautiful in itself than any other body, because it has the intangibility of form: it is the lightest of all bodies, to the point that it is almost intangible. It always remains pure, because it does not hold within itself the other elements that make up matter, whereas all the other elements hold fire within themselves: they, in fact, can be warmed, whereas fire cannot be cooled. Thanks to its nature, only fire has colors and all other things receive form and color from it, and when they move away from the light of the fire they are no longer beautiful.

The works of Pseudo-Dionysius the Areopagite (who lived from the fifth to the sixth century), which influenced all of medieval aesthetics, are Neo-Platonic in nature. This can be seen from the *Celestial Hierarchy* (XV):

> I think, then, the similitude of fire denotes the likeness of the Heavenly Minds to God in the highest degree; for the holy theologians frequently describe the superessential and form-less essence by fire, as having many likenesses, if I may be permitted to say so, of the supremely Divine property, as in things visible. For the sensible fire is, so to speak, in everything, and

passes through everything unmingled, and springs from all, and whilst all-luminous, is, as it were, hidden, unknown, in its essential nature, when there is no material lying near it upon which it may shew its proper energy. It is both uncontrollable and invisible, self-subduing all things.

Together with the concept of proportion, medieval ideas of beauty were dominated by that of *claritas* and light. Films and role-playing games encourage us to think of the Middle Ages as a succession of "dark" centuries, not only metaphorically but in terms of nocturnal colors and gloomy shadows. Nothing could be further from the truth. The people of the Middle Ages certainly lived in dark places, forests, castle halls, and cramped rooms feebly illuminated by firelight; but apart from the fact that they were folk who went to bed early and were more accustomed to the day rather than the night (something that the Romantics liked so much), they portrayed themselves in vivid colors.

In poetry this sense of brilliant color was ever present: grass is green, blood is red, milk is pure white, and, according to the poet Guinizelli, a beautiful woman has a "snow-white face tinged with carmine" (and, later, we find Petrarch's "clear, fresh, sweet waters").

Nor should we forget those visions of dazzling light in Dante's *Paradiso*, whose finest portrayal we owe, oddly enough, to the nineteenth-century artist Doré, who tried (as best he could, but failed) to depict that refulgence, those swirls of flame, those flashes, those suns, the clarity that arises "as the horizon, at the rising sun, grows brighter," those white roses, those rubicund flowers that shine out in the third part of Dante's work, where the vision of God appears as an ecstasy of fire:

In the deep, transparent essence of the lofty Light
there appeared to me three circles
having three colors but the same extent,
and each one seemed reflected by the other
as rainbow is by rainbow, while the third one seemed fire,
equally breathed forth by one and by the other.

The Middle Ages were dominated by a cosmology of light. In the ninth century, in John Scotus Eriugena's *Commentary on the Celestial Hierarchy*, it is said that:

This universal factory of the world is a very great lamp made up of many parts like many lights to reveal the pure species of intelligible things and to see them in the mind's eye, filling the hearts of the wise faithful with divine grace and the aid of reason. This therefore is why the theologian calls God the Father of Lights, since all things come from Him, through which and in which He reveals himself and in the light of the lamp of his wisdom he unifies and makes them.

Between the twelfth and the thirteenth century, the cosmology of light proposed by Robert Grosseteste evolved into an image of the universe formed by a single flow of luminous energy, a source both of beauty and being, leading us to think of a kind of Big Bang. From this single light the astral spheres and the natural zones of the elements were gradually derived through rarefaction and con- densation, and consequently the infinite shades of color and the volumes of things. Saint Bonaventure of Bagnoregio was later to say in his *Commentary on the Sentences* that light is the common nature found in every body, be it celestial or earthly, and is the substantial form of bodies, which, the more light they possess, the more truly and worthily they are a part of being.

Hellfire

But even though fire moves through the sky to reach us, it also erupts from the bowels of the Earth, sowing death and destruction, and this explains why fire has been associated with the infernal realms since earliest times.

In the Book of Job (41:1–27), from the mouth of Leviathan "go burning lamps, and sparks of fire leap out. . . . His breath kindleth coals, and a flame goeth out of his mouth." In the Book of Revelation, when the seventh seal is broken, hail and fire come to devastate the earth, the bottomless pit opens, and smoke and locusts emerge from it; the four angels, released from the river Euphrates to which they were bound, lead countless armies whose soldiers wear breastplates of fire. And when the Lamb reappears and the supreme judge arrives on a white cloud, the sun burns up the survivors. And, after Armageddon, the Beast will be plunged together with the false prophet into a lake of fire and burning sulfur.

According to the Gospels, sinners are hurled into the fires of Gehenna (Matthew 13:40–42):

> As therefore the tares are gathered and burned in the fire; so shall it be in the end of this world. The Son of man shall send forth his angels, and they shall gather out of his kingdom all things that offend, and them which do iniquity; And shall cast them into a furnace of fire: there shall be wailing and gnashing of teeth.

Oddly, there is less fire in Dante's hell than one might think, because the poet does his utmost to come up with a range of diverse torments, but we can be content with heretics lying in fiery graves, men of violence plunged into a river of boiling blood, blasphemers, sodomites, and usurers pelted by fiery rain, simoniacs stuck head down in pits with their feet ablaze, and barrators submerged in boiling pitch.

Hellfire was certainly far more marked in Baroque texts, where descriptions of the torments of hell exceed the violence of Dante, also because they are unredeemed by artistic inspiration. As in this page from Saint Alphonsus Liguori (*Apparecchio alla morte*, 1758, XXVI):

The punishment that most torments the senses of the damned is hellfire. . . . Even in this world the pain of fire is the greatest of all; but there is a vast difference between our fire and the fire of hell, which according to Augustine makes ours seem as if painted. . . . The damned souls will be surrounded by fire, like logs in a furnace. They will find themselves with an abyss of fire below, an abyss above, and an abyss all around. If they touch, see or breathe; they will touch, see or breathe only fire. They will swim in fire as fish swim in water. But this fire will not merely be all around the damned, it will also penetrate their entrails whence it will torment them. Their bodies will become nothing but fire, so that their bowels will burn in their belly, their heart in their breast, their brain in their head, their blood in their veins, even the marrow in their bones: all damned souls will become a furnace of fire in themselves.

And Ercole Mattioli, in *Pietà illustrata* (1694), wrote:

In the opinion of the gravest of theologians, a great prodigy will be that a single fire will contain within itself the cold of ice, the sting of thorns and iron, the gall of asps, the venom of vipers, the cruelty of all wild beasts, the malevolence of all the elements and the stars. . . . A greater prodigy, however, *et supra virtutem ignis,* will be that such fire, even though a single kind, can make distinctions and hence torment most those who have sinned most; Tertullian called this fire *sapiens ignis* and Eusebius of Emesa named it *ignis arbiter,* because as it must match the greatness and diversity of the torments with the greatness and diversity of the sins . . . and almost as if it had reason and full knowledge to distinguish between one sinner and another, the fire will make the harshness of its rigors felt to a greater or lesser degree.

And this brings us to the revelation of the last secret of Fatima on the part of Sister Lucia, former shepherd girl:

The secret comprises three parts, of which I shall reveal two. The first was the vision of hell. Our Lady showed us a huge lake of fire, which seemed to be under the ground. Amid this fire, demons and souls in human form, blackish or bronze in color but transparent, fluttered amid the blaze where, borne up by flames that came from their own bodies together with clouds of smoke, they fell all around like the sparks that fall from great conflagrations, with neither weight nor balance, amid shrieks and groans of suffering and desperation that chilled our blood and made us tremble with fear. The demons could be distinguished by their horrid and revolting resemblance to terrifying unknown animals, but black and transparent.

Alchemical Fire

Midway between heavenly fire and hellfire we find fire as an alchemical agent. Fire and the crucible seem to be essential to the alchemical process, the aim of which is to subject *materia prima*, or first matter, to a series of operations with a view to obtaining from it the philosopher's stone, which can effect projection—that is to say, the transmutation of base metals into gold.

The manipulations of first matter involve three phases, characterized by the color that the matter gradually takes on: the black work, the white work, and the red work. The black work calls for cooking (and therefore the intervention of fire) and the decomposition of the matter; the white work is a process of sublimation or distillation; and the red work is the final stage (red is the color of the sun, which often stands for gold, or vice-versa). The essential instrument of manipulation is the hermetic furnace, the *athanor*, but other equipment used includes alembics, vessels, and mortars, all known by symbolic names such as the philosopher's egg, maternal womb, bridal chamber, pelican, sphere, sepulchre, and so on. The basic substances are sulfur, mercury, and salt. But the procedures are never clear, because the language of alchemists is based on three principles:

1. Since the object of the art is the greatest of secrets and cannot be revealed—the secret of secrets—no expression ever says what it seems to say, and no symbolic interpretation will ever be definitive, because the secret will always lie elsewhere: "Poor fool! Are you so ingenuous as to believe that we would openly teach you the greatest and the most important of secrets? I assure you that anyone wishing to explain the writings of the Hermetic Philosophers in accordance with their

ordinary and literal meaning will soon find himself in the twists and turns of a labyrinth from which he cannot escape, nor will he have an Ariadne's thread to show him the way out" (*The Secret Book of Artephius*, c. 1150).

2. When it seems that they are speaking of ordinary substances, gold, silver, or mercury, they are really talking about the gold and mercury of the Philosophers, which are a different matter altogether.

3. While no account ever says what it seems to say, conversely, all accounts will always regard the same secret. As it says in the thirteenth-century *Turba Philosophorum*: "Know that we are all in agreement, whatever we say. . . . One clarifies what the other has concealed and he who really searches can find everything."

At what point does fire come into the alchemical process? If we take alchemical fire to be analogous to the fire that governs digestion or gestation, it ought to come into play in the course of the black work—that is, when heat, acting on and against viscous, oily, radical, metallic humidity, produces *nigredo*. If we are to believe a text such as the *Dictionnaire Mytho-Hermétique* of Dom Pernety (1787), this is how it goes:

> when heat acts on these materials, they turn first into powder and an oily, viscous water that rises vaporous to the top of the vessel and then falls back down to the base as dew or rain, where it becomes almost like a black, oily broth. That is why this process has been described as sublimation and volatilization, ascension and descension. When it has coagulated, the water becomes first like black pitch, which is why it has been called fetid, stinking earth, and also because it gives off the stench of mold, tomb, and sepulchre.

But the literature contains statements to the effect that the terms distillation, sublimation, calcination, or digestion and cooking, reverberation, dissolution, descension, and coagulation are none other than a single "Operation," carried out in the same vessel—in other words, a cooking of the matter. So, Pernety concludes:

> it is necessary to consider and hold this Operation to be one but expressed in different terms; and it will be understood that all the following expressions always mean the same thing: to distil in the alembic; to separate the soul from the body; to burn, calcinate; to unite the elements; to convert them; to turn one into the other; to corrupt; to fuse; to generate; to conceive; to bring into the world; to attain; to moisten; to wash with fire; to beat with the hammer; to blacken; to putrefy; to rubify; to dissolve; to sublimate; to crush; to reduce to powder; to pound in the mortar; to pulverize on marble—and many other similar expressions all mean merely to cook through the same regime, down to dark red. Care must be taken, therefore, not to remove the vessel and take it off the fire, for if the matter were to cool, all would be lost (*Règles Générales*, 202–206).

So what kind of fire are we talking about, given that different treatises speak variously of fire of Persia, fire of Egypt, fire of the Indies, elemental fire, natural fire, artificial fire, fire of ashes, fire of sand, fire of filings, fire of fusion, fire of flames, fire against nature, Algir fire, Azothic fire, celestial fire, corrosive fire, fire of matter, fire of lion, fire of putrefaction, dragon fire, manure fire, et cetera, et cetera?

Fire keeps the furnace hot at all times, from the beginning to the red work. But could not the term *fire* also be a metaphor for the red matter that appears during the alchemical process? Here, according to Pernety again, are some names for the red stone: red gum, red oil, ruby, vitriol, ashes of tartar, red body, fruit, red stone, red magnesium, starry stone, red salt, red sulfur, blood, poppy, red wine, red vitriol, cochineal, and, naturally, "fire, fire of nature" (*Signes*, 187–189).

Alchemists have always worked with fire and fire is the basis of alchemical practice, yet it is fire that constitutes one of the most impenetrable mysteries of alchemy. Since I have never produced gold, I am unable to provide an answer to this problem and so I will move on to another type of fire, another alchemy, the artistic kind, where fire becomes the instrument of a new genesis and the artist sets himself up as an imitator of the gods.

Fire as the Cause of Art

In *Protagoras*, Plato says:

> Once upon a time, there were gods but no mortal creatures. And when the preordained time of their birth came, the gods molded them within the earth, combining earth and fire and all the compounds of earth and fire. When they were ready to lead the creatures into the light, they ordered Prometheus and Epimetheus to equip them and distribute abilities to each as was fitting. But Epimetheus begged Prometheus to let him make the allotment himself, saying, "When I've made the allotment, you can look it over." Once he'd persuaded him, Epimetheus made the allotment. And in making the allotment, he gave strength without speed to some, but he decked the weaker ones out with speed. He gave weapons to some, but for the weaponless, he came up with some other capacity for

their preservation. Those he'd made small, he gave wings or an underground home as an escape, while those he'd made large—that's just how he kept them safe. He gave out everything else in the same way, ensuring a balance. . . . And when he had supplied them to avoid mutual destruction, he also came up with protection against the elements by covering them with thick hair and solid hides, which were up to the task of staving off winter cold and burning heat alike. And when each creature went to sleep, these same things would serve as its very own natural bedding. And under their feet, he gave some hooves and others firm, bloodless skin. Next, he provided different food for different creatures: for some, the grass of the earth, for others, the fruit of the trees, and for others still, roots. But there were others whom he gave the meat of other animals as food. These he made less fertile, while he made their prey very prolific to ensure the preservation of their kind.

As you know, Epimetheus wasn't exactly the smartest guy around, so he didn't realize that he had already used up all the powers on irrational creatures. He was left with the human race lacking proper arrangements and had no idea what he could do for them. So when Prometheus came to look over the allotment, he found a clueless Epimetheus and saw that the other animals were cared for and had everything, while human beings didn't have clothes or shoes, shelter, or defense. . . . So Prometheus, getting nowhere with figuring out how to save humans, went and stole the technical knowledge from Hephaistos and Athena, along with fire—since you can't get this knowledge or use it without fire—and he gave them as a gift to mankind.

The conquest of fire marked the birth of the arts, at least in the Greek sense of technical skills, and hence mankind's dominion over nature. It is a pity that Plato had not read Lévi-Strauss and had not also said that with the introduction of fire came the cooking of food, but basically cooking is an art and so it was covered by the Platonic notion of *techne*.

Just how much fire has to do with the arts is explained very well by Benvenuto Cellini in his *Life* (1567), where he tells us how he cast his *Perseus*, covering it with a clay tunic and then using a slow fire to draw off the wax,

> which escaped through many air-vents I had made because, the more of them you make, the better the molds will be filled. And once I had finished draining the wax, I made a furnace shaped like a funnel around my Perseus with bricks laid one atop the other in such a way as to leave many spaces so that the fire might breathe better: after that I began to stoke it assiduously with logs and kept it burning constantly for two days and two nights; then, after having drained all the wax, and on seeing that the said mold had been baked perfectly, I immediately began to dig a ditch in which to bury my mold, using all the fine techniques that this beautiful art commands. . . . And having straightened it perfectly so that it was hanging over the center of the ditch, I gradually lowered it to the bottom of the furnace. . . . When I saw it was perfectly stable and that the little tubes for venting the air were in place . . . I turned to my furnace, which I had filled with numerous blocks of copper and pieces of bronze and set them in accordance with the rules of the art, namely one on top of the other to allow the flames of the fire to pass through and

make the metal heat up and liquefy quicker. Then I called out loudly for the fire to be lit. And what with the mass of pine logs full of the oily resin that the tree produces, and because my little furnace was so well made, things worked only too well, so well that . . . the workshop caught fire and we feared the roof might fall in upon us; on the other hand, the heavens sent down so much wind and rain from the side toward the kitchen garden that my furnace cooled down. So, after struggling with these adverse mishaps for several hours, battling fatigue so fiercely that even my strong constitution could no longer resist, I was seized by a sudden and unimaginably high fever, and so I was obliged to take to my bed.

And so, what with accidental fires and artificial fires, after much planning the statue took shape.

While fire is a divine element, at the same time by learning to make fire mankind mastered a power that until then had been reserved for the gods, and so even the fires men lit in the temples are the effect of an act of pride. Greek civilization immediately associated the conquest of fire with this connotation of pride and it is curious how all the celebrations of Prometheus, not only in Greek tragedy, but also in the art that came after it, do not dwell so much on the gift of fire but on the punishment that came in its wake.

Fire as Epiphanic Experience

When artists accept and recognize with pride and hubris that they are similar to the gods, and see the work of art as a substitute for divine creation, then with the advent of the decadent sensibility comparisons between the aesthetic experience and fire and between fire and epiphany begin to make headway.

The concept (if not the term) of epiphany arose with Walter Pater and his "Conclusion" to *The Renaissance* (1873). It is no accident that the famous conclusion begins with a quotation from Heraclitus. Reality is a sum of forces and elements that come into being and gradually decline, and only superficial experience makes them seem solid and fixed in an importunate presence: "But when reflection begins to play upon those objects they are dissipated under its influence; the cohesive force seems suspended like some trick of magic." We are, then, in a world of unstable, fleeting, incoherent impressions: custom is broken, everyday life is rendered vain, and of this, beyond this, there remain only single moments that may be grasped for an instant before they instantly fade away.

> Every moment some form grows perfect in hand or face; some tone on the hills or the sea is choicer than the rest; some mood of passion or insight or intellectual excitement is irresistibly real and attractive to us—for that moment only. . . .
>
> To maintain this ecstasy is success in life . . .
>
> While all melts under our feet, we may well grasp at any exquisite passion, or any contribution to knowledge that seems by a lifted horizon to set the spirit free for a moment, or any stirring of the senses, strange dyes, strange colors, and curious odors, or work of the artist's hands, or the face of one's friend.

All decadent writers describe aesthetic and sensual ecstasy as something radiant. But perhaps the first to link aesthetic ecstasy to the idea of fire was Gabriel D'Annunzio, who we are not so banal as to connect solely with the tired old idea that flame is beautiful. The idea of aesthetic ecstasy as the experience of fire appears in D'Annunzio's novel *The Flame* (1900). The main character, Stelio Effrena, sees the beauty of Venice in terms of fire:

> Every instant, then, pulsed through things like an unbearable flash of light. From the crosses standing on top of cupolas swollen with prayer to the fragile salt crystals hanging beneath the bridges, all things shone in a supreme exultation of light. As the lookout on the battlement's piercing cry warns of the gathering storm below, so, wreathed in flame, the golden angel on the highest tower finally proclaimed His coming. And He came. He came sitting on a cloud as on a chariot of fire, the hem of his purple raiment trailing behind him.

Inspired by *The Flame*, which he had read and loved, here is the greatest exponent of the epiphany, James Joyce: "By an epiphany [Stephen] meant a sudden spiritual manifestation, whether in the vulgarity of speech or of gesture or in a memorable phrase of the mind itself" (*Stephen Hero*, 1944). In Joyce this experience always appears as a fiery experience. The word "fire" appears in *A Portrait of the Artist as a Young Man* (1916) fifty-five times, "flame" and "flaming" thirty-five times, not to mention other associated terms such as "radiance" or "splendor." In *The Flame* Foscarina listens to Stelio and feels "drawn to an atmosphere as fiery as a forge." For Stephen Dedalus aesthetic ecstasy always appears as a blazing radiance, and is expressed through solar metaphors, and it is the same for Stelio Effrena. Let's compare only two passages.

D'Annunzio, in *The Flame*:

The boat veered violently. A miracle caught it. The first rays of the sun pierced the flapping sail, struck the angels on the campaniles of San Marco and San Giorgio Maggiore, set alight the sphere of the Fortuna and crowned with lightning flashes the five domes of the Basilica. . . . Glory to the Miracle! A superhuman feeling of power and liberty swelled the young man's heart, just as the wind swelled the sail that was transfigured for him. In the deep red splendor of the sail he stood as if in the deep red splendor of his own blood.

And Joyce, in the *Portrait*:

His thinking was a dusk of doubt and selfmistrust, lit up at moments by the lightnings of intuition, but lightnings of so clear a splendor that in those moments the world perished about his feet as if it had been fireconsumed: and thereafter his tongue grew heavy and he met the eyes of others with unanswering eyes, for he felt that the spirit of beauty had folded him round like a mantle.

Regenerating Fire

We have seen that, for Heraclitus, the universe is regenerated in all ages through fire. The person who seems to have had greater familiarity with fire was Empedocles, who, perhaps to become a god or to convince his followers that he had become one, threw himself (according to some) into Etna. This final purification, this desire for annihilation in fire, has seduced the poets of all ages. We need only consider Hölderlin's words in *The Death of Empedocles* (1798):

Have you not seen? They are recurring
The lovely times of my entire life again today
And something greater still is yet to come;
Then upward, son, upward to the very peak
Of ancient holy Etna, that is where we'll go,
For gods have greater presence on the heights.
With my own eyes this very day I shall survey
The streams and islands and the sea.
And may the sunlight, hovering golden over all
These waters, deign to bless me in departure,
The splendid youthful light of day, which in
My youth I loved. Then all about us both
Eternal stars will scintillate in silence as
The glowing magma surges from volcanic depths
And tenderly the all-impelling spirit of the ether will
Arrive and touch us. Oh, then!

Between Heraclitus and Empedocles, however, we find another
aspect of fire, seen not only as a creative element but also as one
that destroys and regenerates at the same time. The Stoics talked
of *ekpyrosis* as a universal conflagration (or fire and the end of the
world) in which all things, since they derive from fire, return to
it at the end of their cycle of evolution. In itself the notion of *ekpyrosis* by no means suggests that purification through fire can be
attained by man's design or efforts. But underlying many sacrifices
based on fire there certainly is an idea according to which fire purifies and regenerates things by destroying them. Hence the sa-
crality of the stake.

Past centuries are full of burnings at the stake, and not only of
medieval heretics but also of witches in the modern world, at least

until the eighteenth century. And it is only D'Annunzio's aestheticism that had Mila de Codro say that flames are beautiful. The fires that punished so many heretics were horrible, also because they followed other tortures, and it suffices to read the description (in the *History of Fra Dolcino, Heresiarch*, twelfth century) of Dolcino's torture and execution, when along with his wife Margherita he was handed over to the secular authorities. While the city bells rang the tocsin, they were placed on a cart, surrounded by their torturers and followed by the militia, which made its way clear across the town while at every corner the flesh of the offenders was torn by red hot pincers. Margherita was burned first, in front of Dolcino, whose face remained completely impassive, just as he had not cried out when the pincers tore his limbs. Then the cart continued on its way, while the torturers thrust their irons into vats of burning feces. Dolcino was subjected to other tortures, and never made a sound, except when they cut off his nose, making him shrug a little, and when they tore off his manhood, for at that point he gave a long sigh, like a groan. His last words smacked of impenitence, and he warned them that he would arise again on the third day. Then he was burned and his ashes scattered to the winds.

For the inquisitors of all periods, race and religion, fire purifies not only the sins of humanity, but also those of books. There are many stories of book burnings, some out of neglect, others out of ignorance, but others again, like the Nazi bonfires, in an attempt to purify and eliminate all evidence of degenerate art.

For reasons of morality and for the sake of his sanity, Don Quixote's zealous friends burned his collection of romances. The library in Elias Canetti's *Auto-da-fé* (1935) also burns in a manner reminiscent of Empedocles's sacrifice ("when the flames finally reach him he laughs loudly, as he has never laughed in all his life").

Books condemned to disappear are also burned in Ray Bradbury's *Fahrenheit 451* (1953) while the library in the abbey in my own novel *The Name of the Rose* (1980) meets a similar fate, by chance, although the original cause was censorship.

In his *Universal History of the Destruction of Books* (2007), Fernando Báez asks himself why fire has been the dominant factor in the destruction of books. He answers:

> Fire is salvation, and for that reason, almost all religions dedicate fires to their respective divinities. This power to conserve life is also a destructive power. When man destroys with fire, he plays God, master of the fire of life and death. And in this way he identifies with a purifying solar cult and with the great myth of destruction that almost always takes place through fire. The reason for using fire is obvious: it reduces the spirit of a work to matter.

Contemporary Ekpyrosis

Fire is a destroyer in every episode of war, from the fabled Greek Fire of the Byzantines (a military secret if ever there was one, and I would like to mention the fine novel dedicated to it: Luigi Malerba's *Il fuoco greco* of 1990) to the chance discovery of gunpowder by the monk Berthold Schwarz, who died in a personal and punitive *ekpyrosis*. Fire is the punishment for those who play a double game in times of war and "Fire!" is the command given to all firing squads, as if invoking the origin of life in order to expedite its end. But perhaps the fire of war that has horrified humanity the most—I mean all of humanity, aware for the first time all over the world of what was going on in one part of it—was the explosion of the atomic bomb.

One of the pilots who dropped the bomb on Nagasaki wrote that "suddenly, the light of a thousand suns illuminated the cockpit. Even with my dark welder's goggles, I winced and shut my eyes for a couple of seconds." The Bhagavad-Gita says, "if the radiance of a thousand suns were to burst at once into the sky that would be like the splendor of the Mighty One. . . . I am become Death, the shatterer of worlds." And this was the verse that came to Robert Oppenheimer's mind after the explosion of the first atomic bomb.

And with this, we come close to the dramatic end of my speech and—in a more reasonable span of time, to the end of the human adventure on Earth or Earth's adventure in the cosmos. Because never have three of the primordial elements been so threatened as they are today: the air killed by pollution and carbon dioxide, the water, which is contaminated on the one hand and getting scarcer and scarcer on the other. The only winner is fire, in the form of a heat that is parching the earth and upsetting the seasons, and which by melting the glaciers will invite the sea to invade it. All unawares, we are marching toward the first true *ekpyrosis*. While America and China reject the Kyoto Protocol, we are heading for death by fire. And it matters little to us if the universe will regenerate itself after our holocaust, because it will not be ours.

In his *Fire Sermon,* the Buddha warned:

All things, O priests, are on fire. And what, O priests, are all these things which are on fire? The eye, O priests, is on fire; forms are on fire; eye-consciousness is on fire; impressions received by the eye are on fire; and whatever sensation, pleasant, unpleasant, or indifferent, originates in dependence on impressions received by the eye, that also is on fire. And with what are these on fire? With the fire of passion, say I, with the fire of hatred, with the fire of infatuation; with birth, old age, death, sorrow, lamentation, misery, grief, and despair are they on fire.

The ear is on fire; sounds are on fire ... the nose is on fire; odors are on fire ... the tongue is on fire; tastes are on fire ... the mind is on fire; ideas are on fire ... mind-consciousness is on fire; impressions received by the mind are on fire; and whatever sensation, pleasant, unpleasant, or indifferent, originates in dependence on impressions received by the mind, that also is on fire.

Perceiving this, O priests, the learned and noble disciple conceives an aversion for the eye, conceives an aversion for forms, conceives an aversion for eye-consciousness, conceives an aversion for the impressions received by the eye; and whatever sensation, pleasant, unpleasant, or indifferent, originates in dependence on impressions received by the eye, for that also he conceives an aversion. Conceives an aversion for the ear, conceives an aversion for sounds ... conceives an aversion for the nose, conceives an aversion for odors ... conceives an aversion for the tongue, conceives an aversion for tastes ... conceives an aversion for the body, conceives an aversion for things tangible ... conceives an aversion for the mind, conceives an aversion for ideas, conceives an aversion for mind-consciousness, conceives an aversion for the impressions received by the mind; and whatever sensation, pleasant, unpleasant, or indifferent.

But humankind has been unable (at least in part) to give up its attachment to its own smells, tastes, sounds, and tactile pleasures—and to making fire through friction. Perhaps we should have left its production to the gods, who would have given it to us only occasionally, in the form of lightning bolts.

[La Milanesiana, 2008]

6. The Invisible

Thus far I have developed topics such as the absolute, ugliness, and fire. This time, the theme is the invisible: How can you show what cannot be seen?

In this case, I will talk about the fact that we do see some curious entities that are not *natural*—if by that term we mean beings produced by nature, such as trees and humans. There are other entities that live among us that we talk about as if they were real. I am referring to beings in stories—or better, the fictional characters we encounter in literature.

Fictional characters are inventions of the imagination, and therefore common sense tells us they are nonexistent and cannot be seen. But they are also invisible in the sense that they are not expressed through images but through words, and frequently those words neglect to describe their physical characteristics in much detail.

Yet these characters exist in some way outside the novels that have introduced them to us, and they can live anew through countless images of all kinds. So I am going to resort to images of many invisible things and this will not be a simple rhetorical stratagem. The fact is that some fictional characters have become highly visible because of the many portrayals we have made of them outside the texts in which they came into being. What does it mean for the character created by a text to live outside it? If you think about it, this is no mean problem.

Tolstoy does not tell us much about the physical aspect of Anna Karenina beyond that she was beautiful and charming. Let's read the descriptive passages:

> Vronsky . . . felt he must glance at her once more; not because she was very beautiful, not on account of the elegance and modest grace which were apparent in her whole figure, but because in the expression of her charming face, as she passed close by him, there was something peculiarly caressing and soft. As he looked round, she too turned her head. Her shining grey eyes, that looked dark from the thick lashes, rested with friendly attention on his face, as though she were recognizing him . . . .

> Kitty had been seeing Anna every day; she adored her, and had pictured her invariably in lilac. But now seeing her in black, she felt that she had not fully seen her charm. She saw her now as someone quite new and surprising to her. Now she understood that Anna could not have been in lilac, and that her charm was just that she always stood out against her attire, that her dress could never be noticeable on her. And her black dress, with its sumptuous lace, was not noticeable on her; it was only the frame, and all that was seen was she—simple, natural, elegant, and at the same time gay and eager. . . .

She was fascinating in her simple black dress, fascinating were her round arms with their bracelets, fascinating was her firm neck with its thread of pearls, fascinating the straying curls of her loose hair, fascinating the graceful, light movements of her little feet and hands, fascinating was that lovely face in its eagerness, but there was something terrible and cruel in her fascination.

The description could equally be applied to Sophia Loren, Nicole Kidman, Michelle Obama, or Carla Bruni. And we know how many Kareninas have come down to us from the tradition.

Not bad for an invisible person.

In 1860, after setting sail to join Garibaldi in Sicily, Alexandre Dumas stopped over in Marseilles and visited the Château d'If where, before becoming the Count of Monte Cristo, his character Edmond Dantès had been imprisoned for fourteen years, and had been visited in his cell by the abbé Faria. In the course of his visit, Dumas discovered that visitors were shown the Count's cell and the guides talked about him and Faria as if they had actually existed in history, whereas they neglected to mention real historical figures such as Mirabeau who had been imprisoned there.

Dumas remarked on this in his memoirs: "One of the privileges novelists enjoy is creating characters who kill off those of the historians. The reason is that historians call up mere ghosts while novelists create people in flesh and blood."

The Polish philosopher Roman Ingarden claimed that, in ontological terms, fictional characters are *not fully determined*—in other words, we know few of their properties—whereas real people are *fully determined* and we can predicate their every difference. I think he was wrong: in reality no one can list all the properties of a given individual, because they are potentially infinite, whereas the properties of fictional characters are strictly limited by the text that talks about them—and only those properties mentioned by the text count for their identification.

And in truth, I know Alessandro Manzoni's character in *The Betrothed*, Renzo Tramaglino, better than my father. As far as my father is concerned, there are episodes in his life—goodness knows how many—that I do not know and will never know. There were secret thoughts he never expressed, anxieties he concealed, fears and joys he left unsaid. So, like Dumas's historians, I shall continue to call up this dear ghost to wonder about. Conversely, I know everything about Renzo Tramaglino that I ought to know. Whatever things Manzoni has not told me about him are irrelevant to me, just as they are to Manzoni and for that matter to Renzo, inasmuch as he is a fictional character.

Is this how things really are? Precisely because it tells us about invented things, which are therefore never verified in the real world, a statement in a novel should always be false. Yet we do not consider statements in novels as lies, nor do we accuse Homer or Cervantes of having been liars. We know perfectly well that in reading a work of fiction we make a tacit pact with the author, who *pretends* to say something true and *we pretend* to take him or her seriously. In doing this, every fictional statement designs and constructs a possible world and all our judgments on truth and falsehood will refer not to the real world but to the possible world of the fictional one. So it is false in the possible world of Arthur Conan Doyle to say that Sherlock Holmes lived on the banks of Spoon River, and in Tolstoy's possible world it is false to say that Anna Karenina lived in Baker Street.

There are many possible worlds: for example, there is the possible world of my desires in which I imagine what would happen if I were shipwrecked on an uninhabited Polynesian island with

Sharon Stone. Every possible world is by nature incomplete or chooses as its background many aspects of the real world: in the world of my fantasies, were I shipwrecked in Polynesia with Sharon Stone, the island would certainly have a crown of palm trees around a beach of white sand and other such things that I might encounter in the real world.

Fictional possible worlds never take as their background a universe that is too different from the one in which we live, not even fairy tales, in which the forest—even though there are talking animals in it—is still like the ones in our real world. The Sherlock Holmes stories are set in a London as it is or was, and we would find it disconcerting if Doctor Watson suddenly crossed Saint James Park to visit an Eiffel Tower on the Danube by the corner of Nevsky Prospekt. A writer might even introduce to us a possible world of this kind but she would have to employ many narrative artifices to make us accept it (for example, by introducing a phenomenon such as a space-time warp or something of that sort). Ultimately, if the story is to have any zest, the Eiffel Tower has to be the one in Paris.

Sometimes a fictional world can reveal conspicuous contradictions with respect to the real world. For example, in *A Winter's Tale*, Shakespeare tells us in Act II, scene 2 that the action takes place in Bohemia in a deserted wilderness near the sea—whereas in the real world Bohemia has no beaches, just as there are no Swiss seaside resorts. But it costs us nothing to accept (or pretend to believe) that in that possible world Bohemia is by the sea. Those who subscribe to the fictional pact are usually not hard to please, or are sufficiently uninformed.

Once we have established these differences between the fictional possible world and the real one, we will usually admit that the statement "Anna Karenina committed suicide by throwing herself under a train" is not true in the same way in which the historical statement "Adolf Hitler committed suicide in a bunker in Berlin" *is* true.

Nonetheless, why is it that we would fail a student in a history exam if she said that Hitler was shot on Lake Como but we would also fail a student in a literature exam if he said that Anna Karenina fled to Siberia with Alyosha Karamazov?

The matter is easily resolved in logical and semantic terms, by recognizing that it is true that "Anna Karenina commits suicide by throwing herself under a train" is only a conventionally quicker way of saying "It is true that in the real world Tolstoy wrote that Anna Karenina commits suicide by throwing herself under a train." So it is Tolstoy and Hitler who belong to the same world, not Hitler and Anna Karenina.

So, in logical terms, that Anna Karenina commits suicide would be true *de dicto* while *Hitler committed suicide* would be true *de re*. Or better yet, what happens to Anna Karenina does not concern the meaning of the expression but its signifier. To put it another way, we can make true statements about fictional characters in the same way that we can say that it is true that Beethoven's Fifth Symphony is in C minor (and not in F major like the Sixth) and begins with "G, G, G, E flat." It would be a judgment on the score. Anna Karenina begins with a maxim ("Happy families are all alike; every unhappy family is unhappy in its own way") which is a matter of opinion, but one immediately followed by a factual statement ("Everything was upside-down in the Oblonsky household") with regard to which we must not wonder whether it is true that everything was upside down in the Oblonsky household but whether it is true that in the score called *Anna Karenina* it really says "Everything was upside-down in the Oblonsky household," or its Russian equivalent.

This solution, however, leaves us dissatisfied. A musical score (apart from the infinite problems of interpretation that it implies) is basically a set of instructions for the production of a sequence of sounds, and the real problem of the enjoyment, aesthetic judgment, and the feelings aroused by the Fifth come later. Likewise, what is written on the first page of the novel called *Anna Karenina* makes us think about a state of affairs in the Oblonsky home and it is that state of affairs that determines whether we take something as true or false. In other words, to be strictly obvious, even if we take as true that at the beginning of *Anna Karenina* it says, "Everything was upside-down in the Oblonsky household," we have not yet decided whether it is true or not that everything really was upside down in the Oblonsky house, and especially if, in addition to being true in Tolstoy's possible world, this disorder is not in some way true for us, in our everyday world.

It is true that the score called the *Bible* begins with "Bereshit," but when we say that Abraham was about to sacrifice his son (and we frequently try to interpret this event allegorically, mystically, or morally) we are not referring to the original Hebrew score (which ninety-nine percent of those who talk about Cain or Abraham do not know); further, we are talking about the *meanings* and not the *signifiers* of that book—and those meanings can also be interpreted with other words, frescoes, or films that do not appear in the original score.

The problem as to whether we can make true statements about fictional characters has nothing to do with the problem of the words used to introduce them to us. As children, many young Italians will have read the beautiful books in the Scala d'Oro series, which were abridged versions of the great works of literature written for younger readers by excellent writers. *Anna Karenina* was obviously not one of them, because it is difficult to summarize this work for children or adolescents, but the series did include, for example, *Les Misérables* and *Le capitaine Fracasse*. Thanks to these books, many Italians know who Jean Valjean and the Baron de Sigognac are without having ever seen the scores that were the original texts. How are these characters able to survive, and rather well at that, outside the score that created them?

No one can reasonably deny that Hitler and Anna Karenina are two different entities, with a different ontological status. But we have to admit that many times even our historical statements are *de dicto*—just like those regarding fictional characters. Those students whose modern history essays state that Hitler committed suicide in a bunker in Berlin are not referring to something they know from direct experience, they are simply asserting that this is what it says in their history books.

In other words, with the exception of judgments that depend on my direct experience (such as "it's raining"), all the judgments I can make on the basis of my cultural knowledge depend on information recorded in an encyclopedia, from which I learn both the distance from Earth to the Sun and the fact that Hitler died in a bunker in Berlin. Since I was not there to see if that was true, I trust this information because I have delegated both the information on the Sun and that regarding Hitler to expert scholars.

Moreover, every truth in the encyclopedia is open to revision. If we have a scientifically open mind, we must be prepared to discover new documents one day telling us that Hitler did not die in the bunker but escaped to Argentina, that the body burned in the bunker was not his, that his suicide was invented for propaganda reasons by the Russians or even that the bunker never existed; and in fact even though there is a picture of Churchill sitting where the bunker was, others claim that its location is doubtful. But the fact that Anna Karenina committed suicide by throwing herself under a train cannot and never will be questioned.

Fictional characters have another advantage over historical ones. In history, we are always uncertain about the identity of the Iron Mask, or Kaspar Hauser, and we are not sure if Anastasia Nikolaevna Romanova was murdered with the Russian royal family or whether she survived and was the attractive claimant to the throne later played by Ingrid Bergman. Conversely, when we read Arthur Conan Doyle, we are sure that when Sherlock Holmes refers to Watson, he is always referring to the same person, that there are not two people in London with the same name and the same characteristics, and that the person mentioned in every story will always be the one in *A Study in Scarlet* who is introduced as Watson for the first time by a fellow named Stamford. It is possible that in some unpublished story Conan Doyle might tell us that Watson had lied about being wounded at the battle of Maiwand during the Afghan War, or about holding a degree in medicine, but in this case, too, the man who would be unmasked as a charlatan would still be the person called Watson by Stamford in *A Study in Scarlet*.

The problem of the strong identity of fictional characters is an extremely important one. In 2007, a novel by Philippe Doumenc (*Contre-enquete sur la morte d'Emma Bovary*) was published, in which a police investigation reveals that Madame Bovary did not commit suicide with arsenic but was murdered. It is an amusing little game, but one that becomes interesting only because the readers know that Emma Bovary really did poison herself. If they did not know this irrefutable truth they would not enjoy the counter-story, just as in so-called uchronic novels if we are to appreciate a story in which Napoleon won at Waterloo we must know that it is an encyclopedically accepted truth that he lost.

And so, even though there is an undoubted ontological difference between Hitler and Anna Karenina, I am nonetheless able to underline how novelistic statements, considering the way in which we give credence to them, cite them, and refer to them in our everyday life, are indispensable for the clarification of what we mean by irrefutable truth.

If someone asked us what it means for a statement to be true, we could follow Tarski and reply that the statement "the snow is white" (between quote marks, as a verbal signifier or corresponding proposition) is true if and only if the snow is white. In other words, if the snow is like this or that regardless of the way in which we define it. Nonetheless, while this definition may satisfy logicians, it does not satisfy ordinary people. I would prefer to say that a statement is indubitably true when it is as indubitable as the statement *Superman is Clark Kent* (and vice-versa).

The Pope and the Dalai Lama can debate for years the truth of a statement such as *Jesus Christ is truly the son of God*, but if they are sensible (and informed of the facts), they cannot fail to agree that Superman is the same person as Clark Kent. And so, to know if *Hitler died in a bunker in Berlin* is undoubtedly true, we must check to see if it is as undoubtedly true as *Superman is Clark Kent*.

Thus the epistemological function of novelistic statements is that they can be used as a litmus test for the irrefutability of all other statements.

But what does it mean when we say it is true that Anna Karenina commits suicide instead of saying only that it is true that *in the novel by Tolstoy it says that* Anna Karenina commits suicide? Because it is obvious that if people are moved by the fact that Anna Karenina commits suicide, this does not mean at all that they are moved by the fact that Tolstoy *wrote* that Anna Karenina committed suicide!

This brings us to the reason I began to get interested in these problems. Some time ago, a colleague of mine suggested that I should organize a seminar on why we cry (or, at any rate, feel emotions) about things that happen to fictional characters. At first I told him that it is a matter for psychologists, who have studied the mechanisms of projection and identification. After all, I said, don't we occasionally dream or even fantasize that a loved one dies, and are then moved to tears? So is there any reason why we cannot be moved by what happens to the female lead in *Love Story*?

Then I told myself that, no matter how people may be moved by imagining that their beloved has died, after a while they realize that it is not true, and stop crying; in fact, they are relieved, whereas swarms of young romantics killed themselves after weeping over Werther's suicide, even though they knew both before and after that he was a fictional character. Which means that these readers kept thinking that *in some world* Werther *really* killed himself.

It is probable that none of my readers has wept over the misfortunes of Scarlett O'Hara, but no one can tell me that he was unmoved by those of Medea. I have seen sophisticated intellectuals wiping away stealthy tears during the last act of *Cyrano de Bergerac*, even though they had seen it several times, even though they knew very well how it was going to end and had gone to the theatre only to compare Dépardieu's Cyrano with Belmondo's. As a sensitive lady friend of mine once said: "Whenever I see a flag fluttering on the screen, I cry, and I don't care which country's flag it is."

So there is a difference between pretending that the person we love has died, and pretending that Anna Karenina or Madame Bovary dies. In the first case the delusive state lasts almost no time at all, in the second we continue to talk seriously about the misfortunes of the two women, and we write books about them.

In any case, if we look at two versions of Madame Bovary—Umberto Brunelleschi's 1953 illustrations and the one portrayed by Isabelle Huppert in the 1991 film—at least one of them has nothing directly to do with the novel. It is as if she had left it and gone to live in some other means of expression—the cinema, in this case. Then there is the petit bourgeois Bovary and the risqué Bovary, all the way down to the Bovary used in advertisements for recipes.

Why talk about these versions of the lady? The fact that there are so many types of Bovary who act in ways different from Flaubert's text means that we are no longer dealing with a character from Flaubert's world, but a *fluctuating character*.

Many fictional characters can live outside their own text of origin and act in an area of the universe that is difficult to identify and delimit. Sometimes they even migrate from one text to another, as in novels or films about the sons of the musketeers or Pinocchio the aviator. They no longer belong to the source text. To become a fluctuating character it is not necessary to come from a great work of art, and we should study elsewhere why both Hamlet and Robin Hood, Gargantua and Tintin, Heathcliff and Milady, Leopold Bloom and Superman, Faust and Popeye have all become fluctuating characters, while those who have not include Baron de Charlus, Le grand Meaulnes, Stelio Effrena, and Andrea Sperelli.

A survey showed that 25 percent of Britons believed that Churchill, Gandhi, and Dickens were fictional characters while some percentage (I don't remember how great) believed that Sherlock Holmes and Eleanor Rigby really did exist. So it is possible to become a fluctuating character for a great many reasons. Disraeli does not fluctuate but Churchill does, Scarlett O'Hara does but the Princesse de Clèves does not. (Nicolas Sarkozy has repeatedly stated that he could never read that novel by Madame de La Fayette, and my French friends tell me that this fact has proved a shot in the arm for the unfortunate *Princesse de Clèves* because, out of spite toward Sarkozy, many people have now started to read it.)

Many characters have become so fluctuating that most people know them better through their extratextual avatars than through the text that introduced them in the first place. This is the case with Little Red Riding Hood, for example. Perrault's version differs from that of the Grimms (in Perrault, the hunter does not come to rescue Riding Hood and her grandmother), but the fluctuating story that mothers tell their children, even if they stick to the ending in the Grimms version, merges the two versions and sometimes deviates from both.

Even the three musketeers are no longer those of Dumas.

Every reader of the Nero Wolfe and Archie Goodwin stories knows that Wolfe lived in Manhattan, in a brownstone at a certain number on West 35th Street. In reality, over the years Rex Stout gave us at least ten different numbers on 35th Street—in which, among other discrepancies, there are no brownstones. But at some point a sort of unspoken pact among Wolfe fans convinced everyone that the right number was 454. On June 22, 1996, the city of New York and The Wolfe Pack put up a bronze plaque at 454 West 35th Street to commemorate the fact that the famous brownstone once stood there.

So Medea, Dido, Don Quixote, Monte Cristo, and Gatsby have become individuals who live outside their original scores and even those who have never read those scores hold that they know them and can make correct statements about them. Some characters, in their wanderings outside the original texts, have become muddled amalgams of one another, such as Philip Marlowe, Sam Spade, and the Rick Blaine of *Casablanca* fame. (I should point out that *Casablanca* was originally a play called *Everybody Comes to Rick's*.) These characters, having become independent of the texts of origin, live among us in a certain sense; often they inspire our behavior, and sometimes we elect them as criteria of judgment, saying that someone has an Oedipus complex, for example, or a gargantuan appetite, or the jealousy of an Othello, or Hamletic doubts.

So when we assert that it is true that Anna Karenina committed suicide or that Holmes lived in Baker Street, we make statements not on a given score (that is, what a given author wrote) but on a fluctuating creature, whose ontological status appears fairly bizarre, because it should not exist and yet somehow it moves among us and can occupy our thoughts.

Is it possible to fluctuate without existing in a physical form? Are there any objects that do not necessarily exist in physical form? Of course, it would be enough to define as an object every entity we can conceive of and some of whose properties can be predicated. For example, let's consider the case of the husband and wife, one a history teacher and the other a math teacher, who often talk about both Julius Caesar and the right-angled triangle, but would also like to have a little girl.

So they begin to talk every day not only about Julius Caesar and the right-angled triangle but also about the child they would like to call, as one does, Gessica (with a G of course): how to bring her up, which sports she should play, and how nice it would be if she became a showgirl. So husband and wife are talking (i) about someone who has existed physically but physically no longer exists (Caesar), (ii) about something that some call an ideal object although it is not clear where it exists, unless we assume platonically that there is a world of ideas, and (iii) about someone who hopefully will exist physically but does not yet exist (Gessica). But what happens if, apart from these things, the couple also start talking about freedom and justice?

Freedom and justice are certainly objects of thought, but different from Caesar and Gessica—first and foremost, because they are not so well-defined as Caesar and Gessica, because depending on the various cultures, places, historical periods, and religious beliefs peoples have had contrasting ideas about them, and second, because they are not individuals but concepts. And yet, there are concepts, such as the right-angled triangle, that are better defined than the concept of justice.

Are fictional characters entities like Caesar and Gessica, or the right-angled triangle, or freedom?

They have something in common with Caesar, Gessica, the triangle, and freedom because they are *semiotic objects*—that is to say, sets of properties expressed by a given term, which a culture recognizes by mutual consent and records in its encyclopedia. Examples of semiotic objects are the right-angled triangle, woman, cat, chair, Milan, Everest, Article Seven of the Constitution, the quality of being a horse. Semiotic objects also include those expressed by proper names, and in this sense semiotic objects include not only Julius Caesar (who now exists for us only as a set of properties) but also, assuming they exist somewhere or other, a John Smith or Joe White who, regardless of the fact they are physical entities, are also, when we mention them with a name, sets of properties (and even without ever having met him we could identify Joe White as the son of Tom, born in Slough, currently a cashier with the Bank of such-and-such, living in such-and-such street, and so on). And since the properties expressed by a proper name include those of having existed in the past or existing at present, or those, recorded in any good encyclopedia, of being a mythological entity or a character in a story, so fictional characters are semiotic objects, too.

The boundaries of many semiotic objects are defined so to speak *ab aeterno* (for example, the properties whereby a square is recognized as such are not subject to variation or negotiation in approximate terms); others have defined boundaries (for example, the frontiers between two states) but can take losses or additions of property (Italy has remained identifiable as such even though it has been deprived of Zara or Nice); and a great many others are variously *fuzzy*.

For example, we are able to recognize that German shepherds and chihuahuas are both dogs. They share only some salient properties that for now I will limit myself to define as diagnostics. But this also happens for entities such as the city of Milan—otherwise, those who saw it for the first time, like me, in 1946, half destroyed, without either the Pirelli building or the Torre Velasca, would be unable to identify the modern city as the postwar one. And the same happens, for example, with historical figures, otherwise it would not be possible to make statements such as *if Cleopatra's nose had been a little longer it would have changed the history of Rome* (in other words, we can take our idea of Cleopatra and remove some properties from it without this causing us to stop recognizing it as such—and we can imagine counterfactual situations such as what would have happened if Caesar had not been killed on the Ides of March).

Which diagnostic properties must be kept in order to identify something as belonging to the same species or class is an open problem, and in any case we ought to think that a property becomes or remains diagnostic depending on the context or the universe of discourse.

Fictional characters are fluctuating semiotic objects because they can lose some of their properties without losing their identity—so much so that, in the popular imagination, D'Artagnan is a musketeer while we know that in *The Three Musketeers* he is merely a cadet. If Madame Bovary had lived in Italy rather than in France her story would not have been so different. What then are the truly diagnostic properties of Madame Bovary? One would say that she committed suicide for sentimental reasons. So why can we read a parody like Woody Allen's *The Kugelmass Episode*, where the protagonist uses a time machine to take Madame Bovary from Yonville and carry her off to New York to live the good life she had always dreamed of? Only because the context stresses Madame Bovary's diagnostic property as that of being a provincial petit bourgeois with kitsch passions? In fact, the parody works because the main character hastens to take her back before she commits suicide.

While on the one hand this suicide does not occur in the parody, it remains essential, radically diagnostic, for the identification of Madame Bovary. And this point should be emphasized because, as we shall see at the end, the fascinating thing about fictional characters is that their destiny cannot be changed. We can imagine what would have happened if Napoleon had won at Waterloo, and such a counterfactual exercise would certainly be very interesting, but a story in which Madame Bovary did not kill herself and lived happily ever after somewhere would be insipid to say the least . . .

Why can we be moved by semiotic objects such as fictional characters? We might answer: for the same reason that many people die for justice or liberty. But there is a difference between being moved by Anna Karenina and being moved by the right-angled triangle. (I believe Pythagoras was the only one to experience the latter.)

We are moved by Anna Karenina because, having signed the fictional pact, we pretend to live in her world as if it were ours, and after a while (as if seized by some mystical rapture, certainly due to some qualities of the narrative) *we forget that we are pretending*. Not only that, but since we are not signed up to that world—so to speak—or we are not a relevant presence in it, we instinctively try to take the place of some rightful inhabitant or inhabitants of it with whom we share the most aspects.

If we accept this definition of fictional characters, we see that the gods of all mythologies are semiotic objects, like dwarves, fairies, Santa Claus, and the entities of the various religions. Some may think that comparing religious entities with fairies is merely an expression of atheism, but I invite every believer to try a mental experiment: imagine being a Catholic and believing that Jesus really is the son of God. Fine: in this case, Shiva, the Great Spirit of the prairies, and the Exu of Brazilian cults are merely fictional characters. But imagine now being a Hindu: if Shiva really exists somewhere, then it is obvious that the Great Spirit, Exu, and the God of Israel are fictional characters. And so on, until we have to admit that, whatever our religious belief, all religious entities minus one are fictional characters. And therefore, even if we refuse to decide which one defies the general law, we can be certain that 99 percent of religious entities are fictional characters, who, like Madame Bovary or Othello, are usually born from a text. The only difference is that the number of people sharing opinions and beliefs about Shiva is greater than those who know Madame Bovary—but let's not get involved in quantitative or statistical matters.

The fluctuating characters of fiction are made of the same stuff as the characters of mythology. Oedipus and Achilles were fluctuating entities like Anna Karenina or Pinocchio, except that the former were created in ancient times and the latter were born, as it were, as secular myths. And we feel entitled to say that it is true that Pinocchio was born from a piece of wood just as we feel authorized to say that it is true that Athena was born from the head of Jupiter.

It is not enough to say that the ancients thought that Jupiter and Athena really existed whereas anyone who thinks of Pinocchio as a fluctuating character knows that he never existed. I would say that these are psychological accidents, and I might add that a great number of believers have fairly fuzzy ideas about the degree of existence of their gods—that there have been young shepherdesses who say they have spoken with Our Lady; that some romantic girls killed themselves for love of Jacopo Ortis; that at the Sicilian puppet theatre, the audience used to insult the villain Gano di Maganza; that there are teenagers who are madly in love with a character, not a movie star; that there is no saying that Caesar believed in Jupiter; that Christian poets continued to invoke the Muses—and so we enter a universe of feelings, fantasies, and private emotions where it is difficult draw precise boundary lines.

The kind of existence we have allowed to fluctuating characters also explains their moral function. I know I have already written and talked about this topic, but I cannot overlook it in bringing this contribution to an end.

Although these characters fluctuate, they seem irremediably bound to their destiny. Of course, when we weep at their stories we hope sometimes that things might go differently, that Oedipus might take another path and not meet his father on the road to Thebes, that he might arrive in Athens where he could couple with Phryne, that Hamlet might marry Ophelia and live together happily ever after on the throne of Denmark, that Heathcliff might put up with a little more humiliation and stay on those wuthering heights until he can marry his Catherine and live with her as a perfect country gentleman, that Prince Andrey might get well, that Raskolnikov might not conceive the mad idea of murdering an old woman but finish his studies and become a respectable state official, that when Gregor Samsa is transformed into a horrible insect a beautiful princess enters his room, kisses him, and transforms him into the richest man in Prague. Today, computers could even offer programs that rewrite all these stories to our liking. But do we really want to rewrite them?

Reading fiction means knowing that the character's destiny is ineluctable. If we could change the fate of Madame Bovary, we would no longer have the comforting certainty that the assertion *Madame Bovary committed suicide* is the model of every indisputable truth. Entering a fictional possible world means accepting that things went, and will always go, in a certain way, regardless of our wishes. We must accept this frustrating fact, and through it experience the thrill of destiny.

I believe that this lesson on fate is one of the main functions of fiction, and constitutes the paradigmatic value of fictional characters, saints of the secular community—and also of many believers.

Only the fact that Anna Karenina inevitably dies makes her fondly, imperiously, and obsessively present as the melancholy companion of our existence, even though she never physically existed.

[La Milanesiana, 2009]

7. Paradoxes and Aphorisms

We often hear people say things like "it's paradoxical: he was the one who ran into me and now he claims that I should pay the damages," or "it's paradoxical that Raphael's wife died on the very day of their wedding."

Well, the first case is not paradoxical; it is merely an affront or, at most, absurd. And neither is the second, which is an unusual coincidence and a shocking departure from the norm, like the birth of a two-headed calf.

While both of these naive usages connect to an aspect of a paradox, that it runs counter to what was desired or expected, in neither case are we dealing with a genuine paradox.

If we were reducing paradox to mean something only curious or bizarre, we might even call it paradoxical that there are two distinct meanings of the word paradox. One of them applies in the realm of logic and philosophy, and the other in rhetoric.

Logical paradoxes ought more properly to be called *antinomies*. I saw someone on the internet claiming that the Greeks called them *paralogisms*, but that isn't true. A paralogism is a simple error of reasoning that is easy to correct. For example, it is a paralogism to state that because all Athenians are Greeks, and all Spartans are Greeks, all Athenians are Spartans. In this case, sheer common sense tells us the conclusion is false, but sometimes it helps to diagram the paralogism to find its flaw:

All A's are G's

All S's are G's

Therefore, all A's are S's.

A paralogism is such because in this syllogism the middle term (G) is not quantified, and the lack of quantification of the middle makes the argument fallacious.

On the other hand, what medieval scholars called *insolubilia* are antinomies, which is to say expressions or arguments that cannot be said to be either true or false—because they are are susceptible to two mutually contradictory interpretations.

The most classic antinomy is that of the self-professed liar. The statement "I am lying" cannot be true or false: if it were true, it would mean that I am telling the truth and therefore it is not true that I am lying; and if it were false, then it would not be true that I am lying, and so it would be true that I am telling the truth, and therefore I would really be lying.

The most popular version of this is the paradox of Epimenides, the Cretan who maintains that all Cretans are liars.

St. Paul, a man with many good qualities but no sense of humor, took the saying seriously and, in the Epistle to Titus, he tells us that the Cretans certainly *are* all liars and the proof of this is that a man who knows them well, a Cretan himself, says so. But in that case it is obvious that, since Epimenides is a Cretan, he must be lying. But if he is lying, then it is not true that all Cretans are liars. Therefore, some Cretans tell the truth. But is Epimenides one of them, or not? If he is, then it is true that all Cretans are liars and it is false that some Cretans like Epimenides tell the truth. If Epimenides is one of those who lie, then we go straight back to square one.

But the paradox of Epimenides is not really a paradox, because we can escape that by concluding that Epimenides is the only liar among all the Cretans—in which case, the fact that he does not tell the truth is just normal.

The famous story of Achilles and the tortoise, attributed to Zeno, also passes for a paradox. Let's say the tortoise is one meter ahead of Achilles. To overtake it, Achilles has to close that gap and, after the first half-meter, he has closed half of it. Then he must cover the remaining distance, and after gaining another quarter of a meter, he has accomplished half of that task. And so on ad infinitum, with the logical result that Achilles never passes the tortoise.

Or let's imagine a path that is one kilometer long, from point *P* to point *A*. Then let's imagine a runner, Achilles, who starts from point *P* and runs toward the finish—that is, toward point *A*. Achilles must first cover half the distance between points *P* and *A*, reaching the midpoint between them, which we shall call *M*. Achilles must therefore cover half of the remaining distance between *M* and the finish *A*, arriving at point *S*. This halving process continues ad infinitum, because regardless of how small the distance to cover may be, it can always be halved.

The story of Achilles is not a paradox and Aristotle had already seen the solution when he made a distinction between *potential infinite* and *actual infinite*: among magnitudes there is infinity by addition (I can always find an even number greater than the one before it) but not by division, because the infinity of the subintervals in which a unit of length is divisible is always contained within a limited totality (which is never greater than 1).

Although the process of fractalization (half of the whole, half of the half, half of the half of the half, and so on) continues indefinitely, its result will never be greater than 1—as also happens with irrational numbers. So 3.14, as far as we can analyze it, will never be 4.

If this reasoning is applied to the fractal length of a coast, in which the *potential* division process could be infinite, at least insofar as we can always postulate smaller and smaller microbes, this takes nothing away from the fact that in real terms Achilles can cover this distance in a single step. Achilles will cover his unit of length in his unit of time.

There is also talk of topological paradoxes, and some have said that the Möbius strip is paradoxical. I find nothing paradoxical about it. It may seem improbable that a twist suffices to turn a two-sided surface into a single-sided one, but in fact it happens, and we have seen this; all this means is that topology is a little more complex than Euclidean geometry.

There are far more serious paradoxes, one of the most famous of which is the barber paradox proposed by Bertrand Russell.

It comes in an ingenuous version and a subtler one. The first is: "The village barber shaves all the men who do not shave themselves. Who shaves the village barber?" Obviously, he cannot shave himself because he only shaves those who do *not* shave themselves, and it is presumed that no others in the village are appointed to shave anyone. I put this paradox to my children when they were young and they suggested three solutions: perhaps the village barber is a woman; or the barber does not shave and has a very thick beard; or the barber does not shave but rather burns off his beard, no doubt leaving his face horribly scarred. Actually, the paradox should be stated like this: "Among the inhabitants of a village there is one and only one barber, a well-shaven man. The sign above his shop says, 'the barber who shaves all those who do not shave themselves.' The question at this point is: Who shaves the barber?"

Modern logic and mathematics have proposed many antinomies for the resolution of very subtle problems that I will not deal with here. Rather, I shall limit myself to mentioning some other successful antinomies—for example, this one, cited by Aulus Gellius. The story goes that Protagoras gave legal training to a promising young man, Evatlo, and he required Evatlo to pay only half the fee upfront, saying that the student could pay the rest when he won his first case.

Evatlo, however, did not go on to practice law, but went into politics instead, and so he never won his first case because he never actually had one. Therefore, Protagoras was not paid and finally called on Evatlo to settle the price of his training. The young man decided to defend himself, acting as his own lawyer and thereby creating the following situation of indeterminacy. The possible outcomes according to Protagoras were these: if Evatlo wins, he has to pay Protagoras on the basis of the agreement, because he will have won his first case; if Evatlo loses, he has to pay anyway, by virtue of the sentence. But now look at it from Evatlo's perspective: if Evatlo wins, he does not have to pay Protagoras, thanks to the outcome of the case; but if Evatlo loses, he still does not have to pay Protagoras, because of the terms of the agreement and the fact that he did not win his first case.

This paradox has long served to demonstrate that both lawyers and politicians are untrustworthy people.

Another one is the crocodile dilemma, mentioned by Diogenes Laertius: a crocodile grabs a little boy playing on the banks of the

Nile. The mother begs the crocodile to return her child. "Certainly," says the crocodile, "if you can tell me in advance exactly what I'll do, I'll give you back your son; but if you guess wrong, I'll eat him for lunch." The mother, weeping desperately, calls out her prediction: "you'll devour my baby."

Now the crocodile is in a bind: "I can't give you back the child, because if I do, it means you've guessed wrong, and as I told you, if you guess wrong, I devour him." But the mother shrewdly objects, "It's not like that at all! Quite the opposite, you *can't* eat my baby, because if you devour him, that will mean I guessed correctly. You promised that if I did that, you would return the child, and I know that as an honorable crocodile you will keep your word."

And finally here are some delightful logical paradoxes collected by Raymond Smullyan:

Of course I'm a solipsist, isn't everybody?
Of course I believe that solipsism is the correct philosophy,
   but that's only one man's opinion.
Authorized parking forbidden.
This species has always been extinct.
You've outdone yourself as usual.
God must exist because he wouldn't be so mean as to make
   me believe he exists if he really doesn't.
Superstition brings bad luck.

What, on the other hand, is the rhetorical paradox?

Etymologically, it is only παράδοξος, that which goes *parà ten doxan*—that is, beyond common perception or opinion. So the term originally referred to a statement that was far from everyone's beliefs—odd, bizarre, or surprising. This is the definition of it that we find it in Isidore of Seville; according to him, a paradox occurs when we say that something unexpected has happened, as when Cicero, in his *Defense of Flaccus*, wrote that "he who ought have been the singer of praises has become the one who begs for his release from danger."

We can find rhetorical notions of paradox in various dictionaries, but the basic idea usually contains elements like these:

> a theory, concept, statement or dictum that contrasts with widespread or universally accepted opinion, with common sense and common experience, and with principles and knowledge that are taken as read; but it can possess, in an apparently illogical and disconcerting form, a fundamental validity, which runs counter to the ignorance and the superficiality of those who uncritically follow the opinion of the majority.

So paradox in the rhetorical and literary sense would be a kind of maxim or saying, which at first sight seems to be false but which eventually reveals a nonobvious truth.

In this sense paradox almost always takes the form of a maxim or an aphorism.

There is nothing harder to define than the aphorism. As well as "something set aside for an offering" and "donation," over the years the Greek term came to mean "definition, dictum, concise maxim." Examples include the aphorisms of Hippocrates. According to the Zingarelli Italian dictionary, an aphorism is a "brief maxim that expresses a rule of life or a philosophical judgment."

It has been said that an aphorism is a maxim in which the most important thing is not only the brevity of the form, but also the perspicacity of the content, which puts elegance or brilliance before the acceptability of the assertion in terms of truth. Of course, with regard to maxims and aphorisms, the concept of truth is relative to the aphorist's intentions: to say that an aphorism expresses a truth means to say that its purpose is not only to express what the author understands to be true but also to convince his readers of this. But in general a maxim or aphorism is not necessarily intended to appear witty, nor does it aim to offend current opinions: rather it is intended to expand on a point regarding which current opinion appears superficial, and should be examined in greater depth.

Here is a maxim from Chamfort: "The richest of men is he who lives within his budget; the poorest of men is the miser" (*Maxims and Thoughts*, I, 145). The wit lies in the fact that popular opinion tends to consider the thrifty as those who do not waste their scant resources in order to ensure they can deal with their own needs, and misers as people who amass resources far greater than their needs require. So the maxim would run counter to popular opinion, except that "poor" is also understood in relation to the satisfaction of needs, and not just in the moral sense, while "rich" is understood in relation to resources. The rhetorical game having been revealed, we can see that the maxim does not run contrary to current opinion, but corroborates it.

When, instead, an aphorism goes violently against the conventional view, so that at first sight it appears to be false and unacceptable, and appears to hold some barely acceptable truth only once its hyperbolic form has been judiciously reduced, then we have a paradox.

So, an aphorism would be a maxim intended to be recognized as true, even though it is meant to appear witty, while a paradox would appear to be a maxim that looks false at first sight and, only after mature reflection, seems to express what the author believes to be true, and, because of the hiatus between the expectations of popular opinion and its provocative form, it also appears to be witty.

The history of literature is rich in aphorisms and a little less rich in paradoxes. The art of the aphorism is easy (proverbial expressions are aphorisms, too: your best friend is your mother, its bark is worse than its bite) while the art of the paradox is difficult.

Some time ago I became interested in a master of the aphorism, the Italian writer Pitigrilli, and here are some of his most brilliant maxims. Albeit in a humorous way, some are intended to state a truth that does not run contrary to popular opinion in the slightest:

Gastronome: a cook who went to high school.

Grammar: a complicated instrument that teaches you languages but prevents you from speaking them.

The fragment: a providential resource for writers who can't put together a whole book.

Dipsomania: a scientific word that's so beautiful it makes you want to take to drink.

Others, rather than express a presumed truth, state an ethical choice, a rule of conduct:

Kissing a leper I can understand, but not shaking hands with a cretin.

Be indulgent with those who have done you a wrong, because you don't know what the others have in store for you.

However, in the anthology titled *Dizionario antiballistico* (1962) in which he collected some of his own maxims, sayings, and aphorisms as well as those of others, Pitigrilli, who always wanted to pass for a cynic, even at the cost of candidly confessing his iniquities, realized how insidious playing with aphorisms could be:

Since we are being confidential, I admit that I have encouraged the hooliganism of the reader. Let me explain: when a fight breaks out in the street or a traffic accident occurs, there suddenly emerges from the bowels of the earth an individual who tries to thump one of the two parties with his umbrella, usually the motorist. The unknown thug has vented his latent rancor. It's the same in books: when the reader who has no ideas, or has them in an amorphous state, comes across a picturesque, phosphorescent or explosive expression, he falls in love with it, makes it his own, comments on it with an exclamation mark, with a "good!," a "right!," as if he had always thought so, and that the expression in question was the quintessential extract of his way of thinking, his philosophical system. He "takes a stance," as il Duce used to say. I offer him the way to take a stance without descending into the jungle of the various literatures.

In this sense the aphorism is a brilliant (and new) expression of a commonplace.

To say that the harmonium is "a piano that, disgusted with life, has taken refuge in religion" merely reformulates icastically what we already knew and believed: that the harmonium is a church instrument. To say that alcohol is "a liquid that kills the living and preserves the dead" adds nothing to what we knew about the risks of intemperance and the goings on in schools of anatomy.

When Pitigrilli (*L'esperimento di Pott*, 1929) has his main character say that "intelligence in women is an anomaly encountered exceptionally, like albinism, left-handedness, hermaphroditism or polydactylism" he says exactly, albeit in a witty manner, what the male reader (and probably the female reader, too) of 1929 wanted to hear.

But, in criticizing his *vis aphoristica*, Pitigrilli tells us something more, namely that many brilliant aphorisms can be reversed without losing their power. Let's take a look at examples of such reversal suggested by Pitigrilli himself in his *Dizionario antiballistico*:

> Lots of people hold wealth in contempt but few are generous with it.
> *Lots of people are generous with wealth, but few hold it in contempt.*
> We make promises in accordance with our fears and keep them in accordance with our hopes.
> *We make promises in accordance with our hopes and keep them in accordance with our fears.*
> History is no more than a love affair with liberty.
> *Liberty is no more than a love affair with history.*
> Happiness lies in things and not in our tastes.
> *Happiness lies in our tastes and not in things.*

Pittigrilli also collected maxims by various authors, which although certainly mutually contradictory nonetheless always seemed to express an established truth:

> One only deceives oneself out of optimism. (Hervieu)
> *One is more often deceived by mistrust than by trust. (Rivarol)*

People would be happy if kings were philosophers and
   philosophers kings. (Plutarch)
*The day I wish to castigate a province I'll have it governed
   by a philosopher.* (Frederick II)

I would use the term "interchangeable" for these reversible
aphorisms. The interchangeable aphorism is a disorder of the in-
clination to be amusing—in other words, a maxim that, as long
as it appears witty, is indifferent to the fact that its opposite is
equally true. A paradox is a true reversal of the common point of
view which presents an unacceptable world, one that elicits resistance and rejection, and yet which, if we make an effort to understand it, leads to knowledge; eventually it seems to be witty
because it has to be admitted that this is true. The interchangeable
aphorism contains a highly partial truth and, often, after it has
been reversed, it becomes clear that neither of the two standpoints
it illustrates is true: it seemed true only because it was witty.

Paradox is not a variation on the classical *topos* of the "topsy-
turvy world," which is mechanical. In that universe, animals talk
and humans make animal sounds, fish fly and birds swim, mon-
keys celebrate Mass and bishops swing from tree to tree. It proceeds by *adynata* or *impossibilia* without any logic. It is a game in
the spirit of carnival.

To move on to paradox, this reversal must follow a logic and be
restricted to one portion of the universe. A Persian arrives in Paris
and describes France the way a Parisian would describe Persia.
The effect is paradoxical because it obliges us to see everyday
things from a standpoint outside established opinion.

One of the ways to distinguish paradox from interchangeable
aphorism consists in trying to turn the paradox on its head.

An author who always moved with cynicism and insouciance between paradox and aphorism was Oscar Wilde. Reflecting on the countless aphorisms that he scattered throughout his works, we sense that we are dealing with a flippant author, a dandy who, provided he was able to shock the bourgeoisie, made no distinction between aphorisms, interchangeable aphorisms, and paradoxes. On the contrary, however, he had the cheek to pass off as aphorisms some witty statements that, beneath the wit, are seen to be woeful clichés—or at least clichés as far as the Victorian bourgeoisie and aristocracy were concerned.

An experiment, however, may allow us to see if and to what extent Wilde, an author who made provocative aphorisms the very quintessence of his novels, comedies, and essays, was a true author of dazzling paradoxes or merely a refined collector of witticisms.

Here follows a series of real paradoxes, which I defy you to reverse (without obtaining little more than nonsense or what any sensible person would consider a false maxim):

> Life is simply a 'mauvais quart d'heure' made up of exquisite moments.
> Selfishness is not living as one wishes to live, it is asking others to live as one wishes to live.
> A sensitive person is one who, because he has corns himself, always treads on other people's toes.
> Everybody who is incapable of learning has taken to teaching.
> And of course a *man* who is much *talked* about is always very *attractive*. One feels there must be something in him, after all.
> One can resist everything but temptation.
> Falsehoods are the truth of other people.
> The one duty we owe to history is to rewrite it.

A thing is not necessarily true because a man dies for it.

Relations are simply a tedious pack of people who haven't got the remotest knowledge of how to live nor the smallest instinct about when to die.

Whenever people agree with me I always feel I must be wrong.

But Wilde also produced countless aphorisms that seem easily interchangeable.

To live is the rarest thing in the world. Most people exist.

To exist is the rarest thing in the world. Most people live.

Those who see any difference between soul and body have neither one nor the other.

Those who see no difference between soul and body have neither one nor the other.

Life is far too important a thing ever to talk seriously about it.

Life is not important enough ever to joke about it.

The world is divided into two classes: those who believe the incredible, and those who do the improbable, like me.

The world is divided into two classes: those who believe the improbable, and those who do the incredible, like me.

The world is divided into two classes: those who do the improbable, and those who believe in the incredible, like me.

There is a fatality about all good resolutions. They are invariably made too soon.

There is a fatality about all good resolutions. They are invariably made too late.

To be premature is to be perfect.

To be mature is to be imperfect.

To be perfect is to be premature.

To be imperfect is to be mature.

Ignorance is like a delicate exotic fruit: touch it, and the blossom is gone.

Knowledge is like a delicate exotic fruit: touch it, and the blossom is gone.

The more we study art, the less we care for nature.

The more we study nature, the less we care for art.

Sunsets are quite old-fashioned. They belong to the time when Turner was the last note in art. To admire them is a distinct sign of provincialism of temperament.

Sunsets are in fashion, because they belong to the time when Turner was the last note in art. To admire them today is a distinct sign of modernity.

Beauty reveals everything, because it expresses nothing.

Beauty reveals nothing, because it expresses everything.

No married man is ever attractive, except to his wife. And even then, I've been told, not even to her.

All married men are attractive, except to their wives. And even then, I've been told, even to them.

Dandyism, in its own way, is an attempt to assert the absolute modernity of beauty.

Dandyism, in its own way, is an attempt to assert how absolutely dated beauty is.

Conversation should touch on everything, but should concentrate itself on nothing.

Conversation should touch on nothing, but should concentrate itself on everything.

I love to talk about nothing, it's the only thing I know
   anything about.
*I love to talk about everything, it's the only thing I know
   nothing about.*
Only the great masters of style ever succeed in being
   obscure.
Only the great masters of style ever succeed in being clear.
Anyone can make history, only a great man can write it.
Anyone can write history, only a great man can make it.
The English have everything in common with America
   nowadays except, of course, language.
*The English have nothing in common with America nowadays
   except, of course, language.*
It is only the modern that ever becomes old-fashioned.
It is only the old-fashioned that ever becomes modern.

If we were to stop here, our judgment of Wilde would be fairly severe. The very embodiment of the dandy, but one who came later than Beau Brummel and even his beloved Des Esseintes, he does not trouble to make a distinction between paradoxes, vehicles of outrageous truths, aphorisms, vehicles of acceptable truths, and interchangeable aphorisms, which are merely witty games unconcerned with the truth. And, on the other hand, Wilde's ideas on art would seem to sanction his behavior, since no aphorism ought to be concerned with either utility or truth or morality, but only with beauty and stylistic elegance.

But, if we follow his principles, he should have been sent to jail not for having loved Lord Alfred Douglas but for sending him letters such as: "It is a marvel that those red rose-leaf lips of yours should be made no less for the madness of music and song than for the madness of kissing"—and not only this, but for having maintained during the trial that the letter was an exercise in style and a sort of sonnet in prose.

But can an aphorism that an author puts in the mouth of an inane character be judged inane? Is it an aphorism when Lady Bracknell in *The Importance of Being Ernest* (1895) says: "To lose one parent, Mr. Worthing, may be regarded as a misfortune; but to lose both looks like carelessness"? Hence the legitimate suspicion that Wilde did not believe in some of the aphorisms he uttered or even in the best of his paradoxes; the only thing that interested him was portraying a society capable of appreciating them.

Besides, he says as much himself. Take a look at these lines from *The Importance of Being Earnest*:

ALGERNON. All women become like their mothers. That is their tragedy. No man does. That's his.

JACK. Is that clever?

ALGERNON. It is perfectly phrased! and quite as true as any observation in civilized life should be.

And so Wilde should not be seen as an immoral aphorist but as a satirical author and social critic. The fact that the society in question suited him down to the ground is another matter, and that was his tragedy.

Now let's turn to *The Picture of Dorian Gray* (1890). With a few exceptions, the most memorable aphorisms are put in the mouth of a fatuous character, namely Lord Wotton. Wilde does not offer them to us as maxims for life that he himself stands behind.

Lord Wotton utters, albeit wittily, an intolerable series of commonplaces of the society of his day (and this is precisely why Wilde's readers enjoyed his false paradoxes):

A bishop keeps on saying at the age of eighty what he was told to say when he was a boy of eighteen.

The commonest thing is delightful if one only hides it.

The one charm of marriage is that it makes a life of deception absolutely necessary for both parties.

Nowadays a broken heart will run to many editions.

Young men want to be faithful, and are not; old men want to be faithless, and cannot.

I don't want money. It is only people who pay their bills who want that, Uncle George, and I never pay mine.

I don't desire to change anything in England except the weather.

To get back one's youth, one has merely to repeat one's follies.

Men marry because they are tired; women, because they are curious.

Women are wonderfully practical, much more practical than we are. In situations of that kind we often forget to say anything about marriage, and they always remind us.

When we are happy, we are always good, but when we are good, we are not always happy.

I should fancy that the real tragedy of the poor is that they can afford nothing but self-denial. [I wonder if Wotton had read the *Communist Manifesto* and had learned that workers have nothing to lose but their chains?]

Every effect that one produces gives one an enemy. To be popular, one must be a mediocrity.

Anybody can be good in the country.

Married life is merely a habit.

Crime belongs exclusively to the lower orders. I don't blame them in the smallest degree. I should fancy that crime was to them what art is to us, simply a method of procuring extraordinary sensations.

Murder is always a mistake. One should never do anything that one cannot talk about after dinner.

Alongside this series of commonplaces, which become amusing only because they are fired off in volleys—as in the technique of the list, where the tritest of expressions become admirable for the incongruous relationship they establish with other equally banal expressions—Lord Wotton reveals a particular genius in taking clichés unworthy even of fortune cookies, and making them humorous by reversing them:

Being natural is simply a pose, and the most irritating pose I know.

I adore simple pleasures, they are the last refuge of the complex.

What I want is information: not useful information, of course; useless information.

I assure you there is no nonsense about the Americans. How dreadful!

I can sympathize with everything except suffering.

My dear boy, the people who love only once in their lives are really the shallow people.

There is always something infinitely mean about other people's tragedies.

Whenever a man does a thoroughly stupid thing, it is always from the noblest motives. [But this one is interchangeable: *When a man does a thoroughly noble thing, it is always from the stupidest motives.*]

A man can be happy with any woman, as long as he does not love her.

I think that it is better to be beautiful than to be good.
But . . . it is better to be good than to be ugly. [This is as
common a commonplace as you can get, of the type
popularized on television: It's better to be beautiful, rich,
and healthy than ugly, poor, and ill].
It is only shallow people that do not judge by appearances.
It is perfectly monstrous, the way people go about nowadays
saying things against one behind one's back that are
absolutely and entirely true.
The only difference between a caprice and a lifelong passion
is that the caprice lasts a little longer.

But it cannot be denied that Lord Wotton comes up with some
effective paradoxes, such as:

I choose my friends for their good looks, my acquaintances for
their good characters, and my enemies for their good
intellects.
American girls are as clever at concealing their parents, as
English women are at concealing their past.
Philanthropic people lose all sense of humanity. It is their
distinguishing characteristic.
I can stand brute force, but brute reason is quite
unbearable.
I like Wagner's music better than anybody's. It is so loud that
one can talk the whole time without other people hearing
what one says.
A *grande passion* is the privilege of people who have nothing
to do.
Women inspire us with the desire to do masterpieces and
always prevent us from carrying them out.

The man who could call a spade a spade should be compelled to use one.

But Lord Wotton's paradoxes are more often interchangeable
aphorisms:

Sin is the only real color-element left in modern life.
Virtue is the only real color-element left in modern life.

The truth is that *Dorian Gray* reveals Lord Wotton's fatuous-
ness, but criticizes it at the same time. People say of him: "Don't
mind him, my dear. He never means anything that he says."

Lord Henry played with the idea and grew willful; tossed it
into the air and transformed it; let it escape and recaptured
it; made it iridescent with fancy and winged it with paradox. . . . He felt that the eyes of Dorian Gray were fixed on
him, and the consciousness that amongst his audience there
was one whose temperament he wished to fascinate seemed
to give his wit keenness and to lend color to his imagination.

Some of Wilde's best paradoxes appear in *Phrases and Philosophies for the Use of the Young,* which he published as maxims for life
in an Oxford student magazine:

The well-bred contradict other people. The wise contradict
themselves.
Ambition is the last refuge of the failure.
In examinations the foolish ask questions that the wise
cannot answer.
Only the great masters of style ever succeed in being obscure.

The first duty in life is to be as artificial as possible. What the
  second duty is no one has as yet discovered.
Nothing that actually occurs is of the smallest importance.
Dullness is the coming of age of seriousness.
If one tells the truth, one is sure, sooner or later, to be
  found out.
Only the shallow know themselves.

But the extent to which he considered these real teachings is un-
clear; when some of them were challenged at his trial, he responded: "I rarely think that anything I write is true." It is right
not to require of Wilde a strict distinction between (true) paradoxes, (obvious) aphorisms, and aphorisms that are interchangeable (false, or devoid of any truth value). What he exhibits is *furor
sententialis* (which is an agreeable rhetorical incontinence) rather
than a passion for philosophy.

If this is the case, then we might as well invent a new form of
false paradox, and false aphorism, which would serve only to have
us recognize the existence of commonplaces in which we ourselves
become embroiled every day.

Not so long ago, I came across a delightful little book: *Scusa
l'anticipo ma ho trovato tutti verdi* (Sorry I'm Early, But All the
Lights Were Green). It contains five hundred reversed commonplaces, of which here are just a few:

Sometimes fiction is stranger than truth.
I don't believe in God, but I do believe in the Church.
First he killed himself, then he killed his wife and children
  with the same gun.
Thank you for being so far from me at this time.
My great regret is never having broken off my studies.

It's time Santa Claus realized that children don't exist.

I may be senile, but I'm not old.

They stole my wallet, but it's not about the documents and the keys, it's the money.

Don't sleep, because afterwards you won't drink your Coca-Cola.

It's not the humidity, it's the heat.

Potassium is rich in bananas.

I don't understand ancient art.

After all, Mussolini did some bad things too.

The organizers estimated ten thousand, the police one hundred thousand.

Venice is the Amsterdam of the South.

Albinos have music in their blood.

It used to be all houses round here.

The Chinese are all different.

It seems it's better to sleep with a pillow.

I'd use Linux, but it's too easy.

Now here is a series of famous paradoxes by the Austrian satirist Karl Kraus. I will not try to reverse these; if you think about them, you will see it is not possible. They contain unconventional truths that run counter to popular opinion, and they cannot be twisted to express an opposing truth.

Scandal begins when the police put a stop to it.

To be perfect all one needs is a defect.

The ideal of virginity is the ideal of those who want to deflower.

Penalties serve to deter those who are not inclined to commit any crimes.

> There is an obscure region of the Earth that sends explorers
>   throughout the world.
> Children play at soldiers. But why do soldiers play at being
>   children?

Of course, Kraus also commits the sin of the interchangeable aphorism, so some of his maxims can easily be contradicted, and hence reversed:

> Nothing is more unfathomable than a woman's superficiality.
> *Nothing is more superficial than a woman's unfathomability.*

> I would rather forgive an ugly foot than an ugly stocking.
> *I would rather forgive an ugly stocking than an ugly foot.*

> There are women who are not beautiful but only look that way.
> *There are women who are beautiful but don't look that way.*

> The superman is a premature ideal that presupposes a man.
> *Man is a premature ideal that presupposes the superman.*

The only paradoxes that almost never seem interchangeable are those of the Polish aphorist Stanislaw J. Lec. Here is a brief selection of his *Unkempt Thoughts* (1984):

> If only one could pay the death penalty by sleeping through
>   it in installments.
> I dreamed of reality. What a relief to wake up!
> Open Sesame—I want to get out!
> Who knows what Columbus might have discovered if
>   America hadn't blocked his way!

Horrible is the gag smeared with honey.

The prawn goes red after death. What exemplary refinement in a victim!

If you knock down monuments, spare the pedestals. They can always be used again.

He possessed knowledge, but was unable to make her pregnant.

In his modesty he considered himself a scribbler. But he was merely an informer.

Burning pyres do not light up the darkness.

You can die on Saint Helena without being Napoleon.

They hugged each other so tightly there was no room for feelings.

He covered his head with the ashes of his victims.

I dreamed of Freud. What does that mean?

Frequenting dwarfs is bad for your backbone.

He had a clear conscience. Never used it.

Even in his silence there were grammatical; errors.

I admit that I have a weakness for Lec, but I would like to end with a paradox of his that has always served as a guide for me, even though I have not always followed it, and I hope it will do the same for you:

Reflect, before you think.

[La Milanesiana, 2010]

8. Untruths, Lies, Falsifications

The topic of lying is one of the most controversial matters in the history of logic and the philosophy of language, not to mention ethics and political science, and if you wish to have a rough idea of this huge debate I can recommend a slender volume as essential: Maria Bettetini's *Breve storia della bugia* (Brief History of the Lie). For those who feel like tackling a few hundred pages more, there is Andrea Tagliapietra's *Filosofia della bugia* (Philosophy of the Lie). If I have agreed to stick my nose into this subject (and the allusion to Pinocchio is purely coincidental) it is because, not only have I written novels and essays on falsehood and falsification, many people still cite a passage of mine on the topic. In *A Theory of Semiotics* (1975) I wrote that we must consider anything that can be used to lie as a sign. The smoke that rises from a flame in front of us is not a sign, because it tells us nothing that we do not know already; but the smoke rising from a hilltop is not only a sign of a fire, which we cannot see, it might be used by Indians to signal something. Or someone might be producing it chemically to make us believe in a nonexistent fire, or to convince us that there are Indians on that hilltop when in fact that is not true.

Nonetheless, that definition of mine was too restrictive: I should have said that a sign is anything that can be used to tell not a lie, but, better still, *something that is not the case in the real world*. Because, just as fiction tells us *what is the case* in a possible world different from our own, the lie is only one of the many ways to say *something that is not the case in the real world*.

Let me explain. When Ptolemy claimed that the Sun travels around the Earth he certainly stated something that was not the case, but he said it because he was *mistaken*; he did not tell a lie. To lie is to say the opposite of what one believes to be the case, whereas Ptolemy believed in perfect good faith that the Sun moved. But now let's imagine that Ptolemy had wanted to infiltrate a secret sect of followers of Aristarchus of Samos, who claimed that it was the Earth that revolved around the Sun, and that in order to be accepted by the conspirators he told them all that the Earth definitely revolves around the Sun. Well, by doing so, Ptolemy would certainly have spoken the truth as we know it—and yet, by stating the opposite of what he believed to be true, he would have been lying. So, saying something false is an *aletic* problem, meaning a problem related to the notion of *aletheia*—that is, truth—but lying is more than that, being an ethical or moral problem. You can be a liar regardless of whether you are telling the truth or not. Iago, who accuses the innocent Desdemona, is certainly a liar, but let's assume that, unbeknownst to Iago, Desdemona really has slept with Cassio. Even as he tells Othello the truth, Iago is a liar all the same.

There are some dolts who, if you deal too much with lies or better still with various cases of falsification, as happened to me in my novel *The Prague Cemetery*, immediately challenge you. They say that, if you portray the world as being full of falsifiers and the story itself as the realm of lies, then you are arguing that truth does not exist—and hence you are a relativist. This is complete nonsense, not to be permitted even to those who have never studied philosophy in high school or the seminary.

To say that something is mistaken or false or that it is the result of falsification, you need to have a notion of what is correct or true or authentic. Of course, there are different levels of truth and various ways to verify whether something is actually the case. If I say, "it's raining outside," the truth of my statement can be verified on the basis of personal experience. You need only go outside and hold out your hand. If I say that sulfuric acid is H_2SO_4, you assume that it is true on the basis of notions that we might call textbook, but if you really insist, you can also ask to be admitted to a laboratory where sulfuric acid will be produced before your eyes (even though this does not strike me as a great satisfaction). If someone tells you, "Napoleon died on Saint Helena on May 5, 1821," you are faced with a historical truth that you will believe because your encyclopedia reports that somewhere, let's say in the British admiralty, there is documentation of this event. But there is always a chance that Saint Helena's governor, Hudson Lowe, filed documents that were incorrect (perhaps having misread the calendar) or mendacious (perhaps to conceal the fact that he had let Napoleon escape to Argentina) or that someone in London later forged Hudson Lowe's original report by changing, for reasons we will not be investigating here, the day and the month.

And so we have justified the title of my speech: there are differences among telling untruths, lying, and falsifying, even though this triad actually covers a much wider field of phenomena. For example, is it true or false to say that the Holy Spirit proceeds from both the Father and the Son (*filioque*)? It is true for the Pope, who therefore does not lie when he says so, but it is false for the Patriarch of Constantinople, who accuses the Pope of—at the very least—making a mistake, without which the Great Schism would not have happened. In what sense is it true that Our Lady appeared at Lourdes, since we only have the testimony of Bernadette Soubirous? And if this is so, why does the Roman Catholic Church question whether Our Lady appears in Medjugorje despite the testimony of six visionaries? For truth of this type, the criteria of verification are very different from those used for sulfuric acid.

The Ethics of the Lie

But since any examination of what is true and what is false is a titanic undertaking, let's restrict ourselves to the ethical problems of lying. Lying is prohibited by one of the Commandments, but we know that most of them fall into the category of what the church describes as "less serious matter," which is moreover what makes the difference between mortal sin and venial sin. For example, given *Honor thy father and mother*, there is a difference between telling your mum not to be a bloody nuisance and killing her with a hammer, whereas (so I was taught in my day) less serious matter cannot apply to the commission of impure acts (covered generally by the sixth commandment). In other words, those who rape their grandmothers will go to hell as surely as any adolescent who gets mildly excited by a photo of Monica Bellucci. What happens with *Thou shalt not bear false witness*?

There have been political laxists, like Plato, who admitted that, to educate young people in the path of virtue, it was permissible to tell them (clearly fantastical) myths, all the way down to Machiavelli:

Everyone admits how praiseworthy it is in a prince to keep faith . . . . Nevertheless our experience has been that those princes who have done great things have held good faith of little account, and have known how to circumvent the intellect of men by craft, and in the end have overcome those who have relied on their word. . . . Therefore a wise lord cannot, nor ought he to, keep faith when such observance may be turned against him. . . . If men were entirely good this precept would not hold, but because they are bad, and will not keep faith with you, you too are not bound to observe it with them. . . . Therefore it is necessary for him to have a mind ready to turn itself accordingly as the winds and variations of fortune force it, yet, as I have said above, not to diverge from the good if he can avoid doing so, but, if compelled, then to know how to set about it.

Francis Bacon (*Essays*, 6) pointed out that "dissimulation is but a faint kind of policy, or wisdom; for it asketh a strong wit, and a strong heart, to know when to tell truth, and to do it. Therefore it is the weaker sort of politics, that are the great dissemblers." And Baltasar Gracián noted that "knowing how to dissemble is a great gift for he who rules." Anyone, even today, would think that a general who—under questioning—revealed his plan of attack to an enemy, would be mad—and, from Caesar to Trithemius down to the Enigma code, armies have used various forms of cryptography to communicate through dissimulation.

All the more reason why telling the truth is dangerous and inadvisable in diplomacy. And we make extensive use of diplomatic lies ourselves in our little games of everyday diplomacy, when we say we are pleased to make the acquaintance of someone we would have gladly avoided meeting, or when we turn down an invitation to dinner citing illness to avoid saying that the host's food is notoriously awful.

But rigorists have always maintained that we should never lie for any reason, not even to save a human life. St. Augustine proposed the extreme example of those who have hidden in their own home someone that a vicious murderer is seeking to kill; when the killer asks us if the victim is in our house, good heart if not common sense would require us to lie, yet we must not tell a merciful lie even in that case. The topic was taken up by Immanuel Kant (*On ethical duty toward others, On a supposed right to lie from benevolent motives, On lies*). Benjamin Constant (*Political Reactions*) maintained that, while telling the truth is a duty, nevertheless "no one has the right to a truth that harms others." What we know is like an inheritance we can pass on to others or not, depending on our will. For Kant, instead, veracity was an unconditional duty. "If a man bears false witness he does no wrong to any man in particular but he wrongs humanity, because if his conduct were generalized the natural human desire to know would be thwarted."

As for the murderer who asks you the whereabouts of the victim you are hiding, Kant's argument reveals that the great man was capable of talking nonsense every now and then (as when he claimed that music is an inferior art because even those who do not want to hear it are obliged to listen to it, whereas with a painting you can always look elsewhere). He says: if you lie and say that the victim is not in your house and the killer goes to look for him elsewhere, and it might be that the victim had left your house without your knowledge, then the murderer might come across him nearby and kill him. Whereas if you admit that the victim is in your house and the killer enters, a neighbor might come in and catch the killer before he commits the crime. That it was his duty to capture the murderer never seems to have crossed Kant's mind. The meek professor was waiting for his neighbor.

A more balanced view of lying was held by Thomas Aquinas, who in his *Summa theologiae* (II-II, 110) forgave as a venial fault both the *jocose* lie told for fun, and the *officious* lie, told to serve some useful purpose (for example, one that does not harm anyone but helps save someone's life or chastity). Instead he condemned as a mortal sin the *malicious* lie, which "does not help anyone and harms someone," which "benefits one person by harming another," or "is told solely for the sake of lying and deceiving." And it should be noted, according to almost all authors, that contributing factors in the definition of the lie include not only the awareness that one is saying what is considered to be false, but also the intention to do harm.

Instead, with regard to "white" lies, the Jesuits were later to talk about *peccatum philosophicum* or *peccatillum*, which gave us (Kant suggested) the word *bagatelle*.

But this is no bagatelle. Even today we ask ourselves whether concealing the severity of an illness from a dear one is an act of compassion or an example of deception. And if what Aquinas (II-II, 112, 1 co.) called boastfulness, or getting above oneself, is blameworthy, what about the fact that Kant also condemned false modesty affected to avoid offending the less gifted? And is agreeing with Socrates and saying "I know nothing" in order to get the better of someone who knows less than us the same as telling the taxman "I possess nothing"?

Baroque Simulation

The century that thought about these problems with the greatest subtlety was the age of the Baroque, the century of the birth of absolutism and reasons of state, the century of Mazarin who passed the time not only scanning the faces of others in search of lies but also concealing what he was reading or writing at that time and throwing elaborate little parties where the meat had to look like fish, the fish look like meat, and the fruit look like vegetables because deceitful appearances aroused wonder. This was the century of theatrical liars Iago, Don Giovanni, and Tartuffe, but also the century in which architects like Borromini lied with deceptive and ambiguous perspectives, the century in which appearance was more important than the heart of things because it was the century in which the eye and sight became instruments for the exploration of the universe, the century in which one Giuseppe Battista proposed an *Apologia della menzogna* (Apology for Deception, 1673), a work containing emblematic representations of fraud and simulation.

Torquato Accetto, in his *Dissimulazione onesta* (Honest Dissimulation, 1641), does not praise simulation, which shows something to be what it is not, but dissimulation, which is *not showing something for what it is*—and practices the false modesty that Kant was to condemn. For Accetto (in a century of plots, deceit, threats, and ambushes):

> prudent living comes with purity of spirit . . . on a path strewn with obstacles it is necessary to proceed with slow and sure steps . . . the Gospels invite us to be shrewd as snakes and innocent as doves . . . he who cannot feign cannot live . . . and dissimulation is none other than an industry, that of not letting things be seen as they are, a veil made of honest shadows . . . from which men do not fashion falsehood but give the truth a little rest . . . If someone were to wear a mask every day he would be better known than any other . . . but of the excellent dissimulators of the past and the present we know nothing at all.

Indeed, Accetto, who confesses at a certain point that he published his book in a bloodless sort of way "because writing about dissimulation obliged me to dissimulate," was so successful in this that no one paid any attention to him, and we had to wait until Benedetto Croce rediscovered his book, lying forgotten on a dusty bookshelf.

On the other hand, although Descartes did not shun fame, after Galileo's conviction he decided not to publish the book *Le monde ou traité de la lumière,* which he had been working on since 1630, and so he respected the motto *bene qui latuit, bene vixit,* or one who lives well, lives unnoticed.

It would be easy to say that, while Accetto praises dissimulation, Baltasar Gracián in *The Art of Worldly Wisdom* (1647) praises simulation. But things are not that simple, especially for a baroque Jesuit. Gracián never ceases to assert that politics must not be confused with deception, that "only truth can give true reputation"; he accuses Machiavelli of being a *valiente embustero*—that is to say, a valiant liar—who "seems to have candor on his lips and purity on his tongue but spits out hellfire that sets customs and republics ablaze." At first sight it seems that what he preaches in order to survive in his day is prudence, discretion, and reserve—because one needs "judicious caution in telling the truth that even without lying should not be told all at once" and "nothing requires caution more than the truth; telling it is *like having blood drawn from your own heart. As much skill is required to tell the truth, as is required to keep silent about it."*

But there is only a short step between extreme discretion and timid simulation. Gracián knew (as Machiavelli had already counselled) that you have to be both a fox and a lion, that practical wisdom consists in knowing how to dissimulate, that cunning is more valuable than strength, that "things are held in consideration not for what they are, but for what they appear to be" and that "to be worthy and to be able to show that worth is to be worth double," that "what cannot be seen is as if it did not exist" and "showing your cards is neither useful nor pleasant," that "there is no perfection that does not risk being seen as barbarous if the splendor of artifice does not assist it," that "we should not always act openly because otherwise others will notice this uniformity and will forestall and perhaps frustrate our actions," that we must support others to obtain what we want, not reveal our weaknesses, shift the blame for our mistakes on to others, and never keep the company of those who can belittle us, and that "a good toothpaste perfumes the mouth and knowing how to sell hot air is a great subtlety of life, because most things can be paid for with words . . ."

Finally, "Man's life is a war against the malice of men. Sagacity fights with strategic changes of intention: it never does what it threatens, it aims only at escaping notice. It aims in the air with dexterity and strikes home in an unexpected direction, always seeking to conceal its game. It lets a purpose appear . . . but then turns round and conquers by the unexpected."

Come now, Gracián is not Accetto, and this is why his maxims were so well received in the centuries after him.

Narrative Fiction

Certain phenomenological texts on lying cite narrative fiction as a secondary and admissible case. But *narrative fiction* is not lying. In saying that on Lake Como a curate was threatened by two bravoes, Manzoni does not intend to lie: he pretends that the story he is recounting really happened and he asks us to take part in his fiction, suspending—as Coleridge wished—our disbelief, just like a little boy who pretends that his stick is a rifle and asks us to play along with him by pretending to be the lion he has shot dead.

In narrative fiction we do not say something untrue in order to deceive anyone, or to do them harm: we construct a *possible world* and ask the complicit reader or spectator to inhabit it as if it were a real world and to accept the rules that apply to it as credible (talking animals, magic, humanly impossible deeds).

Naturally, narrative fiction requires the presence of signals of fictionality. Sometimes these signals are given by the "paratext," from the title to the denomination on the cover that says "novel," to the information given in the cover flaps. Within the text itself, the most obvious fictional signal is the introductory formula "once upon a time . . . ," but there are other signals of fictionality such as beginning the narrative *in medias res*, starting off with dialogue, persisting with an individual rather than a general story, and so on. But there are no incontrovertible signals of fictionality.

Narrative fiction often begins with a false signal of veracity. One example may serve for all:

> The author of these Travels, Mr. Lemuel Gulliver, is my ancient and intimate friend; there is likewise some relation between us on the mother's side. About three years ago, Mr. Gulliver growing weary of the concourse of curious people coming to him at his house in Redriff, made a small purchase of land, with a convenient house, near Newark, in Nottinghamshire, his native country; where he now lives retired, yet in good esteem among his neighbors. . . . Before he quitted Redriff, he left the custody of the following papers in my hands. . . . I have carefully perused them three times. . . . There is an air of truth apparent through the whole; and in-

deed the author was so distinguished for his veracity, that it became a sort of proverb among his neighbors at Redriff, when any one affirmed a thing, to say, it was as true as if Mr. Gulliver had spoken it.

If you look at the frontispiece and first page of the first edition of *Gulliver's Travels* (1726): the name Lemuel Gulliver is given as the author of a truthful autobiography whereas there is no mention of Jonathan Swift as the author of the work of fiction it is. This is a bizarre but not infrequent case: if, given the signals of fictionality, everything appearing in the narrative goes under the heading of *pretense*, the cover, which excludes and denies fictionality, would in fact be mendacious. We could say that in those days the public was ready to recognize the fictionality of the "utopian voyage" genre, and that, from the *True History* by Lucian of Samosata (second century) onwards, exaggerated assertions of truthfulness sounded like a signal of fictionality, but often narrative fiction contains such a tightly bound assortment of precise references to the real world that, after spending a little time in a novel, and having become confused by its fantastic elements and references to reality, readers no longer know exactly where they are.

Hence the phenomenon of readers who take novels seriously as if they dealt with things that really happened and who attribute the opinions of the characters to the author. And as a writer of fiction I can assure you that beyond, say, ten thousand copies there is a shift from a public accustomed to reading novels to an unsophisticated public who see novels as a series of true statements; just as in the old Sicilian puppet theatre where, at the end of the show, the spectators would try to lynch the perfidious Gano di Maganza.

Bad Faith

Thus far the lie has seemed to be a dyadic relationship between the deceiver and the deceived. But there is a lie based on a monadic relationship and one based on a triadic relationship.

Bad faith is a monadic relationship, through which someone, who nevertheless knows the truth, lies to himself—and usually ends up believing it. In cases of bad faith the person who is lied to and the person who lies are one and the same, which means that, as a deceiver, I ought to know the truth that I am concealing from myself, the deceived. Perhaps the most beautiful pages on bad faith were penned by Jean-Paul Sartre in *Being and Nothingness* (1943), where he tells us the story of a lady who agrees to go and visit a man who she knows desires her, and who should understand that, from the moment she enters that apartment, her fate is sealed. But she denies this to herself, takes her host's words at face value when he says he admires her, and understands this admiration in a spiritual and not in a carnal sense. She refuses to perceive her host's desire for what it is and recognizes it only insofar as it transcends itself toward admiration. But then at a certain point her host takes her hand. If she leaves it there it means that she has accepted that the relationship has taken a new turn. If she withdraws it, she will break the "troubled and unstable harmony which gives the hour its charm."

> The aim is to postpone the moment of decision as long as possible. We know what happens next; the young woman leaves her hand there, but she does not notice that she is leaving it. She does not notice because it happens by chance that she is at this moment all intellect.... And during this time the divorce of the body from the soul is accomplished; the hand

rests inert between the warm hands of her companion—
neither consenting nor resisting—a thing.

The page in question is perhaps a little male-chauvinistic, but if
we think of Sartre's physical appearance, it is rather pathetic. Who
knows what the lady was like.

Irony

Irony may instead be a triadic relationship, though not necessarily.
With irony we say the opposite of the truth ("That's very clever of
you," "But Brutus is an honorable man"), and irony works if the
interlocutor knows what the truth is. To help him, signals of irony
are used (see Harald Weinrich, *The Linguistics of Lying*) such as
winking, clearing the throat, using a particular tone of voice and,
in writing, the use of quotation marks, italics, or even (the shame
of it) suspension points. And at this point irony becomes fiction.
But if your interlocutor is stupid, no signal of irony is enough, and
so you might as well make fun of him. And this is where irony presupposes a triadic relationship. The victim does not understand
the liar's irony (and therefore gives credence to the lie) and only a
third witness to the exchange understands what the ironist meant
to say—so that the ironist and the witness make fun of the victim.

Falsifying

Is there another case of the triadically structured lie? Yes, in line
with the principle of falsification or counterfeiting.

The counterfeiting of a pseudo-double lends itself to *false identification* that occurs when A (legitimate Author), in historical circumstances t_1, produces O (Original Object) while C (Counterfeiter) in

historical circumstances t_2 produces CO (Counterfeit Object). But CO is not necessarily a forgery because C could have produced CO as an exercise or for fun. It is likely that the Donation of Constantine was initially produced as a mere rhetorical exercise and only in the following centuries was it considered (in good or bad faith) authentic. But we are interested in the intentions of the false identifier (Identifier I) who asserts that CO is indiscernibly identical to O. Only then does CO become a Fake, and that is why false identification brings a triadic relationship into play (in which, of course, Counterfeiter and Identifier may coincide, in which case we are looking at a manifest lie, while if the Identifier is not the Counterfeiter he might make his judgment of identity in good faith, and therefore would not be lying even though he would still be saying something untrue).

For a forgery to be successful, there must be a notion of identity between two objects or individuals. And in order not to lose ourselves in Leibniz's notion of the identity of the indiscernible, let us content ourselves with that of Aristotle's *Metaphysics* (V, 9, 1018a): two things that are supposed to be different are recognized as the same if they occupy the same portion of space at the same time.

The difficulty, in the case of counterfeits, is that normally something present is put on display as if it were the original whereas the presumed original (if it exists) is somewhere else. It is therefore not possible to prove that there are two different objects that occupy two different spaces at the same time.

The counterfeit, obviously, is a success if the copy is in some way similar to the original, or to the community's idea of the original. Otherwise, given Raphael's widely discussed *Vision of Ezekiel*, no one would believe its counterfeit was similar and the problem would not exist. But certainly, with the exception of the experts, people are puzzled by the two works: which of these two paintings is a fake?

In our everyday experience, the commonest case of error owing to similarity is the one where we have difficulty in distinguishing between two tokens of the same type, as when during a party we put our drink down next to another, and then we do not know which one is ours. But in that case we are dealing with confusion between doubles.

A *double* is a physical *token* that possesses all the properties of another physical token, insofar as both have all the pertinent features prescribed by an abstract *type*. In this sense two chairs of the same model or two sheets of A4 printing paper are both doubles of each other. Doubles do not lend themselves to purposes of falsification and deception because, even though they are not indiscernible, they are *interchangeable*. It is true that a microscopic analysis could prove that two sheets of A4 paper have quite significant differences, but we usually consider that, for our purposes, one is worth the other.

Instead, we are dealing with *pseudo-doubles* when only one of the tokens of the type assumes, for one or more users, a particular value. In the case of collecting, particular value is attributed to a token when only one or a very few copies of a certain stamp survive, or the copy of an antique book bears the signature of the author. At this point it becomes interesting to forge a double and this is what happens with rare stamps. For the purpose of everyday trading, two banknotes of the same value should be considered doubles, and therefore interchangeable. But from a legal point of view they are different because they carry a different serial number— even though this difference becomes relevant only when a certain banknote has been used to pay a ransom or is the result of a bank robbery.

Nonetheless, interesting questions such as this one have been posed. Can we consider authentic a banknote printed (with fraudulent intent) on genuine watermarked paper, with the machinery of the issuing authority, by the director of the issuing authority, which is assigned the same number as another banknote, printed legally a few minutes before? If ever it was possible to establish which was printed first, only the first banknote would be authentic—as in the case of the birth of two royal twins, but there, however, it has been insinuated that the twin conceived first is the second to be born. Or should it be decided to destroy one of the two notes at random and consider the remaining one to be the original, which was perhaps the system used for the Man in the Iron Mask?

If the one we have examined is a case of *false strong identification*, we have *false weak identification* or *presumption of interchangeability* when we know perfectly well that *CO* cannot be identified with *O*, but it is held that the two objects are equivalent in terms of value and function and, since there is no precise notion of authorial originality, one is used as the equivalent of the other. This was the case for the Roman patricians who considered themselves aesthetically satisfied with a copy of a Greek statue, and perhaps had it signed "Phidias" or "Praxiteles." And it is the same with tourists who admire a copy of Michelangelo's *David* outside Palazzo Vecchio in Florence, unconcerned by the fact that the original is kept in the Galleria dell'Accademia. Perhaps the Californian visiting public admire the reproduction of the *David* in Forest Lawn cemetery as an original, which means that they do not have a precise idea of what an original is. Again in California I visited a wax museum in Buena Park, where the public probably enjoyed the version of *David* present there as an original.

Sometimes *C* transforms the authentic object into a counterfeit version of itself. For example, unfaithful restorations are carried out on paintings or statues that transform the work, censor parts of the body, and break up a polyptych. Strictly speaking, those ancient works of art that we consider originals have instead been transformed by the action of time or men—and have undergone amputations, restorations, alteration or loss of color. We need only think of the neoclassical ideal of a "white" Hellenism, whereas the original temples and statues were multicolored.

But, given that any material is subject to physical and chemical alterations from the very moment of creation, then every object should be seen as a permanent counterfeit of itself. To avoid this paranoid attitude, our culture has developed flexible criteria for deciding on the physical integrity of an object. For example, from an aesthetic point of view, it is usually said that a work of art lives on its own organic integrity, which is lost if it is deprived of one of its parts. But from an archaeological point of view it is thought that, even if the same work of art has lost some parts, it is still authentically original. It so happens that the Parthenon in Athens has lost its colors, a large quantity of its original architectural features, and some of its stones. But those that remain are presumably the same ones laid down by the original builders. The Parthenon in Nashville, Tennessee, was built in accordance with the Greek model as it appeared at the time of its splendor; it is formally complete, so much so that it is the Greek Parthenon that should be considered an alteration or a counterfeit of the one in Nashville. However, the half-temple located on the Acropolis is considered to be both more "authentic" and more "beautiful" than its American facsimile, not least because it stands in its context. In fact, the fundamental flaw in the Nashville Parthenon is that it stands on a plain and not at the top of an Acropolis.

What happens if the authentic object either no longer exists, or has never existed—in any case, if it has never been seen by anyone? This is the case of *apocrypha* or *pseudepigraphs*. It is maintained that an object *CO* coincides with an authentic object that has never actually existed. This is the case of the great forger Han van Meegeren, whose *Supper in Emmaus*, attributed to Vermeer but actually painted in 1937, was sold (at current values) for two and a half million dollars. When van Meegeren, who was accused of selling Flemish and Dutch works of art to Goering, confessed in the postwar period that these had all been fakes made by his own hand, nobody believed him. To be acquitted of all charges he had to paint another fake in prison to demonstrate his ability.

It is still an open question as to whether such counterfeits are always caused by fraudulent intentions. In theory, a block of marble subjected to the action of water for centuries could be seen as a work by Brancusi, without anyone intending to deceive anyone. Perhaps this was initially the case regarding the fake Modiglianis, if it is true that the persons who made them only did so for fun and then threw them away. But we find an explicit case of pseudepigraphs in the fake Hitler diaries, where the counterfeit is claimed to be an authentic object that never existed.

There are cases in which the counterfeiter knows very well that the original object does not exist, yet believes in good faith that the fake has all the functions that the original object would have had, and presents it as such in its place. This is the typical case of the *diplomatic forgery*. The medieval monks who produced false documents to backdate or expand the possessions of their abbeys believed, on the basis of the tradition, they had really obtained the privileges in question, and sought only to demonstrate this fact publicly. Paradoxically—at least for a mind dominated by unshakeable prejudice—the *Protocols of the Elders of Zion* also belong to this type, in the sense that their authors were aware that the book was a fake but held it to be a sacrosanct one because it formulated what they believed were the real plans of the Jews. This is what the well-known anti-Semite Nesta Webster had to say about it in 1924:

The only opinion to which I have committed myself is that, whether genuine or not, the Protocols do represent the program of world revolution, and that in view of their prophetic nature and of their extraordinary resemblance to the protocols of certain secret societies in the past, they were either the work of some such society or of someone profoundly versed in the lore of secret societies who was able to reproduce their ideas and phraseology.

The Fake Ex Nihilo

It is known that there is a set of different objects, all produced by an author *A* whose fame has been handed down over the centuries (let's say, all the known works of Picasso). From the whole set *A* we can derive an abstract type, which does not take into account all the features of the individual members of that set, but rather presents a sort of generative rule (such as the style, or the type of materials used). A fake is produced and it is claimed to be the work of author *A*. This is the case of the false Picasso sold in 2010 for two million dollars by an antiquarian dealer from Los Angeles, who had paid the counterfeiter a thousand dollars for it. Honestly, on closer inspection, it was worth even less than that, and the victims of the fraud deserve no sympathy. But when, instead, the imitative nature of the object is openly admitted, then we have a work produced *in the manner of* the artist (either as a tribute or as a parody).

The only case of false attribution in which we can know with certainty that two objects are not identical is the one where someone shows us, for example, a reproduction of the *Mona Lisa* while standing in front of the original on show in the Louvre, claiming that the two objects are indiscernibly the same one. This is an admittedly unlikely event, yet even in that case the doubt would remain that the alleged fake is really the authentic *Mona Lisa,* while the one in the Louvre is a fake which has been maliciously (or erroneously) hung on the wall for goodness knows how long—as in, when the painting was found again after the famous theft of 1911.

To prove that a fake is a fake, it is necessary to provide proof of authenticity for the presumptive original.

Proof of Authenticity

Obviously, modern science has many criteria for establishing the authenticity of an original. However, all of these tests seem to aim more at proving that something is fake rather than determining whether it is authentic. A document is false if its material support, such as parchment, does not date from the time of its presumed origins, and today we are able to date finds with considerable accuracy. But while the proof that the Shroud of Turin material dated from the Middle Ages would certainly make it unlikely that the body of Jesus was ever wrapped in it, even if the fabric dated back to the first century of our era, that still would not prove it was used to wrap his body. Modern philologists have shown that the hermetic *Asclepius* was not translated, as was previously assumed, by Mario Vittorino, because in his texts Vittorino always put the word *etenim* at the beginning of the sentence, whereas in the *Asclepius* that word appears second in a sentence in twenty-one cases out of twenty-five. Still, if another text is discovered to have *etenim* always appearing first in the sentence, this does not prove that it was produced by Mario Vittorino.

Sometimes scholars decide to determine whether the conceptual categories, the line of reasoning, the iconological models, and so on, are consistent with the cultural milieu of the presumptive authors.

But while it is reasonable to suppose that a text attributed to, let's say, Plato is false if it contains references to the Gospel of St. John, there is no way to show that a text was written before Christ only because it does not contain any references to the Gospels.

A document is a forgery if the external events it cites could not have been known at the time of its production. Lorenzo Valla denies the authenticity of the Donation of Constantine because, for example, the Donation speaks of Constantinople as a patriarchate when, at the presumed time of its composition, Constantinople went by another name and was not yet a patriarchate. Recent studies on an alleged exchange of letters between Churchill and Mussolini have shown that, despite the genuineness of the paper used, the correspondence must be considered false because, for example, one letter appears to have been written from a house in which by that time Churchill had no longer lived for years; another one deals with events that occurred after the date on the letter.

But if the Donation of Constantine had not mentioned Constantinople, would this prove its authenticity? A text is certainly not by Plato if it mentions the Thirty Years War, but is a text that mentions the Thirty Years War therefore by Descartes?

The prevailing notion of falsification presupposes a "true" original with which the fake should be compared. But we have seen how weak our criteria for determining authenticity are. Moreover, all the aforementioned criteria seem useful only when dealing with "imperfect" fakes. Is there a "perfect fake" that resists any given philological criterion? If today an art forger of the genius of van Meegeren managed to get hold of a poplar board datable to 1500 or thereabouts, if he could get hold of oils and paint identical to those used by Leonardo, and if he replaced the Mona Lisa with a copy that was absolutely perfect in terms of style and execution and capable of reacting positively to all the chemical tests required, would we be able to discover the forgery? And who can say that this has not already happened?

An Optimistic Perspective

Despite this, even though no single criterion is one hundred percent satisfactory, we usually rely on reasonable conjecture based on some balanced assessment of various methods of verification. It is like a trial, where one witness can seem unreliable, but three witnesses who agree are taken seriously; one clue can appear to be weak, but three clues form a system. In all these cases we rely on criteria of interpretative economy. Judgments of authenticity are the result of persuasive arguments, based on proofs that are likely, albeit not entirely irrefutable, and we accept these proofs because it is more reasonably economical to accept them than to spend time casting doubt upon them.

We question the socially accepted authenticity of an object or a document only when some proof to the contrary unsettles our established beliefs. Otherwise, we would have to examine the *Mona Lisa* every time we go to the Louvre, because we have no proof that the *Mona Lisa* seen today is the one seen the day before that has perhaps been replaced overnight.

But such verification would be necessary for every judgment of identity. In fact, there is no guarantee that the friend Tom I meet today is the same one as I met yesterday, because Tom undergoes far more physical (biological) changes than a painting or a statue. In addition, the person I believe to be Tom could be Dick who has mischievously disguised himself as Tom (think of master criminal Diabolik's rubber masks). Tom is not more difficult to counterfeit than the *Mona Lisa*; on the contrary, it is easier to successfully disguise a person than it is to successfully copy a picture—except that it is usually economically more advantageous to forge a banknote or make a fake statue.

In order to recognize Tom every day (or in order to decide that the Cathedral I see today is the same one I visited last year), our parents, husbands, wives, and children must rely on certain instinctive procedures based mainly on the social contract. Such procedures are shown to be reliable because, by using them, our species has managed to survive for millions of years. And this proof, based on adaptation to the environment, is enough for us.

On the other hand, not only is it true that we manage to move around the world with some certainty, asserting that something is true even though we are often wrong, but it is also true that those who lie or falsify are almost always found out. It is possible that there are many unrecognized fakes in our museums, or that Julius Caesar lied to us about how the battle of Alesia unfolded, and to this day we do not know whether Nero really was crazy and set Rome on fire or whether he was the victim of malicious historians. But we do know for sure—and on the strength of philological science—that Constantine made no donation. And it is also true that, if a politician announced a tax cut and then the cut was not made, the massive presence of the facts would tell us that the politician had lied. Hannah Arendt takes a pragmatic view in her 1971 "Lying in Politics":

> secrecy—what diplomatically is called discretion as well as the *arcana imperii*, the mysteries of government—and deception, the deliberate falsehood and the outright lie used as legitimate means to achieve political ends, have been with us since the beginning of recorded history. Truthfulness has never been counted among the political virtues, and lies have always been regarded as justifiable tools in political dealings.

But in the end, when faced with the notorious Pentagon Papers documenting how the American government has lied about various aspects of the conduct of the Vietnam War, she judges the lie to be untenable. Noting that the official line does not stand up in light of the facts, she classifies that form of systematic lying as an offense against factuality that, when it becomes so generalized, engenders a pathological politics. And comparison with the unvarnished facts has led to the recognition that the CIA's allegation that Saddam Hussein was preparing nuclear weapons was a lie.

Along with disavowal as a result of the facts, there is disavowal resulting from the contradictions that the compulsive liar is liable to fall into, and this is why it is said that the truth will out.

Referring to his own time (and not ours) Jonathan Swift (or someone else in his circle, since the attribution remains doubtful) published a pamphlet on the art of political lies in which he wrote:

> There is one essential point wherein a political liar differs from others of the faculty, that he ought to have but a short memory, which is necessary, according to the various occasions he meets with every hour of differing from himself, and swearing to both sides of a contradiction, as he finds the persons disposed with whom he hath to deal. In describing the virtues and vices of mankind, it is convenient, upon every article, to have some eminent person in our eye, from whom we copy our description. I have strictly observed this rule, and my imagination this minute represents before me a certain great man famous for this talent, to the constant practice of which he owes his twenty years' reputation of the most skillful head in England, for the management of nice affairs. The superiority of his genius consists in nothing else but an inexhaustible fund of political lies, which he plentifully distributes

every minute he speaks, and by an unparalleled generosity forgets, and consequently contradicts, the next half hour. He never yet considered whether any proposition were true or false, but whether it were convenient for the present minute or company to affirm or deny it; so that if you think fit to refine upon him, by interpreting everything he says, as we do dreams, by the contrary, you are still to seek, and will find yourself equally deceived whether you believe or not: the only remedy is to suppose, that you have heard some inarticulate sounds, without any meaning at all; and besides, that will take off the horror you might be apt to conceive at the oaths, wherewith he perpetually tags both ends of every proposition; although, at the same time, I think he cannot with any justice be taxed with perjury when he invokes God and Christ, because he hath often fairly given public notice to the world that he believes in neither.

Well, on that occasion, through Swift, the truth spoke out.

[La Milanesiana, 2011]

9. On Some Forms of Imperfection in Art

There is a lot of talk about *imperfection*, but the concept itself is at risk of remaining imperfect. For example, there is an interesting little book from 1988 by Algirdas Greimas which is called *On Imperfection* but does not deal with imperfection, and the same year's *In Praise of Imperfection*, by Rita Levi-Montalcini, is rather a celebration of those limitations of our brain that make it so beautifully creative: it notes the perfection achieved by the cockroach, in that today's insect is the true copy of an ancestor that lived hundreds of millions of years ago. Since then, its brain mechanisms have not evolved: they are perfect. The human brain remains imperfect, and this is why it is capable of evolving.

If we look at it in theological terms, man is certainly imperfect compared to God, but if we go along with Levi-Montalcini's line, perhaps God or nature wanted things this way to guarantee our ongoing creativity.

So let's fly a little lower. Usually, imperfection is defined with respect to a genre, a canon, or a law.

Thomas Aquinas said that the criteria for beauty are *proportio* and *claritas* (and these would seem clear) but also *integritas*. Integritas meant wholeness, and hence *quae diminuta sunt eo ipso turpia sunt* (those who are impaired are by that very fact ugly). In down-to-earth terms, this meant that dwarfs were imperfect because they lacked the right height, and the same went for the crippled whatever they might lack. Likewise, in the thirteenth century, in his *Tractatus de bono et malo,* William of Auvergne held that a person was ugly if he had three eyes or only one, in the first case because the feature was unbecoming and in the second for not having what was proper. A thing is imperfect, therefore, if it has too much or too little with respect to the norm.

The problem of perfection as wholeness obsessed Christian thought when it came to defining how the bodies of the dead would be resurrected on the day of universal judgment. They would be as whole as they were when alive, agreed, but at what point in their life? The way they were at twenty, or at sixty? Let's assume at the moment of their death. But if by the time of their death they were missing an arm or had gone completely bald, would they rise in that state?

In *quaestio* 80 of the *Supplementum,* Aquinas wonders if the intestines will be resurrected. While they are a part of the human body, a person would certainly not be able to rise again full of filth, or even with empty intestines, because nature abhors a vacuum. And what about the arm that was rightly amputated from a thief, who later did penance and was saved—should the arm be recovered given that it did not cooperate in the salvation of the penitent? On the other hand, how could it be eliminated, when its absence would constitute a punishment for someone by this time in a state of bliss? Aquinas responded by saying that, just as a work of art would not be perfect if it lacked something that art requires, so must man be resurrected in perfection—and therefore, it is all the limbs of the body must be reconstituted upon resurrection.

So the intestines will rise again and be full not of ignoble waste but of noble humors. As for the repentant thief, even though that amputated limb played no part in his attaining glory afterwards, nonetheless he deserves to be rewarded with all his parts intact.

But will the hair and nails rise again? It is said that they are produced by superfluous food like sweat, urine, and other excrement, which certainly will not be resurrected with the body. But the Lord has said, "Not a hair of your body will perish." Hair and nails were given to man as ornaments. Now, the human body, especially that of the elect, must be resurrected in all its beauty. So it must rise again complete with hair and nails.

On the other hand, the genitals will not be resurrected, given that in heaven the blessed shall "neither marry nor be given in marriage." The same holds for sperm, which do nothing for the perfection of the individual, as hair does, but only for the perfection of the species. This would suggest that in heaven you can get a shampoo and set, but you cannot have sex.

The other problem, previously raised by St. Augustine, is what would happen to a man devoured by cannibals. In Augustine's view the flesh that has nourished the cannibal is later dissolved, but since God the Almighty can take back what has vanished, it will be returned to the individual who was devoured: it was, so to speak, borrowed by the cannibal and must be returned to whomever it belonged. It would be absurd to think that, while not even a hair of the head can be lost, pounds and pounds of flesh might go missing.

Aquinas was to respond in much the same way, albeit in greater depth. The fact is that this concept of perfection as wholeness was still being preached centuries later by the poet Giacomo Leopardi, who in the *Zibaldone* said that "the perfection of a being is none other than complete conformity with its primordial essence."

Very well. But the stamp known as the Gronchi pink was imperfect, showing Peru with the wrong borders, and indeed it was withdrawn, but precisely because of its imperfection it went on to become a rare and very expensive piece, much sought after by collectors.

The Venus de Milo, which is missing its arms, is also imperfect but crowds flock to see it in the Louvre.

If a fur-covered cup were put on sale in a department store it would be imperfect, because it is not suited to its purpose, but as a work of art by Oppenheim it is certainly perfect.

Sometimes we see seductive glamour in a person marked by a slight squint, a mole, a nose that would look very wrong on a sculpture by Canova, or an asymmetrical face. Montaigne (*Essays* III, II) hailed the attractions of lame women:

'tis a common proverb in Italy, that he knows not Venus in her perfect sweetness who has never lain with a lame mistress. . . . I should have been apt to think; that the shuffling pace of the lame mistress added some new pleasure to the work, and some extraordinary titillation to those who were at the sport; but I have lately learnt that ancient philosophy has itself determined it, which says that the legs and thighs of lame women, not receiving, by reason of their imperfection, their due aliment, it falls out that the genital parts above are fuller and better supplied and much more vigorous; or else that this defect, hindering exercise, they who are troubled with it less dissipate their strength, and come more entire to the sports of Venus. . . . I have formerly made myself believe that I have had more pleasure in a woman by reason she was not straight, and accordingly reckoned that deformity amongst her graces.

Giambattista Marino (*La lira*, 14) found the pallor of a sick woman irresistible:

> My pale little sun,
> Before your sweet pallor,
> Crimson dawn loses her colors.
> My pale little death
> Before your sweet, pale violet
> And amorous purple
> The rose is vanquished.
> Oh, may it please my fate
> That I may grow pale, with you,
> My pale little love!

In Junichiro Tanizaki's 1956 novel *The Key*, we find praise for the legs of Japanese women, which Tanizaki says westerners find imperfect compared to the long, straight legs of western women:

> For the first time I could enjoy the full sight of her, I was able to explore above all the lower part of her body, its secrets so long concealed. Ikuko, who was born in 1911, does not have a western figure, so common among girls today. She is well proportioned for a Japanese woman of her age; yet she does not have particularly full breasts, nor is she large in the buttocks. Her legs, long and graceful as they are, could not be called straight. They swell at the calf, and the ankles are not thin enough. But instead of slender, foreign-looking legs, I have always preferred the rather curved legs of the old-fashioned

Japanese woman, like my mother and aunt. I'm not interested in those thin, tubular legs.

The fact is that when we talk about human beings and even animals, even if we have some criterion of perfection, we are willing to make exceptions in many cases—because we make a distinction between beauty as regularity and attractiveness, which is indefinable and often varies depending on taste.

There can be no argument about attractiveness, and so maybe what we need to clarify better is the criterion of imperfection in art. For a start, at least in our time, we can no longer apply an idea as a rule—otherwise, a face by Picasso would be imperfect—but it is the work of art that applies the rule to itself. What we look for in a work of art (at least these days) is not a correspondence to a canon of taste, but to an internal norm, where economy and formal consistency regulate the text in all its parts. And so, we would define the representation of a human being made by a four-year-old (who would have liked to make a human figure as it appears to us) as imperfect, albeit touching, whereas we would describe Keith Haring's puppets or Cy Twombly's scribbles as perfectly calibrated works within the stylistic criteria adopted by the artist.

Both a painting by Raphael and one by Twombly could conform to this definition of artistic form given by Luigi Pareyson in his *Estetica* (1954):

In a work of art the parts have a dual kind of relationship: each with the others and each with the whole. All the parts are connected together in an indissoluble unity, so that each is necessary and indispensable and has a determined and irreplaceable position, to the point that a single missing part would break up the unity and one variation would spell a return to disorder. . . .

If the alteration of the parts means the dissolution of unity and the disintegration of the whole, this is because the whole itself governs the coherence of the parts among themselves and makes them contribute to form the whole. In this sense the relationships between the parts reflect the relationship that each part has with the whole: the harmony of the parts forms the whole because it is the whole that establishes their unity.

So two forms of imperfection can be attributed to a work of art: the absence of some parts that the whole would require or the presence of more of them. One artwork that certainly has too little is the Venus de Milo, mutilated for centuries. Many imbeciles have tried to make her *perfect* again, and I saw one of these, complete with arms, in a Californian waxworks museum bearing the legend "as it was when conceived by an unknown sculptor."

Why do we consider any attempt to perfect the Venus de Milo to be foolish? Because on contemplating it, we are fascinated by trying to imagine a whole that is now lost. This feeling has something in common with a taste that arose in the eighteenth century, which can be summed up in the term the *aesthetics of ruins*.

Starting from Petrarch's day, and then throughout the sixteenth and seventeenth centuries, ruins were seen as the image of a vanished civilization and they inspired moral reflection on the fragility of human destiny. In his *Record of a Journey from Paris to Jerusalem and Back*, Chateaubriand mediated on the pyramids, witnesses to a challenge to time:

But why see in the pyramid of Cheops only a heap of stones and a skeleton? It is not through a feeling of his own nothingness that man built so tall a sepulchre, but the sense of his own immortality: that sepulchre is not the boundary marker that proclaims the end of a transient existence, it is a monument that marks the entrance to life without end, it is a species of eternal portal built on the edge of eternity.

But, in the *Salon of 1767*, Diderot was to say:

> The effect of these compositions, good or bad as they may be, is to leave you in a state of sweet melancholy. We gaze on the fragments of a triumphal arch, a portico, a pyramid, a temple or a palace and in any event we always come back to ourselves.... Suddenly, solitude and silence reign around us. We are alone, orphans of an entire generation that exists no more.... The ideas that ruins awake in me are grandiose. All things pass, all things perish. Only the world resists. Only time continues to endure. I walk between two eternities.

But moralistic reflection has slowly given way to a contemplation of ruins that appears fascinating precisely because they are ruins and Piranesi's engravings come to mind. A taste for the irregular is a part of this contemplation. The aesthetics of ruins overturns the concept of the formal perfection and completeness of a work of art. Diderot wrote: "Why does a beautiful sketch fascinate us more than a finished painting? It is because it has more life, and fewer forms. When forms are introduced, life flags."

In the aesthetics of ruins the work can be enjoyed in spite of (and perhaps thanks to) its deterioration. Hence the fascination of their malady and the romantic beauty of the death they evoke.

So much for works of art that lack something. But what of those that have something in excess?

This is the problem of the *zeppa*.

According to the dictionary, a *zeppa* (wedge or stopgap) is a wooden element used to stop up a gap or to steady wobbly furniture, but in Italian literary criticism it is a word or phrase added to pad out a line, a stopgap, sometimes for reasons of meter or, in a prose passage, to give a sentence completeness.

Intending to make a distinction between the poetic moments in a literary work and elements concerned with structure or support, Benedetto Croce wrote in *La poesia* (1936):

> The poet (like the moral man for his acts, never exempt from some impurities) suffers when he discovers blemishes in his work and would like to get rid of all of them, even the smallest vestige. . . . But poetry visits the mind with the brilliance of a lightning flash, and the human agency holds on to it, attracted by it, fascinated by it, taking from it what it can and vainly asking it to linger and to let every line of its face be admired, but it has already vanished. . . . Thus Virgil, in order not to lose the whole for a part or a particle, the maximum for the minimum, and not to let the happy moment give him the slip, resigned himself, according to his biographer, to writing some verses that were imperfect or expressed in a provisional manner, and consoled himself by jesting with his friends and calling those verses "props" ("tibicines"), which served to support the construction until he might be able to replace them with solid columns. And those imperfections make the poet suffer indeed, he would like to make them good, and despite this, as if out of a holy reverence for the mystery that is celebrated in him, he very often hesitates to do this, fearing to make things worse, because a cool head is no longer a heated imagination, and the file is a dangerous instrument, which can polish, but can also *exterere*, as Quintilian said, namely remove the best. . . . In poetry one does not come across imperfections alone, which, by definition, are rectifiable . . . but also things that are not poetic yet not

correctable, which do not arouse in the reader . . . displeasure and disapproval, but are regarded with indifference pure and simple. These are the conventional or structural parts, which exist in every poetical work, sometimes barely visible, sometimes eminently visible, especially in very long and complex works. A very well-known case of these conventional and structural parts consists of those additions and fillers that the French call "chevilles" and the Italians "zeppe." . . . What does such padding come from? From the need to maintain the rhythmic uniformity of expression, even at the cost of sacrificing to some extent the coherence of an image or a sound. . . . Those who remember the four marvellous lines with which Ariosto expresses Fiordelisa's dismay and bewilderment when the two barons, Brandimarte's comrades in the hard-fought battle, alone and silent, appear before her:

Tosto che entràro, ed ella loro il viso
vide di gaudio in tal vittoria privo,
senz'altro annunzio sa, senz'altro avviso,
che Brandimarte suo non è più vivo!

(When they enter, and on their faces
she sees no sign of victorious joy
without further notice or warning,
she knows her Brandimarte lives no more)

will note that in the third line "annunzio" and "avviso" are two words that mean the same thing and perhaps that neither of the two is used completely correctly, and that "avviso" was chosen for the rhyme. But the accelerated rhythm obtained through the succession of the two nouns, separated and linked by a caesura, evokes the rapid beating of Fiordelisa's heart and creates a superior poetic image, and the rhyme at the end of the line reconnects that beating with her looks and dismay at the appearance of the two men, at their faces devoid of any sign of joy.

It should be noted that, if this is indeed the case, that *annunzio* and *avviso* are not padding, but precisely the poetically correct words that prompt Croce to say that the four lines are marvelous. But his determination to make a distinction between structure and poetry leads him to continue in this vein:

> But the correct acceptance of these "structural pieces" must not be corrupted by their incorrect acceptance as poetry: which is the error committed by critics of limited understanding, both because they allow themselves to be mastered by a sort of superstitious reverence for the renowned poet (to whom, moreover, they do no honor by putting his poetry on the same level as his activity as an author) and because of a very frequent lack of intelligence and artistic sensibility.

Instead, subparagraph 3.10 of chapter III ("The parts and the whole") of Luigi Pareyson's *Estetica* is titled "The essentiality of every part: structure, padding, imperfections." One of Pareyson's central concerns in *Estetica*, in his polemic against Croce's idealism and its most detrimental effects on militant criticism, was a claim for the totality of artistic form; in other words, a refusal to pluck sporadic moments of poetry from the work as if they were flowers blooming among the brushwood of simple structure, highly functional as it may be. It is not really necessary but it is worth repeating that "structure," in the Italy of those days, was a mechanical artifice that had nothing to do with the moment of poetic intuition, and at best stood out in a Hegelian sense as a negative instance, a conceptual residue, which could at most serve to make the moments of poetry glitter like solitary gems.

In devoting a chapter of his *Estetica* to padding, Pareyson thought instead that structure and padding were essential to the work, which was to be seen as an organic whole in which everything has a function and in the finished work (and indeed from the first moment in which the idea triggers the formative process) *tout se tient*, and it hangs together from the standpoint of the organizational schema that supports it, and of the *forma formante* or "forming form" that obscurely precedes it, controls it in its coming into being, and appears as the result and revelation of the *forma formata* or "formed form."

Perhaps Pareyson was thinking of the idea typical of the Neoplatonic tradition according to which the perfection of the whole is also supported by imperfections that are so to speak redeemed by the totality of the form. See this passage from John Scotus Eriugena (ninth century), in his *De divisione naturae* V:

> What is considered deformed in itself in a part of the whole, not only becomes beautiful in the totality, because it is well ordered, but is also the cause of general Beauty; thus wisdom is illuminated by its comparison with foolishness, science by comparison with ignorance which is only want and privation, life by death, light by the opposition of darkness, worthy things by the deprivation of praise; and to say briefly, all the virtues not only derive praise from the opposite vices but without this comparison they would not deserve praise.... As true reason does not hesitate to affirm, all things that in one part

of the universe are bad, dishonest, ugly and wretched and are considered crimes by those who cannot see all things, in the universal vision, as happens with the Beauty of a picture, they are neither crimes nor foul or dishonest things, nor are they bad. In fact everything that is ordered according to the design of divine Providence is good, beautiful and just. What could be better than the fact that the comparison of opposites leads to the ineffable praise of the universe and of the Creator?

So for Pareyson, if "the whole is a result of parts united in order to constitute a whole there cannot be any negligible or irrelevant detail." And padding is seen as a support required for the outcome of the whole, a sort of bridge or weld "in which the artist operates with less care, with greater impatience or even with indifference, almost rushing through the task as if it were a passage that, precisely because it is imposed by the need to proceed beyond it, may be left to convention without detriment to the whole." Nevertheless, padding is a part of the internal economy of the form, because the whole requires it, albeit in a subordinate position.

Pareyson is telling us that padding is an extremely cunning artifice that allows one part to bind with another; it is an essential coupling. If a door is to open smoothly or with majesty it must have a hinge, as its function is mechanical. The bad architect, addicted to aestheticism, is vexed because a door must be hung on a hinge, and redesigns the latter so that it appears "beautiful" as it performs its function; and by doing this he finds that the door often creaks, jams, and will not open or opens badly. The good architect on the other hand wants the door to open and reveal other spaces, and after having redesigned everything in the building, he does not care if he has to rely on the eternal wisdom of the ironmonger.

Padding can provide a mediocre start, useful for the attainment of a sublime finale. It was three in the morning, on the hill near Recanati immortalized by Giacomo Leopardi in his poem *L'infinito*, where the first words of one of the finest sonnets of all time are carved in the stone, when I realized that *Sempre caro mi fu quest'ermo colle* ("This solitary hill has always been dear to me") is a pretty banal line, which could have been written by any minor romantic poet, and maybe even by poets from other periods or movements. What is a hill supposed to be, in "poetic" language, if not "solitary"? Yet without that humdrum opening the poem would not have got off the ground, and perhaps it was necessary for it to be banal, so that the reader might get a full sense of the sense of panic at the poetically memorable "shipwreck" with which the poem closes.

I would dare say, albeit for the sake of a theory, that a line such as Dante's *Nel mezzo del cammin di nostra vita* (Midway on our life's journey) has the dignified ring of padding. If the *Divine Comedy* had not followed we would not have attached much importance to it, and maybe we would have taken it as a manner of speaking.

I am not identifying padding with a striking start. Some opening bars of Chopin's *Polonaises* are not padding. "That branch of the lake of Como" is not padding; nor is "April is the cruelest month." But let us consider the end of *Romeo and Juliet*, and tell me that the ending would not have been better without the phrase in italics:

A glooming peace this morning with it brings.
The sun, for sorrow, will not show his head.
Go hence, to have more talk of these sad things.
Some shall be pardoned, and some punishèd.
For never was a story of more woe
Than this of Juliet and her Romeo.

But if Shakespeare decided to end with this moralizing platitude, it is because he wished to give the spectators a breather, letting them cool down after the hecatomb they had witnessed. And so that little bit of padding was a good thing.

Il primo ad addormentarsi fu Leo (Leo was the first to fall asleep) is not bad. But then: *l'impreveduta seppure inesperta sfrenatezza di Carla l'aveva spossato* (Carla's unexpected, if inexpert, licentiousness had worn him out). Come on, what do we expect an adult male to be if not "worn out" when subjected to the amorous assault of an adolescent female? Does that "unexpected, if inexpert, licentiousness" not sound like an extract from a court ruling? Nonetheless, without this rather clumsy but necessary passage, chapter 10 of Alberto Moravia's *The Time of Indifference* (1929)— with its splendid description of the sad truth that *post coitum omne animalium triste est*—could not begin.

But what to say about those works that demanding criticism relegates to paraliterature and in seeking to please the reader pay no attention to style and are sometimes made entirely of padding?

Take Dumas's *The Count of Monte Cristo*, for instance.

The Count of Monte Cristo is one of the most exciting novels ever written and on the other hand is one of the most *badly written* novels of all time and in any literature. The book is full of holes. Shameless in repeating the same adjective from one line to the next, incontinent in the accumulation of these same adjectives, capable of opening a sententious digression without managing to close it because the syntax cannot hold up, and panting along in this way for twenty lines, it is mechanical and clumsy in its portrayal of feelings: the characters either quiver, or turn pale, or they wipe away large drops of sweat that run down their brow, they gabble with a voice that no longer has anything human about it, they rise convulsively from a chair and fall back into it, while the author always takes care, obsessively, to repeat that the chair onto which they collapsed again was the same one on which they were sitting a second before.

We are well aware why Dumas did this. Not because he could not write. *The Three Musketeers* is slimmer, faster paced, perhaps to the detriment of psychological development, but rattles along wonderfully. Dumas wrote that way for financial reasons; he was paid a certain amount per line and had to spin things out. Not to mention the need—common to all serialized novels, to help inattentive readers catch up on the previous episode—to obsessively repeat things that were already known, so a character may recount an event on page 100, but on page 105 he meets another character and tells him exactly the same story—and in the first three chapters you should see how often Edmond Dantès tells everyone who will listen that he means to marry and that he is happy: fourteen years in the Chateau d'If are still not enough for a sniveling wimp like him.

Years ago, the Einaudi publishing house invited me to translate *The Count of Monte Cristo*. I agreed because I was fascinated by the idea of taking a novel whose narrative structure I admired and whose style I abhorred, and trying to restore that structure in a faster paced, nimbler style, (obviously) without "rewriting," but slimming down the text where it was redundant—and thereby sparing (both publisher and reader) a few hundred pages.

So Dumas wrote for a certain amount per page. But if he had received extra pay for every word saved would he not have been the first to authorize cuts and ellipses?

An example. The original text says:

Danglars arracha machinalement, et l'une après l'autre, les fleurs d'un magnifique oranger; quand il eut fini avec l'oranger, il s'adressa à un cactus, mais alors le cactus, d'un caractère moins facile que l'oranger, le piqua outrageusement.

A literal translation would go like this:

One after another, Danglars mechanically plucked the blossoms from a magnificent orange tree; when he had finished with the orange tree he turned to a cactus, but the cactus, a less easy character than the orange tree, pricked him outrageously.

Without taking anything away from the honest sarcasm that pervades the excerpt, the translation could easily read:

One after another, he mechanically plucked the blossoms from a magnificent orange tree; when he had finished he turned to a cactus but it, being a more difficult character, pricked him outrageously.

This makes thirty-two words in English, in contrast to forty-two in French. A savings of roughly 25 percent.

Or take expressions such as *comme pour le prier de le tirer de l'embarras où il se trouvait* (as if to beg him to get him out of the difficulty he found himself in). It is obvious that the difficulty someone wants to get out of is the difficulty he actually finds himself in and not another, and it would suffice to say, "as if to beg him to get him out of difficulty." More words saved.

I tried, for a hundred pages or so. Then I gave up because I began to wonder if even the wordiness, the slovenliness, and the redundancies were not part of the narrative apparatus. Would we have loved *The Count of Monte Cristo* as much as we did if we had not read it the first few times in its nineteenth-century translations?

Let's go back to the initial statement. *The Count of Monte Cristo* is one of the most exciting novels ever written. With one shot (or with a volley of shots, in a long-range bombardment), Dumas manages to pack into one novel three archetypal situations capable of tugging at the heartstrings of even an executioner: innocence betrayed, the persecuted victim's acquisition—through a stroke of luck—of a colossal fortune that places him above common mortals, and finally, the strategy of a vendetta resulting in the death of characters that the novelist has desperately contrived to appear hateful beyond all reasonable limits.

On this framework there unfolds the portrait of French society during the "Hundred Days" and later during Louis Philippe's reign, with its dandies, bankers, corrupt magistrates, adulteresses, marriage contracts, parliamentary sessions, international relations, state conspiracies, the optical telegraph, letters of credit, the avaricious and shameless calculations of compound interest and dividends, discount rates, currencies and exchange rates, lunches, dances, and funerals—and all of this dominated by the principal *topos* of the feuilleton, the Superman. But unlike all the other artisans who have attempted this classic locus of the popular novel, the Dumas of the superman attempts a disconnected and breathless state of mind, showing his hero torn between the dizziness of omnipotence (owing to his money and knowledge) and terror at his own privileged role, tormented by doubt and reassured by the knowledge that his omnipotence arises from suffering. Hence, a new archetype grafted on to the others, the Count of Monte Cristo (the power of names) is also a Christ figure, and a duly diabolical one, who is cast into the tomb of the Chateau d'If, a sacrificial victim of human evil, only to arise from it to judge the living and the dead, amid the splendor of a treasure rediscovered after centuries, without ever forgetting that he is a son of man. You can be blasé or critically shrewd, and know a lot about intertextual pit-falls, but still you are drawn into the game, as in a Verdi melo-drama. By dint of excess, melodrama and kitsch verge on the sublime, while excess tips over into genius.

There is certainly redundancy, at every step. But could we enjoy the revelations, the series of discoveries through which Edmond Dantès reveals himself to his enemies (and we tremble every time, even though we already know everything), were it not for the intervention, precisely as a literary artifice, of the redundancy and the spasmodic delay that precedes the dramatic turn of events?

If *The Count of Monte Cristo* were condensed, if the conviction, the escape, the discovery of the treasure, the reappearance in Paris, the vendetta, or rather the chain of vendettas, had all happened within two or three hundred pages, would the novel still have an effect—would it pull us along even in those parts where the tension makes us skip pages and descriptions? (We skip them, but we know they are there, we speed up subjectively but knowing that narrative time is objectively dilated.) It turns out that the horrible stylistic excesses are indeed "padding," but the padding has a structural value; like the graphite rods in nuclear reactors, it slows down the pace to make our expectations more excruciating, our predictions more reckless. Dumas's novel is a machine that prolongs the agony, where what counts is not the quality of the death throes but their duration.

This novel is highly reprehensible from the standpoint of literary style and, if you will, from that of aesthetics. But *The Count of Monte Cristo* is not intended to be art. Its intentions are mytho-poeic. Its aim is to create a myth.

Oedipus and Medea were terrifying mythical characters before Sophocles and Euripides transformed them into art, and Freud would have been able to talk about the Oedipus complex even if Sophocles had never written one word, provided the myth had come to him from another source, perhaps recounted by Dumas or somebody worse than him. Mythopoeia creates a cult and veneration precisely because it allows of what aesthetics would deem to be imperfections.

In fact, many of the works we call cults are such precisely because they are basically *ramshackle*, or "unhinged" so to speak.

In order to transform a work into a cult object, you must be able to take it to pieces, disassemble it, and unhinge it in such a way that only parts of it are remembered, regardless of their original relationship with the whole. In the case of a book, it is possible to disassemble it, so to speak, physically, reducing it to a series of excerpts. And so it happens that a book can give life to a cult phenomenon even if it is a masterpiece, especially if it is a complex masterpiece. Consider the *Divine Comedy*, which has given rise to many trivia games, or Dante cryptography, where what matters for the faithful is to recall certain memorable lines, without posing themselves the problem of the poem as a whole. This means that even a masterpiece, when it comes to haunt the collective memory, can be made ramshackle. But in other cases it becomes a cult object because it is fundamentally, radically ramshackle. This happens more easily with a film than a book. To give rise to a cult, a film must already be inherently ramshackle, shaky and disconnected in itself. A perfect film, given that we cannot reread it as we please, from the point we prefer, as with a book, remains imprinted in our memory as a whole, in the form of an idea or a principal emotion; but only a ramshackle film survives in a disjointed series of images and visual high points. It should show not one central idea, but many. It should not reveal a coherent "philosophy of composition," but it should live on, and by virtue of, its magnificent instability.

And in fact the bombastic *Rio Bravo* is apparently a cult movie, while the perfect *Stagecoach* is not.

"Was that cannon fire? Or is my heart pounding?" Every time *Casablanca* is shown, the audience reacts to this line with the kind of enthusiasm usually reserved for football matches. Sometimes a single word is enough: fans rejoice every time Bogey says "kid" and the spectators often quote the classic lines even before the actors do.

According to the traditional aesthetic canons *Casablanca* is not or ought not to be a work of art, if the films of Dreyer, Eisenstein, and Antonioni are works of art. From the standpoint of formal coherence *Casablanca* is a very modest aesthetic product. It is a hodgepodge of sensational scenes put together in a rather implausible way, the characters are psychologically improbable, and the actors' performance looks slapdash. That notwithstanding, it is a great example of filmic discourse, and has become a cult movie.

"Can I tell you a story?" Ilsa asks. Then she adds: "I don't know the finish yet." Rick says: "Well, go on, tell it. Maybe one will come to you as you go along."

Rick's line is a kind of epitome of *Casablanca*. According to Ingrid Bergman, the film was made up piecemeal as filming progressed. Until the last minute, not even Michael Curtiz knew if Ilsa would leave with Rick or Victor, and Ingrid Bergman's enigmatic smiles were because she still did not know—as they were filming— which of the two men she was really supposed to be in love with.

This explains why, in the story, she does not choose her destiny. Destiny, through the hand of a gang of desperate scriptwriters, chooses her.

When we do not know how to deal with a story, we resort to stereotypical situations since, at least, they have already worked elsewhere. Let's take a marginal but significant example. Every time Laszlo orders a drink (and this happens four times), his choice is always different: (1) Cointreau, (2) a cocktail, (3) cognac, (4) whisky (once he drinks champagne but without having ordered it). Why does a man of ascetic character demonstrate such inconsistency in his alcoholic preferences? There is no psychological justification for this. To my mind, every time this kind of thing happens, Curtiz is unconsciously quoting similar situations in other films, in an attempt to provide a reasonably complete range.

So, it is tempting to interpret *Casablanca* the way Eliot reinterprets *Hamlet*, whose appeal he attributes not to the fact that it is a successful work, because he considers it to be among Shakespeare's less felicitous efforts, but to the imperfection of its composition. According to Eliot, *Hamlet* is the result of an unsuccessful fusion of several previous versions, so the bewildering ambiguity of the main character is due to the difficulty the author had in putting together several *topoi*. *Hamlet* is certainly a disturbing work in which the psychology of the character strikes us as impossible to grasp. Eliot tells us that the mystery of *Hamlet* is clarified if, instead of considering the entire action of the drama as being due to Shakespeare's design, we see the tragedy as a sort of poorly made patchwork of previous tragic material.

There are traces of a work by Thomas Kyd, which we know indirectly from other sources, in which the motive was only that of revenge; and the delay in taking revenge was caused only by the problem of assassinating a monarch surrounded by guards; moreover, Hamlet's "madness" is feigned, the aim being to avert suspicion. In Shakespeare's definitive drama the delayed vengeance is not explained—with the exception of Hamlet's continuous doubts, and the effect of his "madness" is not to lull but to arouse the king's suspicions. Shakespeare's *Hamlet* also deals with the effect of a mother's guilt on the son, but Shakespeare was unable to impose this motif upon the material of the old drama—and the modification is not sufficiently complete to be convincing. In several ways the play is puzzling, disquieting as none of the others is. Shakespeare left in unnecessary and incongruent scenes that ought to have been spotted on even the hastiest revision. Then there are unexplained scenes that would seem to derive from a reworking of Kyd's original play perhaps by Chapman. In conclusion, *Hamlet* is a stratification of motifs that have not merged, and represents the efforts of different authors, where each one put his hand to the work of his predecessors. So, far from being Shakespeare's masterpiece, the play is an artistic failure. "Both workmanship and thought are in an unstable condition. . . . And probably more people have thought *Hamlet* a work of art because they found it interesting, than have found it interesting because it is a work of art. It is the *Mona Lisa* of literature."

On a lesser scale, the same thing happens in *Casablanca*.

Obliged to invent the plot as they went along, the scriptwriters threw everything into the mix, drawing on the tried and tested repertoire. When the choice of tried and tested is limited, the result is merely kitsch. But when you put in *all* the tried and tested elements, the result is architecture like Gaudí's Sagrada Familia: the same dizzying brilliance.

Casablanca is a cult movie because it contains all the archetypes, because every actor reproduces a part played on other occasions, and because human beings do not live a "real" life but a life portrayed stereotypically in previous films. Peter Lorre drags behind him memories of Fritz Lang; Conrad Veidt envelops his German officer with a subtle whiff of *The Cabinet of Dr. Caligari*. *Casablanca* pushes the feeling of déjà vu to such a point that the viewer even adds elements to the film that only appear in later films. It wasn't until *To Have and Have Not* that Bogart took on the role of the Hemingway hero, but here he "already" reveals Hemingwayan connotations for the simple fact that Rick has fought in Spain.

Casablanca stages the powers of narrativity in the natural state, without art stepping in to tame them. And so we can accept that characters have changes of mood, morality, and psychology from one moment to the next, that conspirators cough to break off their talk when a spy approaches, and that ladies of the night weep on hearing the *Marseillaise.*

When all the archetypes shamelessly burst in, we plumb Homeric depths. Two clichés are laughable. A hundred clichés are affecting—because we become obscurely aware that the clichés are talking to one another and holding a get-together. As the height of suffering meets sensuality, and the height of depravity verges on mystical energy, the height of banality lets us glimpse a hint of the sublime.

And in this regard it is possible to justify many cases whose appeal eludes even the most rigorous aesthetics. Take Proust's praise, in *Pleasures and Days* (1896), of bad music. I do not mean unsuccessful symphonies, but popular songs—those catchy tunes that make people cry or dance:

Detest bad music if you will, but don't hold it in contempt. As it is played and sung much more often and much more passionately than good music, so much more than the latter has it gradually been filled with the dreams and tears of mankind. For that reason you should venerate it. Its place, insignificant in the history of art, is huge in the sentimental history of societies. Respect for—I do not say love for—bad music is not merely a form of what might be called the charity of good taste or its skepticism, it is, more than that, the awareness of the importance of the social role of music. How many melodies, worthless in the eyes of an artist, become the confidants chosen by a whole host of romantic young men and of women in love. How many "golden rings" and "Ah! Sleep on, sleep on, mistress mine," the pages of which are tremulously turned every evening by justly celebrated hands, and watered by the most beautiful eyes in the world with tears whose melancholy and voluptuous tribute would arouse the envy of the most stringent maestro in the world—ingenious and inspired confidants who ennoble sorrow and exalt dreams, and, in exchange for the ardent secret confided to them, give the intoxicating illusion of beauty. The working classes, the bourgeoisie, the army, the nobility, just as they have the same postmen to bring news of some grief to afflict them with sorrow or some happiness to fill them with pleasure, have the same invisible messengers of love and the same cherished confessors—in other words, bad musicians. The irritating refrain, for instance, that any refined and well-trained ear will immediately refuse to listen to, has been the repository for the riches of thousands of souls, and keeps the secret of thousands of lives, for which it was the living inspiration, the ever-ready consolation, always lying half-open on the piano's music stand—a source of dreamy grace for those lives, and an ideal. Those arpeggios too, or that "re-entry" of the theme, have aroused in the soul of more than one lover or dreamer an echo of the harmonies of paradise or the very voice of the beloved woman. A book of bad romances, worn out by overuse, ought to touch us like a cemetery or a village. What does it matter if the houses have no style, if the tombs are overladen with inscriptions and ornaments in bad taste? From this dust there may arise, in the eyes of an imagination friendly and respectful enough to silence for a moment its aesthetic disdain, the flock of souls holding in their beaks the still-verdant dream that gave them a foretaste of the other world and filled them with joy or tears in this one.

With this page from Proust, I should like to end my imperfect celebration of imperfection. In grammar, why is the imperfect tense so called? Perhaps it is no accident that, among the tenses which ought to tell us if something is happening, has happened, or will happen (even the imperative nudges us toward the future), and if it has happened more or less time ago, we have one that cannot or will not perform the function of temporal specification that all the other tenses do—one that leaves us uncertain about the temporal collocation of the event. And, in fact, when playing children imagine they are someone else, knowing that they are not, have not been, and never will be that person, they use the imperfect ("So, I was the Indian chief and you were Buffalo Bill . . .").

In discussing Flaubert in *Pleasures and Days*, Proust said, "I confess that certain uses of the imperfect indicative—of this cruel tense that presents life to us as something ephemeral and at the same time passive, which brands our actions as illusion in the very moment in which it calls them up, obliterates them in the past without leaving us, as the simple past does, the consolation of activity—is still an inexhaustible source of mysterious sorrow for me."

And that is how imperfection sometimes becomes essential to art.

[La Milanesiana, 2012]

10. Some Revelations on Secrecy

I ought to begin with a declaration that there is something of great importance I would have liked to convey to you but, as it is a secret, I must keep my mouth shut. By so doing I might acquire great prestige and might even convince you that, as the sixth Imam, Ja'far al-Sadiq, put it, "Our cause is a secret within a secret, the secret of something that remains hidden, a secret that may be disclosed only by another secret, a secret about a secret that is satisfied by a secret."

All mythologies have had a god of secrecy; the figure of Harpocrates, under various names, appears from Egyptian art through the Graeco-Roman world to the Renaissance. But just for the pleasure of disobeying Harpocrates's order, which enjoins silence, I shall offer you some revelations about secrecy.

A secret is information that is not revealed, or must not or should not be revealed, because if it were, that revelation would cause harm to whoever divulged it and sometimes even to those who received it.

Thus we speak of state secrets, official secrets, banking secrets, military secrets, and industrial secrets such as, for example, the recipe for Coca-Cola that is kept hidden away in Atlanta. These secrets (which really do concern something hidden) often wind up being revealed by order of investigating authorities, by the opening of state archives, through imprudence or treason, and especially by espionage.

To guard against espionage and protect their secret communications over the centuries, people have devised cryptographies. These are systems of rules that allow a given message expressed in some natural language to be transformed through a series of substitutions so clever that only a recipient who knows the rules for the substitutions can reverse the process to recover the original message. There are reports of secret writing in ancient India and in the Bible. Julius Caesar speaks of it, too, and we know there was a science of encryption in Arab civilization thanks to an 855 treatise: Abu Bakr Hammad an-Nabati's *Book of the Frenzied Devotee's Desire to Learn About the Riddles of Ancient Scripts*. The practice carries down through the fourteenth century *Muqaddima* of Ibn Khaldun, which mentions a code used by secretaries swapping in names of perfumes, flowers, birds, and fruits to designate the letters.

In the modern era, with the birth of European states, the increasingly complex organization of armies, and military operations over a vast territory (this was the period of the Thirty Years War), the art of cryptography was further developed. One of the first modern systems is that of the moving discs used by Abbot Trithemius, in which a letter from the first circumference replaces a letter from the second. Perhaps the most illustrious example is that of the (far more complex) Nazi Enigma code, deciphered by Alan Turing. Since one of the principles of cryptography is that, no matter how perfect, all codes can be broken sooner or later, cryptographic secrets have a short life. And so we need take no further interest in them.

Likewise, we might take no interest in so-called "open secrets," which, because they have been disclosed to a gossip, are instantly on everyone's lips, except that sometimes secret services deliberately leak false revelations about false secrets to throw an adversary off track—with the result that many pseudo-secrets revealed in this way serve to conceal other secrets that tend to remain such.

In the baroque seventeenth century, the world of absolute powers, the idea gained ground that to survive in society, it was necessary to know how to simulate, either by presenting yourself as the opposite of what you were (as Baltasar Gracián taught) or by concealing your true nature (as Torquato Accetto advised). And a page from Cardinal Mazarin's *The Politicians' Breviary* (1684) offers a lesson for politicians in how to keep secret everything that concerns them:

> If you need to write in a place frequented by many people, put a few sheets of paper you have already written upon on a reading-desk, as if you had to copy them. Let the sheet be evident, and in perspective; but the paper you are really writing on must also be lying on the table, and so protected that the only line that can be read by anyone coming near is the one you are transcribing. But cover what you have written with a book or two, or another piece of paper, or another sheet protected like the first but closer to the written one. If while you are reading, someone should observe you, immediately turn over several papers so that he might not discover what you are about; in fact it would be a good thing to have many open books in front of you, to offer that person with greater deft-

ness one instead of another. If by chance you are writing letters, or reading some book, and a person should approach who might use the presence of that book or those letters to ask questions, then before he can open his mouth, *you* must question *him*.

Reserve

Basically, Mazarin's behavior was an almost paranoid form of reserve, but reserve also covers personal secrets that sometimes vanish with the death of their possessor. Such secrets may concern acts that cannot be confessed, but not only those, because some people may wish legitimately not to make known their illnesses, sexual proclivities, or origins. Society recognizes the right to confidentiality and a sociologist such as Georg Simmel, in his study on secrecy, recognized this right as an important part of the social contract.

If anything, it is interesting to note that this right to privacy is gradually losing more and more value in our mass media society, where giving up confidentiality takes the form of exhibitionism. The largely beneficial safety valve that was gossip is disappearing. Classic gossip, the kind that went on in the village, in the porter's lodge, or at the inn, was an element of social cohesion because not infrequently the gossips, instead of enjoying the misfortunes of those gossiped about, felt or showed pity.

This worked if the victims were not present and were unaware that they were victims (or saved face by pretending not to know). And so, for the value of the social safety valve of gossip to remain intact, everyone—tormentors and victims—was required to maintain reserve as much as possible. The first variation came along with specialist publications, which traded in gossip about people (actors and actresses, singers, monarchs in exile, playboys) who willingly exposed themselves to the gaze of photographers and journalists. This kind of gossip, once a whisper, became a shout, conferring fame upon the victims and thus arousing the envy of the nonfamous. Consequently television came up with programs in which anyone could become a famous victim by showing up to gossip about himself or herself. And the screens filled with people squabbling with their spouse about mutual infidelities, or desperately calling upon lovers or mistresses who had dumped them, or staging divorce proceedings in which their sexual incapacities were pitilessly analyzed.

It was fitting that, anticipating this social change, the reserved Piedmontese Cesare Pavese would commit suicide leaving a memorable message: "And don't gossip too much." But no one paid him any heed and by now we know everything about his unhappy love affairs.

But the abandonment of privacy has recently taken other forms. On the one hand we are aware but, all things considered, we do not seem to care that through credit card checks, phone records, and medical records anyone can know our every little move and everything about us; on the other hand the WikiLeaks case has persuaded us that making public the *arcana imperii* is a democratic operation, while every state and government should be allowed to keep some things confidential because making certain information, contacts, or projects public immediately is liable to cause them to fail, often with harmful consequences for the community. One example of this is the desire to make public consultations for the formation of a government immediately available in streaming, a situation in which people feel observed and so to avoid losing face they can only reiterate their official positions without conceding anything to negotiation—which is the soul of political relationships.

Secrecy and the Mysteries

The age of reserve has ended, but the idea of the mystery secret—or the hermetic and occult secret—has lived on for thousands of years now. The doctrine of Pythagoras presented itself as a knowledge of arcane truths, the fruit of a revelation received from the Egyptians. In a period marked by the crisis of classical rationalism, during the second century AD the pagan world tended more and more to identify truth with the secret, or with what is said in an obscure way. To be truly secret a form of wisdom had to be exotic and ancient. In particular, the East was ancient and spoke unknown languages, what is unknown is secret, and therefore must contain a part of that secret that only the divinity knows.

This attitude was the reverse of the attitude typical of the classical Greek intellectual, who saw the barbarians—*oi barbaroi*—as stutterers or, in other words, people who could not even articulate words. But later, it was precisely the alleged stuttering of the foreigner that went on to become a sacred language.

At this point we witness the birth of the notion that the truth is a secret, possessed by the guardians of a tradition now lost. And it was to be typical of all Renaissance texts on magic to point out that access to revelation comes through the utterance of tongues incomprehensible even to those who pronounce them, invented or modeled on a second-rate version of Hebrew.

The Rosicrucians

With regard to the fortunes of every doctrine that presents itself as a secret, the history of the Rosicrucians is worth examining. At the beginning of the seventeenth century, the idea was making headway that a Golden Age was beginning, just when Europe was ablaze with national conflicts and denominational hatreds. In different forms, this climate of expectation pervaded both Catholic and Protestant regions and projects appeared for ideal republics, or for a hoped-for universal monarchy, and for a general renewal of customs and religious sensibility. In 1614 a manifesto appeared, the *Fama fraternitatis*, followed in 1615 by a second text, the *Confessio fraternitatis Roseae crucis. Ad eruditos Europae*. In these manifestos the mysterious Rosicrucian confraternity revealed its existence, gave information on its mythical founder, Christian Rosenkreutz, and predicted that an order would arise in Europe that possessed an abundance of gold, silver, and precious stones that would be distributed to kings to satisfy their legitimate needs and aims. The manifestos stressed the secret character of the confraternity and that their members cannot reveal their nature ("our edifice—even if a hundred thousand people had seen it from close to—will forever be intangible, indestructible and hidden from the ungodly world"). However, an appeal was made to all the scholars of Europe to make contact with the adepts of the order: "Even though we have not yet revealed our names, nor when we shall meet . . . anyone who sends us his name may confer with one of us in open speech or, were there any impediment, in writing."

Almost immediately, from every part of Europe, people began writing appeals to the Rosicrucians, starting with an influential occultist such as Robert Fludd. No one claimed to know them, no one called themselves Rosicrucians, everyone tried to make them understand that they were in perfect accord with their program. Michael Maier in *Themis aurea* (1618) claimed that the confraternity really existed, but said that he was too humble a person to have ever been a part of it. Everyone allowed that the group was secret, and for this reason those who claimed to be members of the Rose-Cross (thereby failing to respect the commitment to confidentiality that binds the adepts) were not: "The usual behavior of Rosicrucian writers is to say that they are not themselves Rosicrucians" according to Frances Yates (1972). And this is what is believed to this day, at least if we are accept the view of an author who took the Rosicrucian idea very seriously, Réné Guénon: "It is probable that most of the so-called Brothers of the Rose-Cross were really only Rosicrucians. . . . Indeed, we can even be certain that they were not [Brothers] solely from the fact that they belonged to such associations; this may seem paradoxical and even contradictory at first glance, but can nonetheless be easily understood" (*Perspectives on Initiation*, 2014).

Consequently, not only is there no historical evidence of the existence of the brotherhood of the Rose-Cross, and at best we have clear historical evidence of the existence of successive groups—each of which claims to be the sole true heir of the original brotherhood, one example being AMORC, the *Anticus et mysticus ordo rosae crucis* whose pseudo-Egyptian temple you can still see in San José, California. But a Rosicrucian organization that claims to be part of a tradition going back thousands of years will be the first to tell you that the documents relating to that tradition cannot be accessed: "Naturally, you will understand," the *Manuel Rosicrucien* (1984) says to this day "that the Grand Brotherhood and the Grand White Lodge are not visible organizations." And in the official documents of the *Anticus et mysticus ordo rosae crucis* it is stated that the original texts that legitimize the order certainly exist, but for obvious reasons they are locked up in inaccessible archives.

In 1623, anonymous posters appeared in Paris announcing the arrival of the Rosicrucians in the city, and this announcement triggered fierce controversy, including the suspicion that the Rosicrucians were Satan worshippers. Even Descartes, who during a trip to Germany had tried—it was said— to approach them (obviously without success), on his return to Paris was suspected of belonging to the confraternity. He got out of trouble with a master stroke: as it was commonly believed that the Rosicrucians were invisible, he made sure he was seen on many public occasions, and so debunked the rumors about him, as Adrien Baillet tells us in his *Vie de Monsieur Descartes* (1691).

Poor Descartes's bright idea tells us what Georg Simmel was to repeat in his essay on secrecy, namely that the typical characteristic of secret societies is invisibility—and come to think about it, secret associations like those of the Carbonari always desired invisibility, to such an extent that, as happened with the mysterious Illuminati of Bavaria (and as still happens today with some terrorist groups), each small group of followers knows only their group leader, but not the members of the hierarchies above them.

That many of the Carbonari ended up on the guillotine or in front of a firing squad does not depend so much on their secret having been leaked, but on the fact that if the aim of a secret association is to bring about an uprising, the secret ceases to be such when the uprising breaks out. There are secrets, such as that of a group planning a takeover bid for the conquest of a stock, but such things cease to be secret when the bid is a success or a spectacular failure. The secrets of groups intent on a specific purpose must have a very short life, otherwise the members of the group are just happy-go-lucky types incapable of accomplishing anything.

But things were very different with the Rosicrucians, who did not intend to achieve anything in the immediate future. In any event, to explain how this invisibility did not exclude their existence, a certain Neuhaus published in 1623, *Pia & utilissima admonitio de Fratribus Rosae-Crucis* in which he wondered if they existed, who they were, how they got their name, and to what purpose they publicly revealed themselves; and he concluded with the extraordinary argument that "since they change and make anagrams of their names, and conceal their age, and come without being recognized, there is no logic that can deny that they necessarily exist."

The reason for the great popularity of the Rosicrucians is that they announced a secret but talked about everything, bar the nature of the secret.

Connected in some way with the Rosicrucian tradition, symbolic masonry arose in the seventeenth century. With Anderson's Constitution, this movement sought to legitimize itself by tracing its origins to the builders of the Temple of Solomon. In the following years, with the so-called Scottish rite, the relationship between the builders of the Temple and the Templars, whose secret tradition was to come to modern Freemasonry through the mediation of the Rosicrucian brotherhood, was added to the origin myth. In support of this theory many Masonic organizations—almost always in conflict with the Grand Lodge of London—chose symbols and rites that might emphasize the link with the Templar and Rosicrucian traditions. And so the degrees of initiation (which had to correspond to degrees of knowledge of the secret and which were originally three) swelled to thirty-three. See, for example, the series of high degrees of the Ancient and Primitive Rite of Memphis-Misraim founded by Cagliostro:

> Knight of the Planispheres, Prince of the Zodiac, Sublime Hermetic Philosopher, Supreme Commander of the Stars, Sublime Pontifex of Isis, Prince of the Sacred Hill, Philosopher of Samothrace, Titan of the Caucasus, Child of the Golden Lyre, Knight of the True Phoenix, Knight of the Sphinx, Sublime Sage of the Labyrinths, Mystic Guardian of the Sanctuary, Architect of the

Mysterious Tower, Sublime Prince of the Sacred Curtain, Interpreter of the Hieroglyphics, Orphic Doctor, Guardian of the Three Fires, Guardian of the Incommunicable Name, Beloved Shepherd of the Oasis of Mysteries, Doctor of the Sacred Fire, Knight of the Luminous Triangle.

The degrees represent successive phases in the initiation to the Masonic Secret. The author of one of the finest definitions of the Masonic Secret was Giacomo Casanova:

> Those who enter Freemasonry only to ferret out the secret may find themselves disappointed: they may indeed happen to live for fifty years as Master Masons without succeeding. The mystery of Freemasonry is by its nature inviolable: the Freemason knows it only by intuition, not by having learned it.... When he has known it, he takes good care not to share the discovery with anyone, not even his best Mason friend, because if the latter has been unable to penetrate the mystery, neither will he be able to profit from it if he learns it from others.... What happens in the Lodge must remain secret, but whoever is so indiscreet and unscrupulous as to reveal it does not reveal its essence: how could he, if he does not know it? If he knows it, he would not reveal it.

The initiatory secret, therefore, cannot be revealed and so it cannot be betrayed.

Giuliano Di Bernardo, former Grand Master of the Gran Loggia Regolare d'Italia, has expatiated upon the Masonic secret. An expert on logic, he is not inclined to occult interpretations of Masonic symbolism. In his *Filosofia della massoneria* he writes:

There are ... those who seek esoteric truths [in the symbols], the secrets of alchemy, the philosopher's stone: in such cases, the symbols are inadequate and barely express a semblance of the deep meanings of the esoteric life. These and other interpretations of Masonic symbolism are erroneous and therefore incapable of grasping its true nature, which can be thus enunciated: in Freemasonry, the symbols express only one secret, which is the initiatory one. ... Those incapable of understanding this will always be in the situation of the uninitiated person who, on chancing to enter the Masonic temple, observes objects that are not familiar to him, such as a setsquare, a compass, a hammer, a book, etc., but without understanding their symbolic significance. In order to interpret what he sees he needs Masonic light, which can only be granted to him by initiation. Then, and only then will he have understood the Masonic secret. ... If the secret is revealed and is destructured from its symbolism, the foundation of Freemasonry is immediately destroyed. A Freemasonry without its initiatory foundation is nothing but an ordinary society with philanthropic aims.

As if to say (I interpret) that Freemasonry without the secret is merely another Rotary Club. Naturally, and for obvious reasons, Di Bernardo's book does not say what the Masonic secret is.

From the eighteenth century onwards, as a consequence of the concealment of the secret and the invisibility of the secret society, we come to the myth of the Unknown Superiors, who controlled the destiny of the world. In 1789, the Marquis de Luchet (in his *Essai sur la secte des illuminés*) warned: "In the bosom of the deepest darkness there has formed a society of new beings who know one another without ever having seen one another. ... This society has adopted the blind obedience of the Jesuit rule, the trials and external ceremonies of Freemasonry, and the subterranean mysteries and incredible audacity of the Templars."

Between 1797 and 1798, in response to the French Revolution, Abbé Barruel had written his *Mémoires pour servir à l'histoire du jacobinisme*, in which we are told how, after being destroyed by Philip the Fair, the Templars had transformed themselves into a secret society for the destruction of the monarchy and the papacy. In the eighteenth century they took over Freemasonry and created a sort of academy whose diabolical members were Voltaire, Turgot, Condorcet, Diderot, and d'Alembert—and it was from this coterie that the Jacobins originated. But the Jacobins themselves were controlled by an even more secret society, the Illuminati of Bavaria, regicides by vocation. The French revolution was the final result of this conspiracy.

Barruel's book contained no reference to the Jews. But in 1806, Barruel received a letter from a certain captain Simonini, reminding him how Freemasonry was founded by the Jews and that they had infiltrated all secret societies. Hence, and this is another story that we cannot deal with now, the birth of the Jewish conspiracy myth that was eventually to lead to the infamous *Protocols of the Elders of Zion*, abundant traces of which, unfortunately, can still be found today on many internet sites.

There are, however, some today who still think that secret groups covertly dominate the development of world events and all you need do is go on the internet to find various discussions on the Trilateral, the Bilderberg Group, or the Davos meetings, as if politicians, industrialists, and bankers could not meet privately whenever they wish, to decide on economic strategies that are unfortunately before everyone's eyes—and as if speculation about derivatives were not enough to explain the ruin of many small savers, but it was necessary to discover a more hidden plan.

On the internet you can find references to other disturbing secrets, such as the insinuation that Pope Francis, through the backing of Cardinal Martini, has links with Masonic groups.

The conspiracy syndrome developed with greater imagination in the case of the destruction of the the World Trade Center, a plot variously attributed to Bush's secret plans, to the Jews, and so on.

If you make a search on the internet you will find that New York City has 11 letters, Afghanistan has 11 letters, Ramsin Yuseb, the terrorist who had threatened to destroy the Towers, has 11 letters, George W. Bush has 11 letters, the twin towers formed an 11, New York is the eleventh state of the United States, the first plane to crash into one of the towers was flight number 11, this flight carried 92 passengers and 9 + 2 make 11, flight 77 which also crashed into the towers carried 65 passengers and 6 + 5 = 11, the date 9 / 11 is the same as the American emergency number, 911, the sum of whose digits gives 11. The total number of victims in all the hijacked planes was 254, the sum of whose digits gives 11, September 11 is the 254th day of the annual calendar and 2 plus 5 plus 4 make 11. And so on and cabalistically so forth.

What are the objections to these apparently prodigious coincidences?

New York has 11 letters if you add City, Afghanistan has 11 letters although the hijackers were not Afghans but men hailing from Saudi Arabia, Egypt, Lebanon, and the United Arab Emirates, Ramsin Yuseb has 11 letters only if you deliberately use a certain transliteration, but if Yuseb had been transliterated as Yussef the game would not work, George W. Bush has 11 letters only if you include his middle initial, the Twin Towers form an 11 but also a

2 in Roman numerals, Flight 77 did not hit one of the towers but the Pentagon and did not carry 65 but 59 passengers, the total number of victims was not 254 but 265, and so on.

Again, on the internet, it is explained that if you write the flight number of the first plane that crashed into the first tower (Q33NY, incidentally the initials of New York), space this formula out and ask the computer to transcribe it, not in a normal font like Times or Garamond but in those more or less cabalistic signs called Wingdings, you get amazing secret messages.

The only problem is that neither of the planes that crashed into the towers had the flight number Q33NY, and it was necessary to invent those initials to obtain the alleged secret message.

Then there are so-called secrets that are very disappointing once revealed. This is the case with the third secret of Fatima, which, delivered in an envelope sealed in 1944 by Sister Lucia, was to be revealed only after 1960. Pope John XXIII and his successors did not consider it appropriate to divulge its contents, but they were eventually made public in 2000 by order of John Paul II. It seems that only Benedict XVI already knew the message, and he showed a certain common sense in advising that it should remain where it was because it contained nothing interesting. But the allure of the secret had grown beyond measure. Once the message was opened it was seen to contain descriptions that were definitely tragic, but inspired by the images of some Iberian-flavored Book of Revelation, and any prophetic content it had lay in the fact that in subsequent years (but also in the years before it was written, in Spain—a stone's throw from Sister Lucia's homeland) some very ugly things would happen, but these were known about or could be imagined without having seen the Virgin Mary.

Unlike many lovers of the cryptic who would have sought to find hidden meanings in the message, including alleged relationships between the secrets of Fatima and the secrets of Medjugorje, the future Pope Benedict—then Cardinal-Prefect of the Congregation for the Doctrine of the Faith—while immediately warning that a private vision is not a matter of faith, and that an allegory is not a prophecy, explicitly pointed out the analogies with The Book of Revelation. "The conclusion of the 'secret' evokes images which Sister Lucia may have seen in devotional books," he noted, "and whose content derives from ancient notions of faith." So, in a chapter significantly titled "The Anthropological Structure of Private Revelations," he wrote that the visionary "sees with his concrete possibilities, with the modalities accessible to him of representation and knowledge." And this, in simple terms, means that Sister Lucia had seen in ecstasy what she had read in the books in her convent and in texts two thousand years old. The content of the third secret of Fatima had already been on sale for a very long time in all specialist religious bookshops, including the *Pia Società San Paolo.*

A Secret Revealed Is Worthless

As a Rosicrucian occultist like Joséphin Péladan once said, an initiation secret revealed is worthless. Yet people are eager for secrets, and those who are believed to possess a secret that has not yet been revealed always acquire a form of power, because goodness knows what he or she might disclose one day. It has always been a principle of the police and secret services of half the world that the more things you know, or demonstrate that you know, the more your power grows. It does not matter whether something is true or not. What matters is to make people believe that you possess a secret. And it spells ruin for a secret service when government files are opened or some agency like WikiLeaks violates them. Then it turns out that the secret reports of the services and the embassies were usually made up of folders in which press cuttings had been transcribed, stuff that circulated freely before spies and agents turned them into confidential revelations, and that—from the ambassador down to the lowliest office boy—it was not really worth paying them a salary, because all they were good for was a cut and paste job.

So how can we maintain the power that derives from the possession of a secret, while preventing the so-called secret from becoming public? You must boast about an empty secret. Having a secret and not revealing it does not mean lying, if anything it is an extreme form of reserve. But to say you have a secret, while there is none, is *to lie about the secret*. Georg Simmel has pointed out that this happens with children, where "it is often a matter of pride and boasting when one child says to another 'I know something you don't know', and this is widely expressed as a means of downgrading the other, even when . . . there is no secret."

Children's pseudo-secrets have an effect only on other children, but the pseudo-secret of many initiatic groups (and many secret services) has an effect on those adults who are eager to penetrate secrets and are therefore always ready to admit that there actually are secrets.

Perhaps some will know that I dealt with the syndrome of the empty secret in my novel *Foucault's Pendulum*, where three friends who are playful scholarly types, or scholarly playful types, invent a universal plan taking their cue from all the rubbish on the shelves of occult bookshops (the kind of stuff that Dan Brown's characters draw on, though not in jest, in *The Da Vinci Code*). The three friends do not know what the ultimate secret of the plan may be, and indeed they have fun by leaving it unspecified, but a pack of full-time professional occultists takes them seriously and, in the tempestuous finale, Jacopo Belbo is hanged on Foucault's pendulum. But even before this, fascinated by his empty secret—and by now wholly absorbed in his game—he writes on his computer.

> Believe there is a secret and you will feel like an initiate. It costs nothing. To create an immense hope that can never be uprooted, because it has no root. Ancestors who do not exist will never appear and say that you have betrayed. . . . Like Andreae: to create, in jest, the greatest revelation of history and, while others are destroyed by it, swear for the rest of your life that you had nothing to do with it.

And after the death of Belbo, his friend Casaubon, the narrator of the novel, notes in dismay:

> We invented a nonexistent Plan, and They not only believed it was real but . . . identified the fragments of their muddled mythology as moments of our Plan, moments joined in a logical, irrefutable web of analogy, semblance, suspicion. But if you invent a plan and others carry it out, it's as if the Plan exists. At that point it does exist. Hereafter, hordes of Diabolicals will swarm through the world in search of the map. We offered a map to people who were trying to overcome a deep, private frustration. What frustration? Belbo's last file suggested it to me: There can be no failure if there really is a Plan. Defeated you may be, but never through any fault of your own. To bow to a cosmic will is no shame. . . . You don't complain about being mortal, prey to a thousand microorganisms you can't control; you aren't responsible for the fact that your feet are not very prehensile, that you have no tail, that your hair and teeth don't grow back when you lose them, that your arteries harden with time. It's because of the Envious Angels.

The same applies to everyday life. Take stock-market crashes. They happen because each individual makes a wrong move, and all the wrong moves put together create panic. Then whoever lacks steady nerves asks himself: Who's behind this plot, who's benefiting? He has to find an enemy, a plotter, or it will be, God forbid, his fault. If you feel guilty, you invent a plot, many plots. And to counter them, you have to organize your own plot.

But the more you invent enemy plots, to exonerate your lack of understanding, the more you fall in love with them, and you pattern your own on their model.... God blinds those He wishes to destroy; you just have to lend Him a helping hand. A plot, if there is to be one, must be a secret. A secret that, if we only knew it, would dispel our frustration, lead us to salvation; or else the knowing of it in itself would be salvation. Does such a luminous secret exist? Yes, provided it is never known. Known, it will only disappoint us. Hadn't Agliè spoken of the yearning for mystery that stirred the age of the Antonines? Yet someone had just arrived and declared himself the Son of God, the Son of God made flesh, to redeem the sins of the world. Was that a run-of-the-mill mystery? And he promised salvation to all: you only had to love your neighbor. Was that a trivial secret? And he bequeathed the idea that whoever uttered the right words at the right time could turn a chunk of bread and a half-glass of wine into the body and blood of the Son of God, and be nourished by it. Was that a paltry riddle? And then he led the Church fathers to ponder and proclaim that God was One and Triune and that the Spirit proceeded from the Father and the Son, but that the Son did not proceed from the Father and the Spirit. Was that some easy formula for hylics? And yet they, who now had salvation within their grasp—do-it-yourself salvation—turned deaf ears. Is that all there is to it? How trite. And they kept on scouring the Mediterranean in their boats, looking for a lost knowledge, of which those thirty-denarii dogmas were but the superficial veil, the parable for the poor in spirit, the allusive hieroglyph, the wink of the eye at the pneumatics. The mystery of the Trinity? Too simple: there had to be more to it.

Someone—Rubinstein, maybe—once said, when asked if he believed in God: "Oh, no, I believe . . . in something much bigger." . . . But everything is not a bigger secret. There are no "bigger secrets," because the moment a secret is revealed, it seems little. There is only an empty secret. A secret that keeps slipping. . . . The universe is peeled like an onion, and an onion is all peel. Let us imagine an infinite onion, which has its center everywhere and its circumference nowhere. Initiation travels an endless Möbius strip. The true initiate is he who knows that the most powerful secret is a secret without content, because no enemy will be able to make him confess it, no rival devotee will be able to take it from him. . . . Belbo had claimed to possess a secret, and because of this he had gained power over Them. . . . And the more Belbo refused to reveal it, the bigger They believed the secret to be; the more he vowed he didn't possess it, the more convinced They were that he did possess it, and that it was a true secret, because if it were false, he would have revealed it. Through the centuries the search for this secret had been the glue holding Them all together, despite excommunications, internecine fighting, coups de main. Now They were on the verge of knowing it. But They were assailed by two fears: that the secret would be a disappointment, and that once it was known to all, there would be no secret left. Which would be the end of Them. Agliè then thought: If Belbo spoke, all would know, and he, Agliè, would lose the mysterious aura that granted him charisma and power. . . . Thus he forced Belbo to raise the tone of his refusal and to say no definitively. The others, out of the same fear, preferred to kill him. They might be losing the map—they would have centuries to continue the search for it—but they were preserving the vigor of their base, slobbering desire.

This, in conclusion, is the true secret: the reaching out at all costs toward an inviolable and unattainable secret is slobbering desire. It is not enough to know that some Al-Qaeda suicide bombers destroyed the twin towers. We will never be satisfied by what is before all our eyes, because we are the children of a blundering scoundrel of a Demiurge.

[La Milanesiana, 2013]

11. Conspiracy

When they asked me to give a talk on manias and obsessions, my thought was that one of the great obsessions of our time is undoubtedly with conspiracy. A quick look at the internet will show you just how many (mostly phony) conspiracies allegedly exist. The obsession with conspiracies, however, does not concern our day alone but also the past.

That some conspiracies do exist and have existed in history seems clear to me, from the plan to assassinate Julius Caesar to the Gunpowder Plot and from the infernal machinations of Georges Cadoudal down to modern financial plots to take over this or that corporation. But the tendency of real conspiracies is that they quickly come to light, whether they succeed, as in the case of Julius Caesar, or fail, as in Orsini's plot to kill Napoleon III, or the so-called "golpe dei forestali"—an attempted 1969–1970 coup d'état organized by Junio Valerio Borghese—or Licio Gelli's other machinations. The real plots, therefore, are not as mysterious and neither are they relevant on this occasion.

What *is* relevant is the phenomenon of the conspiracy theory, and especially those fabulous tales of cosmic plots with which the internet abounds. These remain mysterious and unfathomable because they share the characteristics of the secrets discussed by the early sociologist Georg Simmel; he observed that a secret is more powerful and seductive the emptier it is. An empty secret looms menacingly and can be neither unveiled nor disputed, and this is precisely what allows it to become an instrument of power.

This brings us to the principal conspiracy circulating on the internet: the one focused on September 11, 2001. Theories about the attacks are legion. There are the most extreme ones (found on Arab fundamentalist or neo-Nazi sites), according to which the conspiracy was organized by the Jews—the "proof" being that all the Jews who worked in the two skyscrapers were warned not to go to work that day. That news, reported by the Lebanese television station al-Manar, was clearly false; in reality, at least two hundred Israeli citizens died in the conflagration, together with many hundreds of American Jews.

Then there are the anti-Bush theories, according to which the attack was staged to provide a pretext for invading Afghanistan and Iraq. Other theories attribute the event to various more or less rogue American secret service agendas. And there is also a theory that, while the conspiracy was originally an Arab fundamentalist one, the American government discovered the plot in advance yet allowed things to happen so that there would be cause to invade Afghanistan and Iraq (not unlike the theory that Roosevelt was informed of the imminent attack on Pearl Harbor but did nothing to save his fleet because he wanted a reason to declare war on Japan). In all these cases, supporters of the theories believe that the official reconstruction of the facts is false, fraudulent, and puerile.

Anyone wanting to have an idea about these various conspiracy theories can read the book *Zero. Perché la versione ufficiale sull'11/9 è un falso* (Zero: Why the Official Version of 9/11 is a Fake), edited by Giuletto Chiesa and Roberto Vignoli. You may not believe this, but the names of some highly respected colleagues appear in this book, whom I will not identify here out of respect.

Those who want to hear the other side of the story should also thank Piemme Editions, because with admirable equanimity (and demonstrating how to capture two distinct sectors of the market), they have published a book against conspiracy theories, too: *11/9. La cospirazione impossibile* (9/11: The Impossible Conspiracy) by Massimo Polidoro, featuring views of equally respectable colleagues. I will not go into the details of the arguments advanced on either side, all of which can seem persuasive, and will rather appeal only to what I would call the "proof of silence." A model of the proof of silence is its use, for example, against those who speculate that the Americans' televised moon landing was a fake. Let's say the American spacecraft did not arrive on the moon. In that case, there was a party in a position to check the matter out which even had an interest in exposing any fraud: the Soviet Union. So the fact that the Soviets stayed silent is the proof that the Americans really did land on the Moon. And that's that.

As regards plots and secrets, experience (historical experience, too) tells us two things. First, if there is a secret, even if it is known to only one person, this person, maybe in bed with a lover, will reveal it sooner or later. (Only naive Masons and the adepts of some fake Templar rite believe in secrets that remain inviolate.) Second, if there is a secret, there will always be a sum of money adequate to persuade its holder to reveal it. (It took only a few hundred thousand pounds, in the form of a book advance, to persuade an officer of the British Army to spill what he got up to in bed with Princess Diana. And if he had instead done it with the princess's mother-in-law, it would have been sufficient to double that sum, and a gentleman of that kind would have told the story anyway). Now, to organize a fake attack on the twin towers (to mine them, to warn the air force not to intervene, to conceal any embarrassing evidence, and so on) would have required the collaboration of hundreds of people at least, if not thousands. Especially given that the people used for such enterprises are not usually gentlemen, it is impossible to believe that at least one of these would not have talked. In short, there is no Deep Throat in this story.

The conspiracy syndrome is as old as time and the man who gave us a superb outline of the thinking behind it was Karl Popper. As long ago as the early 1940s, Popper shared his thoughts in *The Open Society and its Enemies*:

> The "conspiracy theory of society" is the view that an explanation of a social phenomenon consists in the discovery of the men or groups who are interested in the occurrence of this phenomenon (sometimes it is a hidden interest which has first to be revealed), and who have planned and conspired to bring it about. This view of the aims of the social sciences arises, of course, from the mistaken theory that, whatever happens in society—especially happenings such as war, unemployment, poverty, shortages, which people as a rule dislike—is the result of direct design by some powerful individuals and groups. This theory is . . . a typical result of the secularization of a religious superstition. The belief in the Homeric gods whose conspiracies explain the history of the Trojan War is gone. The gods are abandoned. But their place

is filled by powerful men or groups—sinister pressure groups whose wickedness is responsible for all the evils we suffer from—such as the Learned Elders of Zion, or the monopolists, or the capitalists, or the imperialists.

I do not wish to imply that conspiracies never happen. On the contrary, they are typical social phenomena. They become important, for example, whenever people who believe in the conspiracy theory get into power. And people who believe that they know how to make heaven on earth are most likely to adopt the conspiracy theory, and to get involved in a counter-conspiracy against nonexisting conspirators.

In 1969, Popper revisited the subject in *Conjectures and Refutations*:

This theory, which is more primitive than most forms of theism, is akin to Homer's theory of society. Homer conceived the power of the gods in such a way that whatever happened on the plain before Troy was only a reflection of the various conspiracies on Olympus. The conspiracy theory of society is just a version of this theism, of a belief in gods whose whims and wills rule everything. It comes from abandoning God and then asking: "Who is in his place?" His place is then filled by various powerful men and groups—sinister pressure groups, who are to be blamed for having planned the great depression and all the evils from which we suffer. . . . Only when conspiracy theoreticians come into power does it become something like a theory which accounts for things which actually happen (a case of what I have called the "Oedipus Effect"). For example, when Hitler came into power, believing in the conspiracy myth of the Learned Elders of Zion, he tried to outdo their conspiracy with his own counterconspiracy.

The psychology of conspiracy springs from the fact that the most obvious explanations for many disturbing events do not satisfy us, and often they do not satisfy us because it hurts us to accept them. Consider the theories that cropped up after the 1978 kidnapping and murder of the former Italian prime minister Aldo Moro: How is it possible, people wondered, that a few thirty-year-olds could plan and carry out such a perfect scheme? There had to be some shrewder *grande vecchio* (grand old man) behind the operation. Never mind that, at that time, other thirty-year-olds were running companies, piloting jumbo jets, and inventing new electronic devices. It was easier to ask how thirty-year-olds were able to kidnap Moro in Via Fani than to face the reality that those thirty-year-olds were the offspring of the kind of people who dream up grand old man stories.

After Popper, the conspiracy syndrome was studied by many other authors, and I shall mention only Daniel Pipes's book, *Conspiracy* (subtitled *How the Paranoid Style Flourishes and Where It Comes From*). It opens with a quotation from Metternich who is said to have asked, on learning of the death of the Russian ambassador: "What could have been his purpose?"

Humanity has always been fascinated by imaginary plots. Popper cited Homer, but in a more recent century we find Abbé Barruel, who attributed the French Revolution to a plot hatched by members of the ancient Knights Templar. Adding to his theory that they had survived and infiltrated Masonic sects was a mysterious letter he received from a Captain Simonini, who also brought the Jews into the picture, thereby preparing the way for the future *Protocols of the Elders of Zion*.

Recently I found on the internet a site that attributes every abomination of the last two centuries to the Jesuits. This site hosts a long text: *Le monde malade des jésuites*, by Joël Labruyère. As the title suggests, it is a wide-ranging review of world events, and not just recent ones either, ascribable to the universal conspiracy of the Jesuits.

The Jesuits of the nineteenth century, from Abbé Barruel to the founders of the Jesuit periodical *La Civiltà Cattolica* and the novelist Father Bresciani, were among the main propagators of the Judeo-Masonic conspiracy theory, and it was only right that they be repaid in the same coin by liberals, Mazzinians, Freemasons, and anticlerical movements. The theory of the Jesuitical plot was popularized to some degree by pamphlets and books—from *Lettres provinciales* by Blaise Pascal and *Il gesuita moderno* by Vincenzo Gioberti to the writings of Jules Michelet and Edgar Quinet—but much more so by Eugène Sue's serialized novels *The Wandering Jew* and *The Mysteries of the People*.

Nothing new here, then: Labruyère's website stokes the Jesuit obsession to fever pitch. I shall give only a quick overview, because Labruyère's conspiratorial fantasy is of Homeric dimensions: The aim of the Jesuits has always been to set up a world government, controlling both the Pope and the various European monarchies. Through the notorious Illuminati of Bavaria (a group the Jesuits themselves had created before later denouncing them as communists) they tried to bring down the monarchies that had outlawed the Company of Jesus. It was the Jesuits who sank the *Titanic* because that incident made it possible to found the Federal Reserve Bank, through the mediation of the Knights of Malta whom they controlled. And it is no accident that among those who died on the *Titanic* were the three richest Jews in the world, John Jacob Astor, Benjamin Guggenheim, and Isidor Straus, who had opposed the foundation of that bank. Working with the Federal Reserve, the Jesuits then financed the two world wars, which clearly yielded only advantages to the Vatican. As for the assassination of Kennedy, if we bear in mind that the CIA came into being as a Jesuit program inspired by the spiritual exercises of Saint Ignatius Loyola, and that the Jesuits controlled it through the Soviet KGB, it emerges that Kennedy was killed by the same people who sent the *Titanic* to the bottom.

Naturally, all neo-Nazi and anti-Semitic groups are of Jesuit origin; the Jesuits were behind Nixon and Clinton; the Jesuits were responsible for the Oklahoma City bombing; and the Jesuits were behind Cardinal Spellman, who fomented the Vietnam War which brought 220 million dollars into the Jesuit Federal Bank. This is not to forget, of course, Opus Dei, which the Jesuits controlled through the Knights of Malta.

And this brings us straight to the *Da Vinci Code* by Dan Brown, a novel whose raw material is the conspiracy syndrome and one that has prompted legions of credulous readers to visit places in France and England (where, obviously, the things described are not to be found). Brown cheerfully dots his narrative with countless errors. He writes, for example, that the Priory of Sion was founded in Jerusalem by "a French king called Godfrey of Bouillon," but it is known that Godfrey never accepted the title of king. He writes that Pope Clement V, in a bid to eliminate the Templars, "had sent sealed secret orders to be opened simultaneously by his soldiers throughout Europe on Friday, October 13, 1307," when it is a matter of historical fact that the messages to the bailiffs and seneschals of the kingdom of France were sent not by the Pope but by Philip the Fair (and it is hardly clear how the Pope could have had "soldiers throughout Europe"). He confuses the manuscripts found at Qumran in 1947 (which speak neither of the "true story of the Grail" nor "of the ministry of Christ") with the manuscripts of Nag Hammadi, which contain some Gnostic gospels. And as for his claims about the church of Saint Sulpice in Paris, that a gnomon in it is "a vestige of the pagan temple that once stood in that exact spot" and that a Rose Line would appear corresponding to the Paris meridian, and that this line runs on to the cellars of the Louvre, below the so-called inverted pyramid, where the Holy Grail has found its final resting place—pure fiction. To this day, numerous mystery hunters make a pilgrimage to Saint Sulpice to see the Rose Line, and consequently the church authorities have felt obliged to put up a notice:

> The meridian constituted by the brass strip set in the floor of the church is part of a scientific instrument made in the eighteenth century. This was done with the full agreement of the ecclesiastical authorities by the astronomers of the recently established Paris Observatory. Contrary to fanciful allegations in a recent best-selling novel, this is not a vestige of a pagan temple. No such temple ever existed in this place. It was never called a "Rose-Line." It does not coincide with the meridian traced through the middle of the Paris Observatory which serves as a reference for maps where longitudes are measured in degrees East or West of Paris. . . . Please also note that the letters "P" and "S" in the small round windows at both ends of the transept refer to Peter and Sulpice, the patron saints of the church, and not an imaginary "Priory of Sion."

Why are such canards successful? Because they promise knowledge denied to others. Frédéric Lordon, writing in *Le monde Diplomatique*, suggests that the conspiracy syndrome is the reaction of people who would like to know what is going on but have noticed that they are often denied access to the whole story. Lordon cites Spinoza's *Tractatus Theologico-Politicus* (written back in the sixteenth century) where it is said: "It is not surprising that the common people have neither truth nor justice, since affairs of state are taken care of without their knowledge." But there is a certain difference between state secrets, reticence, and conspiracy. In his 1964 book *The Paranoid Style in American Politics*, Richard Hofstadter says that the taste for conspiracy should be interpreted by applying a psychiatric framework to social thinking. It is a matter of two forms of paranoia. In a psychiatric case of paranoia, the individual thinks the world is plotting against him, whereas the mark of social paranoia is the belief that sinister powers are targeting one's group, nation, or religion. The social paranoiac, I would say, is more dangerous than the psychiatric one because he perceives that his persecution is shared by many, perhaps millions of other people and has the impression that he is acting against the conspiracy in a selfless way. This explains a great deal that happens in the world today, as well as much that has happened in the past.

Pasolini once wrote that conspiracies make us think crazy thoughts because they free us from the burden of having to face the truth. The fact that the world is full of conspirators could be a matter of indifference: if someone believes that the Americans did not go to the moon, that's his problem. In a 2013 article, "The Social Consequences of Conspiracism," Daniel Jolley and Karen Douglas conclude that "exposure to information supporting conspiracy theories reduced participants' intentions to engage in politics, relative to participants who were given information refuting conspiracy theories." In fact, if you are convinced that the history of the world is directed by secret societies—be they the Illuminati or the Bilderberg group—that are about to establish a new world order, what do you do? You give up, and you fret and fume. So every conspiracy theory directs the public imagination toward nonexistent dangers and away from genuine threats. As Chomsky once suggested, imagining what was almost a conspiracy of conspiracy theories, those who get the greatest advantage from fantasies about a supposed plot are the very institutions that the conspiracy theory aims to strike. This amounts to saying that, in thinking that Bush ordered the destruction of the Twin Towers to justiᶠ intervention in Iraq, people flit between a variety of delusions and stop analyzing the real reasons that prompted Bush to intervene in Iraq, and the influence that the Neocons had on him and his politics.

But what I wish to engage with here is not so much the spread of the conspiracy syndrome, which is clear to all, but with what I would call the pseudo-semiotic techniques used to prove and justify conspiracies.

Usually a conspiracy theory makes use of random coincidences that become dense with meaning, and of connections made between completely unconnected facts. Just to give some examples, here is a fine series of coincidences that, if they have not yet degenerated into conspiracy theories, are on the borderline. I read on the internet that Lincoln was elected to Congress in 1846, Kennedy was elected in 1946, Lincoln was elected president in 1860, Kennedy in 1960. Both their wives lost a child while living in the White House. Both were shot in the head by a Confederate southerner on a Friday. Lincoln's secretary was called Kennedy, and Kennedy's secretary was called Lincoln. Lincoln's successor was Andrew Johnson (born 1808) and Lyndon B. Johnson, Kennedy's successor, was born in 1908. John Wilkes Booth, who murdered Lincoln, was born in 1839, and Lee Harvey Oswald was born in 1939. Lincoln was shot at Ford's Theater. Kennedy was hit in a Ford Lincoln car. Lincoln was shot in a theatre and his killer hid in a warehouse. Kennedy's assassin shot from a warehouse and went to hide in a theatre. Both Booth and Oswald were killed before the trial. The (rather vulgar) icing on the cake: one week before his death Lincoln was in Monroe, Maryland. A week before he was killed, Kennedy was "in" Monroe, Marilyn.

Speculation in a similar vein has surrounded the collapse of the twin towers and the recurrence of the number 11.

Again, on the internet, and just to add a little more fuel, it is explained that, if you fold a $50 bill following a procedure similar to that of origami, you get the image of the two towers in flames, a sign that Masonic conspirators had been planning that disaster for a very long time. (It is customary to find Masonic symbols on American banknotes, and not by chance, because most of the signatories of the Declaration of Independence were Freemasons.)

Some time ago, taking my cue from such fantasies, I wrote a parody of Dan Brown's *Da Vinci Code*. If we observe Leonardo's *Last Supper* we see that there are thirteen at the table. However, if we eliminate Jesus and Judas (who were both to die shortly afterwards) this leaves eleven guests. Eleven is the sum of the letters in the names Petrus and Judas, 11 is the number of letters in the word *Apocalypsis*, there are also 11 letters in *Ultima Coena* (Last Supper), on either side of Jesus one apostle appears with hands spread open and another with the index finger extended, in both cases forming an eleven. Finally, the sum of the panels at the sides and the windows shown in the fresco comes to eleven. Moreover, following an elementary cabalistic principle, if we assign a progressive number to the 26 letters of the alphabet, substituting each letter with a number, the name Leonardo da Vinci gives $12 + 5 + 15 + 14 + 1 + 18 + 4 + 15 + 4 + 1 + 22 + 9 + 14 + 3 + 9 = 146$, and the sum of the digits 1, 4 and 6 makes 11. Now do the same operation with the name of Matteo (Matthew): the sum of the numerical values of the letters is equal to 74, and 7 plus 4 makes 11. Eleven times eleven makes

121—but if we subtract the ten commandments from this figure, we get 111.

The sum of the numerical values of the letters of Giuda (Judas) is 42, and 4 plus 2 makes 6. This appearance of the number 6 leads us to multiply 111 by 6, and we get 666, the Number of the Beast.

So, at the same time as it denounces the betrayal of Christ, *The Last Supper* announces the coming of the Antichrist.

Of course, to make the figures add up I had to call Peter by his Latin name, Petrus, and Matthew by his Italian name, Judas once in Italian and once in English, *Ultima coena* in Latin (there was no way round that) and to get 111 I had to subtract the 10 commandments from 121 and not the 5 holy wounds of the Lord or the 7 works of corporal mercy. But that's the way it goes in numerology.

But I would like to end by reconstructing a phony conspiracy that still leads thousands of curious people to the village of Rennes-le-Château. This notion is based on the idea that Christ married Mary Magdalene thereby founding the Merovingian dynasty and then the imaginary Priory of Sion, purportedly still active today. The conspiracy is linked, how could it be otherwise, to the mystery of the Grail.

The legendary relic has traveled a tortuous route, now in one place now in another, and according to one of the most recent legends, which sprang from the books of the Nazi Otto Rahn, it was in Montségur, in southern France. The area was right for a revival of the legend: all that was needed was a pretext. And the pretext came with the story of Abbé Bérenger Saunière, parish priest from 1885 to 1909 of Rennes-le-Château, a small village about forty kilometers from Carcassonne. Saunière had restored the local church inside and outside, built a house, Villa Bethania, and a tower on the hill, the Magdala Tower, which resembled the Tower of David in Jerusalem.

It was calculated that the cost was 200,000 francs at the time, corresponding to about two hundred years of salary for a provincial priest, so the bishop of Carcassonne launched an investigation and then transferred Saunière to another parish. Saunière refused and retired to private life, before dying in 1917.

After his death a whole range of theories arose. It was said that during the renovation works to the parish church, Saunière had found a treasure trove. In reality, the wily priest had been advertising for people to send money in exchange for promised masses for their deceased relatives, thereby amassing a fortune for hundreds of masses that he had never celebrated—and it was for precisely this reason he was put on trial by the bishop of Carcassonne.

On his death, Saunière left everything to his housekeeper, Marie Dénarnaud, who, to add value to the properties she inherited, continued to fuel the legend of the treasure. When he inherited Marie's estate in 1946, a certain Noël Corbu opened a restaurant in the village and used the local press to spread news of the "billionaire priest," thereby prompting several treasure hunters to show up in the village.

At that point, enter Pierre Plantard, a character who had been active in extreme right-wing groups, had founded anti-Semitic groups, and at the age of seventeen had launched Alpha Galates, a movement siding with the collaborationist Vichy regime. This had not stopped him, after the liberation, from claiming that his organizations were partisan resistance groups.

In December 1963, after six months in prison for breach of trust (he was later sentenced to a year for the corruption of minors), Plantard presented his Priory of Sion, boasting that it was almost two thousand years old, on the basis of documents that Saunière had allegedly found. These documents demonstrated the survival of the Merovingian royal line, and Plantard claimed he was a descendant of Dagobert II.

Plantard's scam crossed paths with a book by Gérard de Sède, who in 1962 had written about the mysteries of the Castle of Gisors, in Normandy, where he had met Roger Lhomoy, half tramp and half lunatic, who had worked for a time as a gardener and custodian at the castle. There he spent two years digging at night in the cellars where he found old tunnels. Lhomoy claimed he had entered a room where he supposedly saw a stone altar, images of Jesus and the twelve apostles on the walls, and, lined up along the walls, stone sarcophagi and thirty coffers in precious metal.

Despite the discovery of a few tunnels, none of the subsequent research, encouraged by de Sède, led to the fabulous room. In the meantime, de Sède had been approached by Plantard, who claimed to have not only secret documents that unfortunately he could not show, but also a map of the mysterious room. In reality, he had drawn the map himself following the statements made by the said Lhomoy, but this had encouraged de Sède to write his book and to surmise, as always happens in these cases, that the Templars had had a hand in the affair. In 1967, de Sède published *L'Or de Rennes* (The Treasure of Rennes) and with this book he definitively brought the myth of the Priory of Sion to the attention of the media, including the reproduction of the fake parchments that Planchard had been able to distribute in some libraries in the meantime. In fact, as Plantard himself later confessed, the fake parchments had been drawn up by Philippe de Cherisey, a French radio humorist and actor, who in 1979 had finally declared that he was the author of the forgeries and that he had copied the uncial script from documents found in the Bibliothèque Nationale in Paris.

In these documents De Sède found a disquieting reference to a famous painting, Poussin's *The Arcadian Shepherds*, where (as had already happened in a painting by Guercino) some shepherds open a tomb with the words *Et in Arcadia ego* on it. It is a classic *memento mori*, in which death announces its presence even in happy Arcadia. But Plantard maintained that the phrase had been on his family coat of arms since the thirteenth century (unlikely, given that Plantard was the son of a waiter), that the landscape in the paintings resembled that of Rennes-le-Château (whereas Poussin was born in Normandy and Guercino had never been in France), and that the tombs in Poussin's and Guercino's paintings resembled a sepulchre visible until the 1980s, on a road between Rennes-le-Château and Rennes-les-Bains. Unfortunately it has been proved that the tomb was not built until the twentieth century.

In any case he deduced from this the proof that Guercino's and Poussin's paintings had been commissioned by the Priory of Sion. But the deciphering of Poussin's painting did not stop there: by anagramming *Et in Arcadia ego* he derived the command *I! Tego arcana Dei*. In other words, "Begone! I conceal the mysteries of God." Hence the "proof" that the tomb was that of Jesus.

De Sède observed that in the church restored by Saunière there appears the inscription *Terribilis est locus iste*, which thrilled mystery lovers. Actually, it is a quotation from *Genesis* 24 that appears in many churches and refers to Jacob's vision when he dreamed of ascending to heaven and, on waking up, he says in the Latin version of the Vulgate: "How terrible this place is!." But in Latin *terribilis* also means worthy of veneration, awe inspiring—and therefore there is nothing menacing about the expression.

The font in the church rests on a kneeling demon, thought to be Asmodeus, and here too we could cite many Romanesque churches

philosophy can at best recognize its existence, or at least its apparition as a psychological constant of the human mind. Simply put, a lightning strike that incinerates a tree accompanied by a clap of thunder would in itself be only a frightening accident and sensation were it not seen and justified as a manifestation of some transcendent entity or will—without this, though the event would remain impressive in memory, it would not have tremendous import.

The sacred is therefore presented as the *numinoso, mysterium tremendum et fascinans* (the numinous, terrible yet fascinating mystery) which confounds reason, which overwhelms and arouses wonder, amazement, and dismay, but which at the same time gives rise to forces of both repulsion and attraction—and as such, it resists immediate description in conceptual terms but is instead experiential, to use Friedrich Schleiermacher's term, involving an ingrained awareness of the infinite, and a feeling of dependence, weakness, impotence, and insignificance in its presence.

Sometimes the experience of the sacred, the presence of which is felt without our being able to define it, prompts people to react with practices of submission or of sacrifice, even human sacrifice. At other times, and this happens with simpler folk in particular, people want to *see* the sacred, hence the need for a hierophancy—a system of priests who interpret the sacred mysteries, and in that way allow the sacred to take the visible forms that will make it understandable. Those who experience the presence of the sacred, to be able to speak of it, want to see the numinous. Otherwise, there are only its effects to observe (and they are effects we like to escape)—namely, wonder, amazement, dismay, and terror.

The sacred does not always appear in anthropomorphic forms; in certain cultures it can assume a variety of vicarious forms. It can be a tree or a rock in which, in some way, people perceive something "other."

Clearly, simpler people attempt to confer a recognizably human or animal likeness on the sacred, either in the form of a totemic image or in the way that has always scandalized mystics and theologians the most, by giving it an anthropomorphic form.

So the fundamental problem with the sacred is that, to allow it to appear and be something that gives meaning to our experience, it may be talked about and made evident in the guise of *idola* or *amalgamata*, images—but how is it possible to make images of the sacred if the sacred is by definition something that lies beyond our experience?

There is a rather disconcerting text in which William of Ockham says that an image can only be a sign that allows us to recall something we have already known as an entity in and of itself; otherwise, the image would not strike us as similar to whatever is represented. So seeing a statue of Hercules would not make me think of Hercules if I had not already seen Hercules.

This text assumes (and this was a matter on which there was general agreement) that we are not capable, starting from an icon, of imagining something that until then was unknown to us. This would seem to contradict our experience, since people constantly use paintings, photographs, or Identi-Kit facial composites to be able to envision people, animals, or things still unknown—and even in Ockham's day, when monarchs wanted to marry off daughters to cousins living in another country they would send images of them in advance. There is, however, an epistemological explanation for such an embarrassing statement. For Augustine, a sign was something which, while presenting itself to the senses, conveyed *aliquid ex se faciens in cogitationem venire*—something else to the intellect. For the Aristotelian tradition, at least until Thomas Aquinas, the sign referred directly to the concept, which was in its turn an image of the thing. But for Ockham, the true *signum* of the thing was the concept, not the word that referred to it. Concepts are the natural signs that *signify* things, while words are imposed by direct relation to things, he explains in *Summa logicae*: *voces sunt signa secundario significantia illa quae per passiones animae primario importantur*. Words signify the same things signified by concepts, yet they do not signify concepts!

If the only sign of individual things is the concept, and the physical expression (be it a word or a picture) is only a symptom of the inner image, then without a preliminary *notitia intuitiva* of an object, the physical expressions cannot mean anything. Words and images neither create nor bring into being anything in the mind of the addressee (as could happen in Augustine's semiotics) if that mind does not already contain the only possible sign of the experienced reality—in other words, the mental one.

We might object to Ockham that any representation (such as an Identi-Kit composite) stimulates our mind to produce a mental sign thanks to which we can recognize the corresponding thing, and this is why we can imagine Hercules or Hitler even though we have never met them. But Ockham's text gives rise to an interesting problem: the police officer could not put together that image of the suspect if the witness providing the input had not really met or seen the corresponding individual, just as Pietro Annigoni could not have made the portrait of Queen Elizabeth if she had not been sitting in front of him. The indisputable consequence is that there cannot be an image of something no one has *ever* seen. Even when something new is created, as is the case with centaurs, it results from putting together parts of things that are already known. And this is why we can make images of Hitler and even Mickey Mouse, but we cannot make images of a circle whose center is everywhere and circumference is nowhere. The Ockhamist theory of the image can be challenged as regards images of things attainable through experience, but holds up perfectly well for images of things that transcend experience.

Perhaps the first to pose the problem of the impossibility of representing or naming the sacred was Dionysius the Areopagite, known since the nineteenth century as Pseudo-Dionysius. He conceived of the deity as unfathomable and contradictory, describing something that is "not a material body, and therefore does not possess outward shape or intelligible form, or quality, or quantity, or solid weight; nor has It any local existence which can be perceived by sight or touch. . . . It is not soul, or mind, or endowed with the faculty of imagination, conjecture, reason, or understanding . . . nor is It number or order, or greatness . . . nor is It personal essence, or eternity, or time . . . nor is it darkness, nor is It light, or error, or truth . . ." and so on, for pages and pages of dazzling mystic aphasia. Not knowing how to name it otherwise, Pseudo-Dionysius calls the divinity "the luminous dimness, a silence which teaches secretly" and "luminous darkness." But even these are images that refer to data of experience. How can we base on data drawn from experience something that should instead be the foundation of such data?

Pseudo-Dionysius held that God is ineffable, and the only way to address this satisfactorily is with silence. When someone speaks, it can only conceal the divine mysteries from those who cannot accept them.

This mystical attitude is, however, constantly contradicted by the opposite one, the theophanic conviction that, as God is the cause of all things, all names befit him, in the sense that every effect refers to its Cause. God can therefore be given the form and figure of man, of fire, or of amber. People can praise the ears, eyes, hair, face, hands, shoulders, wings, and arms, the back and the feet, and fashion crowns, thrones, goblets, volcanoes, and other objects full of mystery.

Pseudo-Dionysius warns, however, that such naming drawn from various symbols will never be adequate. Hence the need for those making such representations to dispense with what can only be extremely understated hyperbole (the oxymoron being appropriate here). Instead, the deity should only be named using "dissimilar similarities" or "incongruous dissimilarities" such that, for the divine "sometimes the images are of the lowliest kind, such as sweet-smelling ointment, and corner stone. Sometimes the imagery is even derived from animals so that God is described as a lion or a panther, a leopard or a charging bear. Add to this what seems the lowliest and most incongruous of all, for the experts in things divine gave him the form of a worm." Elsewhere Dionysius refers to another supreme case of dissimilitude, citing the part of Psalm 78 where a wrathful Lord is "awaked as one out of sleep, and like a mighty man that shouteth by reason of wine."

But here, too, the allusion to the inexpressible sacred is through representations of things attainable in experience—and they are no greater than attempts to anthropomorphize the deity (depicting God with a beard and triangular halo), or for that matter to animalize the Holy Spirit.

And therefore, since we cannot really formulate a negative theology that says only what God is not, in trying to find one that is positively affirmative, we end up accepting representations of God as if he were one of us. This emerges even at the beginning of the Book of Genesis: if God made us in his own image and likeness, this means that *we* can imagine God in *our* own image and likeness.

Christianity has overcome this impossibility to a certain extent by speaking of an incarnate deity. Incarnation would be the semiotic artifice through which God is rendered thinkable and representable, understandable even to the humble—not only through the image of Jesus but also through the likeness of those who have been in some way mediators of the sacred, such as the Virgin Mary and the saints.

But the Ockhamist predicament arises in these cases, too, because none of the artists who have painted or sculpted portraits of Jesus and the Virgin ever saw them—given that the portraiture of evangelical characters began centuries after the death of Christ—and the Mandylion, the Veil of Veronica, and the Shroud of Turin (to the extent we wish to lend them credence) also appeared in much later periods.

If anyone has had direct experience of God, it is the mystics and, precisely out of faithfulness to the idea of the non-perceivable nature of the sacred and the impossibility of translating it into images, they have always described the experience of divinity in the form of darkness, dark night, emptiness, and silence. Yet all the great mystics have affirmed that, even in the mystical vision, which is an ineffable gift, it is possible to provide an image of God. To the mystic, God appears as a Great Void.

Dionysius the Carthusian, a fifteenth-century Flemish theologian, said: "O most benign God, you are the light and the sphere of light, where your elect go sweetly to rest, where they fall asleep and sleep. You are like a vast desert, perfectly flat and incommensurable, in which the truly devout heart, purified of all particular love, illuminated from on high, and full of ardor, wanders without getting lost, blissfully succumbs and together heals."

The thirteenth-century German mystic Meister Eckhart speaks of a silent and empty deity as an abyss devoid of mode and form, and describes how the soul "wants to go into the simple ground, into the quiet desert, into which distinction never gazed, not the Father, nor the Son, nor the Holy Spirit . . . For this ground is a simple silence, in itself immovable, and by this immovability all things are moved." Only in this way does the soul attain supreme bliss, by plunging into the deserted divinity where there is neither work nor image. Eckhart's disciple Johannes Tauler in his own *Sermons* writes:

> The purified and clarified spirit sinks into the divine darkness, in a mute silence and in an unfathomable and ineffable union, and in this sinking all equality and all inequality are lost, and in that abyss the spirit loses itself and knows nothing either of God or of itself, it knows not either the equal or the unequal, or any thing; since it has plunged into the unity of God and has forgotten all differences.

And Tauler says that one arrives at true simplicity through closed senses, the absence of images, and contempt for oneself. In every event and in every external act, we must be the master of our senses, because in truth the senses lead us out of ourselves and cause extraneous images to come to us. We read of a holy man who, having to leave his cell in the month of May, pulled the hood of his habit over his eyes. Asked why he did this, he said: "I am defending my eyes from the sight of the trees, so that the visions of my spirit might not be obstructed. O my dear children, if the sight of the wild wood created an impediment for that man, how harmful the variety of worldly and frivolous things must be!"

In *The Ascent of Mount Carmel*, Saint John of the Cross says:

> For, in order that one may attain supernatural transformation, it is clear that he must be plunged into darkness and carried far away from all contained in his nature that is sensual and rational. For the word supernatural means that which soars above the natural self; the natural self, therefore, remains beneath it. For, although this transformation and

union is something that cannot be comprehended by human ability and sense, the soul must completely and voluntarily void itself of all that can enter into it. . . .

With respect to all these there may come, and there are wont to come, to spiritual persons representations and objects of a supernatural kind. With respect to sight, they are apt to picture figures and forms of persons belonging to the life to come—the forms of certain saints, and representations of angels, good and evil, and certain lights and brightnesses of an extraordinary kind. And with the ears they hear certain extraordinary words, sometimes spoken by those figures that they see, sometimes without seeing the person who speaks them. As to the sense of smell, they sometimes perceive the sweetest perfumes with the senses, without knowing whence they proceed. Likewise, as to taste, it comes to pass that they are conscious of the sweetest savors, and, as to touch, they experience great delight—sometimes to such a degree that it is as though all the bones and the marrow rejoice and sing and are bathed in delight; this is like that which we call spiritual unction, which in pure souls proceeds from the spirit and flows into the very members. And this sensible sweetness is a very ordinary thing with spiritual persons, for it comes to them from their sensible affection and devotion to a greater or a lesser degree, to each one after his own manner.

And it must be known that, although all these things may happen to the bodily senses in the way of God, we must never rely upon them or accept them, but must always fly from them, without trying to ascertain whether they be good or evil; for, the more completely exterior and corporeal they are, the less certainly are they of God. For it is more proper and habitual to God to communicate Himself to the spirit, wherein there is more security and profit for the soul, than to sense, wherein there is ordinarily much danger and deception . . . .

So he that esteems such things errs greatly and exposes himself to great peril of being deceived; in any case he will have within himself a complete impediment to the attainment of spirituality . . . .

For over and above the difficulty that there is in being sure that one is not going astray in respect of locutions and visions which are of God, there are ordinarily many of these locutions and visions which are of the devil; for in his converse with the soul the devil habitually wears the same guise as God assumes.

In the early seventeenth century, Jakob Böhme had a fundamental mystical experience that brought him into contact with the very core of the universe, thanks to a sort of dazzling epiphany when one morning he saw a ray of sunlight reflected in a tin tub. What he saw is not known, nor did he tell us, and all the editions that have tried to illustrate his mystical perceptions are made up of circular, spindly structures that are difficult to decipher.

The bottomless abyss of the Divinity, Böhme writes in *The Incarnation of Jesus Christ* (1620), is none other than a quietude devoid of essence. It can give nothing. It is eternal peace with no peer, an abyss with neither beginning nor end. It is neither purpose nor place, it is not seeking or finding, nor anything where there is possibility. It resembles an eye, its own mirror. It has no essence, or light or darkness; it is above all a magic, and it has a will, which we must neither seek nor follow, for it perturbs us. By this will we mean the foundation of the Divinity, without origin. It comprises itself in itself, beyond nature; therefore we must keep silent

And yet (even though I am not an expert in the history of mysticism and I make this suggestion with great caution) while I have the impression that the experience of pure and ineffable nothing-ness is proper to male mysticism, it does not seem to me that many mystical women have referred to God as Pure Nothingness; on the contrary, the most important among them have spoken of Christ as an almost carnal presence. Female mysticism is dominated by hierophany, and the woman who sees the divine image expatiates on her subject in pages of undoubted erotic ecstasy, and on her amorous feelings for the Cross.

The following quotation from Saint Maddalena de' Pazzi's "The Forty Days" (*I quaranta giorni*, 1558) ought to suffice:

> Love, love, Oh love, give me a great voice so that when I call you Love I may be heard from the East to the West, and in all parts of the world, even unto hell, so that you may be known and beloved of all; Love, love, You are strong, and powerful love. Love, love only you penetrate, and pierce; you break and vanquish all things. Love, love. You are heaven and earth, Fire and Air, Blood and Water. Oh Love you are God and man, love and hate, Joy of nobility, Divine, Old and new Truth. Oh Love neither loved nor known. But I see one person who has known this love.

Then there are the pages in which Saint Teresa of Ávila speaks of the wine of love that penetrates her veins and inebriates her, of the divine spouse that in an instant makes her enjoy all the beauty, all the glory of paradise in such an ineffable way:

> on some occasions I am in such transports I do not realize, were it not for my uttering amorous moans with all my spirit. . . . Once an angel appeared before me in tangible, bodily

form. He was most beautiful and I saw in his hand a long spear of gold, and at the point there seemed to be a little fire. He appeared to me to be thrusting it at times into my heart, and piercing my very entrails; when he drew it out, he seemed to draw them out also, and to leave me all on fire with a great love of God. . . . The pain was so sharp that it made me utter several moans; and so excessive was the sweetness caused me by this intense pain that one can never wish to lose it, nor will one's soul be content with anything less than God. It is not bodily pain, but spiritual, though the body has a share in it— indeed, a great share.

Among the poems of Teresa of Ávila, we also find this:

> When the gentle hunter
> Shot me and made me surrender
> My soul fell into the arms of love . . .
> What joy my beloved
> To be close to you
> Eager to see you
> I wish to die. And when you deign
> To enter my breast
> Oh then my God, in that moment
> I fear losing you.

At fifteen, the French Salesian nun Marguerite Marie Alacoque (1647–1690) began to believe she was "betrothed to Jesus" and even reported that one day Jesus lay himself upon her with all his weight. "Let me use you at my pleasure because there is a time for all things," he told her when she protested. "Now I want you to be the object of my love, yielding to my will, without resistance on your part, so that I may enjoy you." It is worth quoting much more from her autobiography:

> One day, having a little more leisure—for the occupations confided to me left me scarcely any—I was praying before the Blessed Sacrament, when I felt myself wholly penetrated with that Divine Presence, but to such a degree that I lost all thought of myself and of the place where I was, and abandoned myself to this Divine Spirit, yielding up my heart to the power of His love. He made me repose for a long time upon His Sacred Breast, where He disclosed to me the marvels of His love and the inexplicable secrets of His Sacred Heart, which so far He had concealed from me. Then it was that, for the first time, He opened to me His Divine Heart in a manner so real and sensible as to be beyond all doubt, by reason of the effects which this favor produced in me, fearful, as I always am, of deceiving myself in anything that I say of what passes in me. It seems to me that this is what took place: "My Divine Heart," He said, "is so inflamed with love for men, and for thee in particular that, being unable any longer to contain within Itself the flames of Its burning Charity, It must needs spread them abroad by thy means, and manifest Itself to them (mankind) in order to enrich them with the precious treasures which I discover to thee, and which contain graces of sanctification and salvation necessary to withdraw them from the abyss of perdition. I have chosen thee as an abyss of unworthiness and ignorance for the accomplishment of this great design, in order that every thing may be done by Me." After this He asked me for my heart, which I begged Him to take. He did so and placed it in His own Ador-

able Heart where He showed it to me as a little atom which was being consumed in this great furnace, and withdrawing it thence as a burning flame in the form of a heart, He restored it to the place whence He had taken it saying to me: "See, My well-beloved, I give thee a precious token of My love, having enclosed within thy side a little spark of its glowing flames, that it may serve thee for a heart and consume thee to the last moment of thy life; its ardor will never be exhausted, and thou wilt be able to find some slight relief only by bleeding. . . .

On the First Friday of each month, the above-mentioned grace connected with the pain in my side was renewed in the following manner: The Sacred Heart was represented to me as a resplendent sun, the burning rays of which fell vertically upon my heart, which was inflamed with a fire so fervid that it seemed as if it would reduce me to ashes. It was at these times especially that my Divine Master taught me what He required of me and disclosed to me the secrets of His loving Heart. On one occasion, whilst the Blessed Sacrament was exposed, feeling wholly withdrawn within myself by an extraordinary recollection of all my senses and powers, Jesus Christ, my sweet Master, presented Himself to me, all resplendent with glory, His Five Wounds shining like so many suns. Flames issued from every part of His Sacred Humanity, especially from His Adorable Bosom, which resembled an open furnace and disclosed to me His most loving and most amiable Heart, which was the living source of these flames.

I was so extremely dainty that the least want of cleanliness made me feel inclined to vomit. He reproved me for this with such severity, that, on one occasion, being about to remove what a sick person had vomited, I was constrained to take it up with my tongue and to swallow it, saying: "Had I a thousand bodies, O my God, a thousand loves and a thousand lives, I would immolate them all to Thy service!" I experienced such delight in this action that I would have wished to meet every day with similar occasions, that I might thus learn to conquer myself, having God alone as witness. And He, Whose goodness alone had given me the strength to overcome myself did not fail to manifest to me the pleasure He had taken therein. For the following night, if I mistake not, He kept me for two or three hours with my lips pressed to the Wound of His Sacred Heart. It would be difficult for me to explain what I then felt, and what marvellous effects this grace produced in my soul and in my heart. . . .

Thus did this Divine Love deal with His unworthy slave. It happened once, when I was tending a patient who was suffering from dysentery, I was overcome by a feeling of nausea; but He gave me so severe a reprimand, that I felt urged to repair this fault and I felt obliged, as I went to throw away what the woman had done, to thrust my tongue in it and fill my mouth. I would have swallowed it all if He had not reminded me of obedience, which did not permit me to eat anything without permission.

Why women would have erotic traffic with the (male) divine image while men (who could experience ecstasies of equal intensity with the Virgin) would not, I am unable to explain. The nineteenth-century physician Jean-Martin Charcot would have said that hysteria is a uniquely feminine disorder, but this has been denied; one might say that women have greater bodily sensitivity; or even that the reasons are purely cultural: men were not denied the possibility of erotic relationships and chose chastity of their own free will, while women were forcibly kept away from any sexual experience that was not sanctioned by marriage and perhaps through hierophanic sex they could satisfy many repressed desires. I do not know and I do not wish to deal with this topic here.

All I can say is, since it was the female saints who saw the sacred in an anthropomorphic manner, it is to their experience we must necessarily turn. In the *noche oscura* of St. John of the Cross we are lost and silent.

It is therefore beyond doubt that the sacred, while it is by definition inexpressible, comes to be expressed because human beings (except the most heroic mystics) need to see it. But, inasmuch as it is unattainable, either by its essence or due to the lack of experience of the individuals who have embodied it, it can only be *represented*—and not just anthropomorphically, but also and solely with reference to models with precise locations in history.

And this is what I intend to deal with now: how the sacred takes on different forms depending on the historical period and the artistic tastes of that time.

In the Middle Ages they maintained that *pulchra enim sunt ubera quae paululum supereminent et tument modice* (breasts that stand out little and swell moderately are beautiful). This was another way of referring to small breasts supported by a tight corset—and this is how the ladies and the Madonnas of the secular imagination were portrayed.

In the Renaissance, the opulence of Holbein's and Raphael's ladies recalls the opulence of certain Virgins by Lorenzo Lotto, and the almost cellulitic emphasis with which Rubens represents the beauty of Venus also shows through the garments of the Virgin Mary or at least becomes evident in the appealing angelic cellulite of the putti.

We could go on to reflect on how the style of different eras is reflected in the sacred representations of Asian cultures, but I think we can limit ourselves here to also citing the romantic and decadent portrayals of masculine beauty in the nineteenth and twentieth century and how this ideal is also realized in images of the Sacred Heart—not to mention how the languor of the fin-de-siècle aesthete is reflected in the languor of the saints.

With regard to the mysticism of the Sacred Heart as an epiphany of divine love, Raymond Firth, in *Symbols Public and Private*, notes that Saint Marguerite Marie Alacoque had her mystical visions at a time when it had become known that the seat of affections is not the heart. But either Jesus in appearing to her, or the confessor who helped her express her mystical experience in visible terms, did not take into account the science explaining the world God made as it truly works, but rather chose to align with common opinion about those workings. And to this day, common opinion still talks in terms of heartfelt love and broken hearts—as if to suggest that our only mediator with the sacred is popular song.

Our Lady appeared to Bernadette in Lourdes in 1858, so we know how Bernadette Soubirous actually looked from photos of that time. But because ecclesiastical authorities gave permission to take photographs of her on various occasions, we can also see how at a certain point, as her reputation for holiness grew, the photographers of the time managed to make her more seductive. By the 1950s, Hollywood was presenting her in the form of Jennifer Jones—and I remember the scandalized reaction in the Catholic world when, a few years later, the very same Jennifer Jones, the face of Bernadette, appeared in the erotically charged scenes of *Duel in the Sun*.

The shepherd girls of Fatima were no models of grace and beauty but, again, 1950s Hollywood transformed them. And then came the transformation of the Blessed, and later Saint, Dominic Savio: after appearing in the first portrayals as a boy dressed appropriately but inelegantly, with trousers made baggy by kneeling, he gradually became increasingly good-looking and emerged in modern times as a handsome and virile young man. He even appeared, as if part of an engaged couple, with a young woman who, like him, died very young in the odor of sanctity: the Blessed Laura Vicuña.

This is not to mention the transformations of the Virgin Mary. An old statue of Our Lady in Lourdes resembles the women painted by Francesco Hayez in the nineteenth century, and the faces of certain statues of the Madonna of Fatima have the beauty of other times, but just imagine how Our Lady of Medjugorje must appear to the faithful who see her today: probably far closer to the fashion-model looks of a Monica Bellucci than to the grief-stricken Virgins of the distant past.

Saint Maria Goretti has also been subjected to similar changes as her kitsch devotional iconography has gradually been transformed by analogy with the actresses of the day.

Now we come to a curious case: the publication of the Three Secrets of Fatima in the twentieth century.

On reading Sister Lucia's document on the third secret of Fatima, it can be seen that the text—which the good sister wrote not as an illiterate little girl in 1917 but in 1944, by then a mature nun—is full of highly recognizable quotations from the Book of Revelation. Sister Lucia says that on the left-hand side of Our Lady and a little higher up she and her cousins saw an Angel with a sword of fire in his left hand; the glittering sword emitted flames that looked as though they might set the world on fire; but they were extinguished on contact with the splendor that Our Lady emanated from her right hand toward him. And pointing to the earth with his right hand, the angel cried out in a loud voice: "Penance, Penance, Penance!" And the children then saw in the immense light of God "rather like how you see people in a mirror when they pass in front of it," a bishop dressed in white ("we had the impression that it was the Holy Father"), various other bishops, priests, and religious men and women all going up a steep mountain, at the top of which there was a big Cross of rough-hewn tree trunks as if made of the wood of the cork tree complete with bark; before reaching that place the Holy Father passed through a big city half in ruins, and with trembling, halting steps, afflicted by pain and sorrow, he prayed for the souls of the dead bodies he encountered on his way; once he reached the top of the mountain, on his knees at the foot of the big Cross, he was killed by a group of soldiers who shot him with bullets and arrows, and in the same way, one after another, the other bishops, priests, religious men and women, and various secular people of different ranks and positions were all killed. Beneath the two arms of the Cross there were two Angels, both with glass "watering cans" in their hands in which they gathered up the blood of the martyrs and used it to bathe the souls that were making their way to God.

So Lucia saw an angel with a sword of fire who seemed to want to set the world on fire. In the Book of Revelation, angels also spread fire throughout the world, for example in 9:8, with the angel of the second trumpet. True, this angel does not have a flaming sword, but we will see later where the sword comes from (perhaps assisted by traditional iconography, which offers a wealth of archangels with burning swords). Then Lucia sees the divine light as in a mirror: here the suggestion does not come from Revelation, but from the first epistle of St. Paul to the Corinthians (13:12): "For now we see through a glass, darkly, but then face to face."

After this, behold a bishop dressed in white. He is alone, whereas in Revelation the gentleman in white has many servants, all ready to be martyred, appearing multiple times (in 6:11, in 7:9, and in 7:14), but never mind. Then we see bishops and priests going up a steep mountain, and we are at Revelation 6:15, where the powerful of the Earth hide in the dens and rocks of a mountain. Then the Holy Father arrives in a "half ruined" city, and on his way encounters the souls of the dead; the city is mentioned in Revelation 11:8, corpses included, while it collapses and falls into ruin in 11:13 and, again, in the form of Babylon, in 18:21.

Let's go on to where the bishop and many other faithful are killed by soldiers with arrows and firearms. While Sister Lucia is innovating when she mentions firearms, massacres with sharp weapons are performed by locusts wearing warriors' breastplates in 9:7, at the sound of the fifth trumpet. Finally, we come to the two angels pouring blood from a glass watering can (*regador* in Portuguese). Revelation surely abounds in angels that spill blood, but in 8:5 they do it with a censer, in 14:20 the blood overflows from a vat, and in 16:3 it is poured from a vial. Why a watering can? We might recall that Fatima is not far from the Asturias, where in the Middle Ages they first made those splendid Mozarabic miniatures of the Apocalypse that were afterwards reproduced many times. In some of the images of angels sounding trumpets, the trumpets may be taken for swords of fire or, just as readily, if associated with the sort of spouts that appear below, might be mistaken for some kind of watering can. In other images, we see angels pouring blood from goblets of indeterminate design, as if they were watering the world.

The interesting thing is that, if you read the theological commentary written by then Cardinal Joseph Ratzinger, you see that, in pointing out that a private vision is not a matter of faith, and that an allegory is not a prophecy to be taken literally, he explicitly points out the analogies with Revelation's images, and notes: "The concluding part of the 'secret' uses images which Lucia may have seen in devotional books and which draw their inspiration from long-standing intuitions of faith." So, in a chapter significantly titled "The Anthropological Structure of Private Revelations" in the theological commentary on the *Message of Fatima*, he writes:

> In this field, theological anthropology distinguishes three forms of perception or "vision": vision with the senses, and hence exterior bodily perception, interior perception, and spiritual vision (*visio sensibilis–imaginativa–intellectualis*). It is clear that in the visions of Lourdes, Fatima and other places it is not a question of normal exterior perception of the senses: the images and forms which are seen are not located spatially, as is the case, for example, with a tree or a house. This is perfectly obvious . . . especially since not everybody present saw them, but only the "visionaries." It is also clear that it is not a matter of a "vision" in the mind, without images, as occurs at the higher levels of mysticism. Therefore we are dealing with the middle category, interior perception. . . . Interior vision does not mean fantasy, which would be no more than an expression of the subjective imagination. It means rather that the soul is touched by something real, even if beyond the senses. It is rendered capable of seeing that which is beyond the senses, that which cannot be seen—seeing by means of the "interior senses." . . . Perhaps this explains why children tend to be the ones to receive these apparitions: their souls

are as yet little disturbed, their interior powers of perception are still not impaired. . . . "Interior vision" is not fantasy. . . . But it also has its limitations. Even in exterior vision the subjective element is always present: We do not see the pure object, but it comes to us through the filter of our senses, which carry out a work of translation. This is still more evident in the case of interior vision, especially when it involves realities which in themselves transcend our horizon. The subject, the visionary, is still more powerfully involved. He sees insofar as he is able, in the modes of representation and consciousness available to him. In the case of interior vision, the process of translation is even more extensive than in exterior vision, for the subject shares in an essential way in the formation of the image of what appears. He can arrive at the image only within the bounds of his capacities and possibilities. Such visions therefore are never simple "photographs" of the other world, but are influenced by the potentialities and limitations of the perceiving subject.

This can be demonstrated in all the great visions of the saints; and naturally it is also true of the visions of the children at Fatima. The images described by them are by no means a simple expression of their fantasy, but the result of a real perception of a higher and interior origin. But neither should they be thought of as if for a moment the veil of the other world were drawn back, with heaven appearing in its pure essence, as one day we hope to see it in our definitive union with God. Rather the images are, in a manner of speaking, a synthesis of the impulse coming from on high and the capacity to receive this impulse in the visionaries—that is, the children.

This, in rather more secular terms, means that visionaries see only what their culture has taught them to see and allows them to imagine. It seems to me that the approval of the retired Pontiff puts a reasonable seal on my brief observations on the iconography of the sacred.

[Prepared for La Milanesiana, 2016]

BIBLIOGRAPHY

INDEX

Bibliography

Listed here are published works explicitly mentioned in the text, presented alphabetically by chapter. In his remarks, Eco himself did not indicate specific editions used or recommended. For the convenience of English-language readers, information is presented for English-language editions rather than the Italian-language editions that Eco is more likely to have known.

1. On the Shoulders of Giants

Aldhelm of Malmesbury. "Letter to Eahfrid." In James Ussher, *Veterum Epistolarum Hibernicarum Sylloge*, letter no. 13, 37–41. Dublin: Societatis Bibliopolarum, 1632.

Apuleius. *Florida*. In *Apologia. Florida. De Deo Socratis*. Trans. Christopher P. Jones. Loeb Classical Library, no. 534. Cambridge, MA: Harvard University Press, 2017.

Aristotle. "Logic." In *The Works of Aristotle*, vol. 1, trans. William David Ross. London: Encyclopædia Britannica, 1971.

Auraicept na n'Eces: The Scholar's Primer [7th century]. Trans. George Calder. Edinburgh: John Grant, 1917.

Dante Alighieri. *De vulgari eloquentia* [1304–1307]. "On the Eloquence of the Vernacular." In *De Vulgari Eloquentia: Dante's Book of Exile*, trans. Marianne Shapiro. Lincoln: University of Nebraska Press, 1990.

Diderot, Denis, and Jean Baptiste le Rond d'Alembert. *Encyclopédie ou dictionnaire raisonné des sciences, des arts et des métiers.* Paris: Briasson-David-Le Breton-Durand, 1751–1780.

Gregory, Tullio. *Scetticismo ed empirismo: Studio su Gassendi* [Skepticism and Empiricism: A Study of Gassendi]. Bari: Laterza, 1961.

Horace. *Epistles.* In *Satires. Epistles. The Art of Poetry.* Loeb Classical Library, no. 194. Cambridge, MA: Harvard University Press, 1926.

Jeauneau, Édouard. *Nani sulle spalle di giganti.* Naples: Guida, 1969.

Jerome, Saint. *Adversus Jovinianum* [c. 390]. "Against Jovinianus." In *Nicene and Post-Nicene Fathers,* trans. W. H. Fremantle, G. Lewis, and W. G. Martley, ed. Philip Schaff and Henry Wace, 2nd ser., vol. 6. Buffalo, NY: Christian Literature Publishing, 1893.

John of Salisbury. *The Metalogicon of John of Salisbury: A Twelfth-Century Defense of the Verbal and Logical Arts of the Trivium.* Trans. Daniel D. McGarry. London: Peter Smith, 1971.

Merton, Robert K. *On the Shoulders of Giants.* New York: Free Press, 1965.

Nietzsche, Friedrich. *Untimely Meditations* [1876]. Cambridge: Cambridge University Press, 1997.

Ovid. *Ars amatoria.* Trans. B. P. Moore. London: Folio Society, 1965.

Ortega y Gasset, José. *Man and Crisis.* Trans. Mildred Adams. New York: W. W. Norton, 1958. Ortega y Gasset. *En torno a Galileo* [1933]. In *Obras completas,* vol. 5. Madrid, 1947.

Rifkin, Jeremy. *Entropy: A New World View.* New York: Viking, 1980.

Virgil the Grammarian [Virgilius Maro Grammaticus]. Epitomae; Epistolae. In *Virgilio Marone Grammatico: Epitomi ed Epistole,* trans. G. Polara. Naples: Liguori, 1979.

William of Conches. "Commentaries on Priscian's Institutiones grammaticae." In *Glosulae de magno Prisciano* [*Institutiones I–XVI*]. Versio altera, ed. Édouard Jeauneau Turnhout: Brepols.

2. Beauty

Barbey d'Aurevilly, Jules. *Léa* [1832]. In *Le cachet d'Onyx; Léa.* Paris: La Connaissance, 1919.

Bernard of Clairvaux. *Apologia ad Guillelmum. Cistercians and Cluniacs: St. Bernard's Apologia to Abbot William.* Trans. Michael Casey. Kalamazoo, MI: Cistercian Publications, 1970.

Burke, Edmund. *A Philosophical Enquiry into the Origin of Our Ideas of the Sublime and Beautiful* [1757]. A new ed. London: printed for J. Dodsley, 1787.

Clement of Alexandria. *The Stromata, or Miscellanies.* In *Ante-Nicene Fathers,* vol. 2: *Fathers of the Second Century: Hermas, Tatian, Athenagonas, Theophilus, and Clement of Alexandria.* Ed. A. Roberts and J. Donaldson, rev. and arr. A. Cleveland Coxe, 299–368. New York: Christian Literature Publishing, 1885.

Formaggio, Dino. *L'arte.* Milan: ISEDI, 1973.

Guido Guinizelli. *Vedut'ho la lucente stella diana.* "I've Got the Bright Star Diana." In *An Anthology of Italian Poems 13th–19th Century,* trans. Lorna de' Lucchi. New York: Alfred A. Knopf, 1922, 28–32, 348.

Hildegard of Bingen. *Selected Writings* [12th century]. Trans. Mark Atherton. London: Penguin, 2001.

Pacioli, Luca. *De divina proportione* [1509]. Sansepolcro: Aboca Museum, 2009.

Physiologus: A Medieval Book of Nature Lore [2nd–5th century]. Trans. Michael J. Curley. Chicago: University of Chicago Press, 2009.

Piero della Francesca. *De perspectiva pingendi,* 1472–1475. "On Perspective in Painting," Aboca Museum Editions, facsimile of the Treatise stored in the Panizzi Library in Reggio. http://www.codicesillustres.com /catalogue/de_prospectiva_pingendi/.

Plato. *Timaeus.* Trans. Benjamin Jowett. New York: Macmillan, 1959.

Pliny the Elder. *Natural History.* Trans. Horace Rackham; W. H. S. Jones. Loeb Classical Library. Cambridge, MA: Harvard University Press.

Proust, Marcel. *In Search of Lost Time* [1909–1922]. London: Everyman's Library, 2001.

Pseudo-Callisthenes. *The Romance of Alexander the Great* [3rd century]. Trans. Albert Mugrdich Wolohojian. New York: Columbia University Press, 1969.

Pseudo-Dionysius the Areopagite. *On the Divine Names and On the Mystical Theology.* Trans. C. E. Rolt. London: SPCK, 1920.

Shaftesbury, Anthony Ashley Cooper, Third Earl of. *Characteristics of Men, Manners, Opinions, Times.* Ed. Lawrence E. Klein. Cambridge: Cambridge University Press, 1999.

Sue, Eugène. *The Mysteries of the People, Or, History of a Proletarian Family across the Ages.* Trans. Daniel De Leon and Solon De Leon. New York: NY Labor News, 1904. Sue. *Les Mystères de Paris.* Originally serialized in ninety parts in *Journal des débats,* June 1842 to October 1843.

Thomas Aquinas. *Summa Theologiae: Latin Text and English Translation.* New York: McGraw-Hill, 61 vols., 1964–. Repr. New York: Cambridge University Press, 2006.

Xenophanes of Colophon. *Fragments.* Trans. J. H. Lesher. Toronto: University of Toronto Press, 1992.

3. Ugliness

Aesop Romance: The Book of Xanthus the Philosopher and Aesop His Slave, or the Career of Aesop. Trans. Lloyd W. Daly. In *Anthology of Ancient Greek Popular Literature,* ed. William F. Hansen. Bloomington: Indiana University Press, 1988.

Baudelaire, Charles. *Les fleurs du mal* [1857]. *The Flowers of Evil.* Trans. Marthiel Mathews and Jackson Mathews. New York: New Directions, 1955.

Bonaventure of Bagnoregio. *Commentaria in quattuor libros sententiarum Magistri Petri Lombardi. Bonaventure on the Eucharist: Commentary on the 'Sentences.'* Trans. Junius Johnson. Wilsele, Belgium: Peeters, 2017.

Broch, Hermann. "Kitsch" (1933) and "Notes on the Problem of Kitsch" (1950). In *Kitsch: The World of Bad Taste,* ed. Gillo Dorfles. New York: Universe Books, 1968.

Brown, Fredric. "Sentry" [1954]. In *From These Ashes: The Complete Short SF of Fredric Brown,* ed. Ben Yalow. Framingham, MA: NESFA Press, 2001.

Burton, Robert. *The Anatomy of Melancholy* [1624]. Ed. Floyd Dell and Paul Jordan-Smith. New York: Tudor, 1948.

Céline, Louis-Ferdinand. *Bagatelles pour un massacre.* Paris: Éditions Denoël, 1937.

Choniates, Niketas. *O City of Byzantium: Annals of Niketas Choniates.* Dayton, OH: Wayne State University Press, 1984.

Collodi, Carlo. *The Adventures of Pinocchio* [1881]. Trans. Nicolas J. Perella. Berkeley: University of California Press, 1986.

De Amicis, Edmondo. *Cuore (Heart): An Italian Schoolboy's Journal.* Trans. Isabel F. Hapgood. New York: Thomas Y. Crowell, 1887.

de Vitry, Jacques. *The Exempla or Illustrative Stories from the Sermones Vulgares of Jacques de Vitry.* Trans. Thomas Frederick Crane. London: David Nutt, 1890.

Dickens, Charles. *Hard Times.* London: Bradbury and Evans, 1854.

Encyclopædia Britannica, ed. 1798.

Fleming, Ian. *Dr. No.* London: Jonathan Cape, 1958.

Fleming, Ian. *From Russia with Love.* London: Jonathan Cape, 1957.

Fleming, Ian. *Goldfinger.* London: Jonathan Cape, 1959.

Fleming, Ian. *Live and Let Die.* London: Jonathan Cape, 1954.

Gozzano, Guido. "Grandmother Speranza's Friend." In *The Man I Pretend to Be: The Colloquies and Selected Poems of Guido Gozzano,* trans. Michael Palma. Princeton, NJ: Princeton University Press, 1981.

Gryphius, Andreas. *Notte, lucente notte. Sonetti* [17th century]. Venice: Marsilio, 1993.

Guerrini, Olindo [nom de plume Lorenzo Strecchetti]. *Postuma: Il canto dell'odio e altri versi proibiti.* Rome: Napoleone, 1981.

Hegel, G. W. F. *Aesthetics: Lectures on Fine Arts.* Trans. T. M. Knox. Oxford: Clarendon Press, 1975.

Hildegard of Bingen. *Scivias* [12th century]. Trans. Columba Hart and Jane Bishop. New York: Paulist Press, 1990.

Homer. *The Iliad.* Trans. Caroline Alexander. New York: Ecco / Harper Collins, 2015.

Hugo, Victor. *Cromwell* [1827]. Trans. George Burnham Ives. Boston: Little, Brown, 1909.

Hugo, Victor. *L'Homme qui rit* [1869]. *The Man Who Laughs.* Trans. unknown. Boston: Little, Brown and Co., 1888.

Iamblichus. *Life of Pythagoras.* Trans. Thomas Taylor. Rochester, VT: Inner Traditions / Bear, 1986.

Lautréamont, Comte de [Isidore Ducasse]. *The Songs of Maldoror.* Trans. Alexis Lykiard. New York: Thomas Y. Crowell, 1972.

Lombroso, Cesare. *L'Uomo delinquente* [1876]. *Criminal Man.* Trans. Mary Gibson and Nicole Hahn Rafter. Durham, NC: Duke University Press, 2006.

Marinetti, Filippo Tommaso. "Technical Manifesto of Futurist Literature" [1912]. In *Modernism: An Anthology,* ed. Lawrence Rainey. Malden, MA: Blackwell, 2005.

Marx, Karl. *Economic and Philosophic Manuscripts of 1844.* Trans. Martin Milligan. Amherst, NY: Prometheus Books, 1988.

Nietzsche, Friedrich. *The Gay Science* [1882/1886]. Mineola, NY: Dover, 2006.

Palazzeschi, Aldo. *Il controdolore* [1913]. Florence: Salimbeni, 1980.

Perrault, Charles. *Little Red Riding Hood* [1697]. London: Moorfields, 1810.

Rosenkranz, Karl. *The Aesthetics of Ugliness: A Critical Edition* [1853]. Trans. Andrei Pop and Mechtild Widrich. London: Bloomsbury, 2015.

Rostand, Edmond. *Cyrano de Bergerac* [1897]. Trans. Christopher Fry. New York: Oxford University Press, 1975.

Sade, Donatien-Alphonse François de. *The 120 Days of Sodom* [1785]. In *The 120 Days of Sodom, and Other Writings,* trans. Austryn Wainhouse and Richard Seaver. New York: Grove Press, 1966.

Segneri, Paolo. *The Panegyrics of Father Segneri, of the Society of Jesus.* Trans. Rev. William Humphrey. London: Washbourne, 1877.

Shakespeare, William. *The Tempest* [1610]. New York: Simon and Schuster, 2004.

Shakespeare, William. *Macbeth* [1605–1608]. New York: Simon and Schuster, 2003.

Shelley, Mary. *Frankenstein* [1818]. Boston: Cornhill, 1922.

Sontag, Susan. *Against Interpretation.* New York: Farrar Straus and Giroux, 1966.

Spillane, Mickey. *One Lonely Night.* New York: E. P. Dutton, 1951.

Testamentum Domini [4th–5th century]. *The Testament of Our Lord.* Trans. from Syriac by James Cooper and Arthur John Maclean. Edinburgh: T. and T. Clark, 1902.

Thomas Aquinas. *Summa Theologiae: Latin Text and English Translation.* New York: McGraw-Hill, 61 vols., 1964–. Repr. New York: Cambridge University Press, 2006.

Wagner, Richard. "Judaism in Music" [1850]. In *Judaism in Music and Other Essays,* trans. William Ashton Ellis. Lincoln: University of Nebraska Press, 1995.

4. The Absolute and the Relative

Dante Alighieri. *The Divine Comedy.* Trans. James Finn Cotter. New York: HarperCollins, 1989.

Hegel, G. W. F. *Hegel's Preface to the Phenomenology of Spirit.* Trans. Yirmiyahu Yovel. Princeton, NJ: Princeton University Press, 2005.

Jervis, Giovanni. *Contro il relativismo.* Rome-Bari: Laterza, 2005.

John Paul II, Pope. *Encyclical Letter Fides et Ratio of the Supreme Pontiff John Paul II to the Bishops of the Catholic Church on the Relationship between Faith and Reason.* September 14, 1998. Vatican City: Libreria editrice vaticana, 1998. http://w2.vatican.va/content/john-paul-ii/en/encyclicals /documents/hf_jp-ii_enc_14091998_fides-et-ratio.html.

Joyce, James. *A Portrait of the Artist as a Young Man* [1916]. New York: B. W. Huebsch, 1922.

Keats, John. "Ode on a Grecian Urn" [1819]. In *John Keats: The Complete Poems,* ed. John Barnard. London: Penguin Classics, 1977.

Lecaldano, Eugenio. *Un'etica senza Dio.* Rome-Bari: Laterza, 2006.

Lenin, Vladimir Ilich. *Materialism and Empirio-Criticism* [1909]. Moscow: Progress Publishers, 1970.

Nicholas of Cusa. *De docta ignorantia* [1440]. *On Learned Ignorance.* Trans. Germain Heron. London: Routledge and Kegan Paul, 1954.

Nietzsche, Friedrich. "On Truth and Lies in an Extra-Moral Sense" [1873]. In *Friedrich Nietzsche On Truth and Lying,* trans. Sander L. Gilman, Carole Blair, and David J. Parent. New York: Oxford University Press, 1989.

Peirce, Charles Sanders. "A Syllabus of Certain Topics of Logic." In *Collected Papers.* Cambridge, MA: Harvard University Press, 1965.

Pera, Marcello, and Joseph Ratzinger. *Senza radici: Europa, relativismo, cristianesimo, islam.* Milan: Mondadori, 2004.

Pseudo-Dionysius the Areopagite. *The Heavenly Hierarchy and The Ecclesiastical Hierarchy.* Trans. John Parker. London: James Parker and Co., 1899.

Ratzinger, Joseph. *Doctrinal Note on Some Questions Regarding the Participation of Catholics in Political Life.* November 24, 2002. http://www.vatican .va/roman_curia/congregations/cfaith/documents/rc_con_cfaith_doc _20021124_politica_en.html.

Ratzinger, Joseph. *Il monoteismo.* Milan: Mondadori, 2002.

Thomas Aquinas. *De aeternitate mundi. On the Eternity of the World.* Trans. Cyril Vollert, Lottie Kendzierski, and Paul Byrne. Milwaukee, WI: Marquette University Press, 1965.

5. Beautiful Flame

Anonymous. *History of Fra Dolcino, Heresiarch* [13th century].

Aristotle. *The Physics, Books I–IV.* Loeb Classical Library, no. 228. Cambridge, MA: Harvard University Press, 1957.

Artephius, The Secret Book of the Blessed Stone Called the Philosopher's [c. 1150]. London: Tho. Walkley, 1624.

Bachelard, Gaston. *Psychoanalysis of Fire.* Trans. Alan C. M. Ross. London: Routledge and Kegan Paul, 1964.

Báez, Fernando. *A Universal History of the Destruction of Books: From Ancient Sumer to Modern Iraq.* New York: Atlas, 2008.

Bhagavad-Gita: Krishna's Counsel in Time of War. Trans. Barbara Stoler Miller. New York: Columbia University Press, 1986.

Bonaventure of Bagnoregio. *Commentaria in quattuor libros sententiarum Magistri Petri Lombardi. Bonaventure on the Eucharist: Commentary on the 'Sentences.'* Trans. Junius Johnson. Wilsele, Belgium: Peeters, 2017.

Buddha. "Adittapariyaya Sutta: The Fire Sermon" (SN 35.28). Trans. Ñanamoli Thera. Access to Insight (BCBS Edition), 2010, http://www .accesstoinsight.org/tipitaka/sn/sn35/sn35.028.nymo.html.

Canetti, Elias. *Auto-da-Fé* [1935]. Trans. C. V. Wedgwood. New York: Stein and Day, 1946.

Cellini, Benvenuto. *My Life* [1567]. Trans. Julia Conaway Bondanella. Oxford: Oxford University Press, 2002.

D'Annunzio, Gabriele. *Il Fuoco* [1900]. *The Flame.* Trans. Susan Bassnett. New York: Marsilio, 1995.

Dante Alighieri. *The Divine Comedy.* Trans. Robert Hollander and Jean Hollander. New York: Doubleday, 2000–2007. (*Inferno,* 2000; *Purgatorio,* 2003; *Paradiso,* 2007.)

Eco, Umberto. *The Name of the Rose.* Trans. William Weaver. New York: Harcourt, 1983. Eco, *Il nome della rosa.* Milan: Bompiani, 1980.

Heraclitus. *Fragments*. In *The Art and Thought of Heraclitus: An Edition of the Fragments with Translation and Commentary*, trans. Charles H. Kahn. Cambridge: Cambridge University Press, 1979.

Hölderlin, Friedrich. *The Death of Empedocles* [1798]. Trans. David Farrell Krell. Albany, NY: SUNY Press, 2009.

John Scotus Eriugena. *Eriugena's Commentary on the Celestial Hierarchy*. Trans. Paul Rorem. Toronto: Pontifical Institute of Mediaeval Studies, 2005.

Joyce, James. *Portrait of the Artist as a Young Man*. New York: Viking and B. W. Huebsch, 1916.

Joyce, James. *Stephen Hero* [1944]. New York: Vintage / Ebury div. Random House, 1969.

Liguori, Alfonso M. de'. *Apparecchio alla morte, cioè considerazioni sulle massime eterne utili a tutti per meditare ed a' sacerdoti per predicare* [1758]. Cinisello Balsamo: Edizione San Paolo, 2007.

Malerba, Luigi. *Il fuoco greco* [1990]. Milan: Mondadori, 2000.

Mattioli, Ercole. *La pietà illustrata*. Venice: appresso Nicolò Pezzana, 1694.

Pater, Walter. *The Renaissance*. London: Boni and Liveright, 1873.

Pernety, Dom. *Dictionnaire Mytho-Hermétique* [1787]. Milan: Archè, 1980.

Plato. *Protagoras*. In *Laches, Protagoras, Meno, Euthydemus*. Trans. W. R. M. Lamb. Loeb Classical Library, no. 165. Cambridge, MA: Harvard University Press, 1977.

Plotinus. *The Enneads*. Ed. Lloyd P. Gerson. Cambridge: Cambridge University Press, 2018.

Pseudo-Dionysius the Areopagite. *The Heavenly Hierarchy and The Ecclesiastical Hierarchy*. Trans. John Parker. London: James Parker and Co., 1899.

Ratzinger, Joseph. *The Message of Fatima*. June 26, 2000. http://www.vatican .va/roman_curia/congregations/cfaith/documents/rc_con_cfaith_doc _20000626_message-fatima_en.html.

Turba Philosophorum, Or Assembly of the Sagas [13th century]. Trans. Arthur Edward Waite. London: George Redway, 1896.

6. The Invisible

Allen, Woody. "The Kugelmass Episode." *New Yorker,* April 24, 1977.

Doumenc, Philippe. *Contre-enquete sur la morte d'Emma Bovary* [Counterinvestigation into the Death of Emma Bovary]. Paris: Actes Sud, 2009.

Doyle, Arthur Conan. *A Study in Scarlet* [1887]. New York: Random House, 2003.

Dumas, Alexandre. *The Count of Monte Cristo* [1844]. New York: Random House / Modern Library, 1996.

Dumas, Alexandre. *The Three Musketeers* [1844]. London: Wordsworth Editions, 1997.

Eco, Umberto. "On the Ontology of Fictional Characters." *Sign Systems Studies* 37, no. 1 / 2 (2009): 82–97.

Flaubert, Gustave. *Madame Bovary* [1856]. Trans. Eleanor Marx-Aveling. London: Jonathan Cape, 1930.

Gautier, Théophile. *Le capitaine Fracasse* [1863]. *Captain Fracasse.* Trans. F. C. de Sumichrast. New York: Collier, 1902.

Hugo, Victor. *Les misérables* [1862]. Trans. Lascelles Wraxall. London: Hurst and Blackett, 1862.

Isidore of Seville. *The Etymologies of Isidore of Seville.* Trans. Stephen A. Barney, W. J. Lewis, J. A. Beach, and Oliver Berghof. Cambridge: Cambridge University Press, 2006.

Shakespeare, William. *A Winter's Tale* [1611]. New York: Simon and Schuster, 2005.

Tolstoy, Lev. *Anna Karenina* [1873–1877]. Trans. Constance Garnett. New York: Thomas Y. Crowell, 1899.

7. Paradoxes and Aphorisms

Aristotle. *The Physics, Books I–IV.* Loeb Classical Library, no. 228. Cambridge, MA: Harvard University Press, 1957.

Chamfort, Nicolas de. *The Cynic's Breviary: Maxims and Anecdotes from Nicolas de Chamfort* [1795]. Trans. William G. Hutchison. London: Elkin Mathews, 1902.

Kraus, Karl. *From Half-Truths & One-and-a-Half-Truths: Selected Aphorisms.* Trans. Harry Zohn. Chicago: University of Chicago Press, 1990.

Isidore of Seville. *The Etymologies of Isidore of Seville.* Trans. Stephen A. Barney, W. J. Lewis, J. A. Beach, and Oliver Berghof. Cambridge: Cambridge University Press, 2006.

Lec, Stanisław J. *Unkempt Thoughts* [1957]. Trans. Clifton Fadiman. New York: St. Martin's Press, 1962.

Pitigrilli [Dino Segre]. *Dizionario antiballistico* [1953]. Milan: Sonzogno, 1962.

Pitigrilli [Dino Segre]. *L'esperimento di Pott.* Milan: Sonzogno, 1929.

Scusa l'anticipo ma ho trovato tutti verdi. Ed. A. Bucciante. Turin: Einaudi, 2010.

Smullyan, Raymond. *To Mock a Mockingbird: And Other Logic Puzzles.* New York: Alfred A. Knopf, 1985.

Wilde, Oscar. *The Importance of Being Ernest* [1895]. London: Leonard Smithers, 1899.

Wilde, Oscar. *The Picture of Dorian Gray* [1890]. In *The Picture of Dorian Gray: An Annotated, Uncensored Edition,* ed. Nicholas Frankel. Cambridge, MA: Belknap Press of Harvard University Press, 2011.

Wilde, Oscar. *The Writings of Oscar Wilde: Epigrams: Phrases and Philosophies for the Use of the Young.* London: A. R. Keller & Co., 1907.

8. Untruths, Lies, Falsifications

Accetto, Torquato. *Della dissimulazione onesta* [1641; On Honest Dissimulation]. Ed. S. S. Nigro. Turin: Einaudi, 1997.

Arendt, Hannah. "Lying in Politics: Reflections on The Pentagon Papers." *New York Review of Books,* November 18, 1971.

Aristotle. *The Metaphysics.* London: Penguin Classics, 1999.

Bacon, Francis. Essay 6: "Of Simulation and Dissimulation" [1625]. In *The Essays of Francis Bacon.* Ed. Clark S. Northrup. Boston: Houghton Mifflin, 1908.

Battista, Giuseppe. *Apologia della menzogna* [1673]. Palermo: Sellerio, 1990.

Bettetini, Maria. *Breve storia della bugia: Da Ulisse a Pinocchio.* Milan: Raffaello Cortina, 2010.

Constant, Benjamin. *Des réactions politique* [1797]. "On Political Reactions." In *Political Writings*, trans. Biancamaria Fontana. Cambridge: Cambridge University Press, 1988.

Descartes, René. *Le monde ou traité de la lumière* [1667]. "The Treatise on Light." In *The World and Other Writings*, trans. Stephen Graukroger. Cambridge: Cambridge University Press, 1998.

Eco, Umberto. *The Prague Cemetery*. Trans. Richard Dixon. Boston: Houghton Mifflin Harcourt, 2011. Eco, *Il Cimitero di Praga*. Milan: Bompiani, 2010.

Eco, Umberto. "Strategies of Lying." In *On Signs*, ed. Marshall Blonsky. Baltimore: Johns Hopkins University Press, 1985.

Eco, Umberto. *A Theory of Semiotics*. Bloomington: Indiana University Press, 1976. Eco, *Trattato di semiotica generale*. Milan: Bompiani, 1975.

Gracián y Morales, Baltasar. *The Art of Worldly Wisdom*. Trans. Christopher Maurer. New York: Doubleday, 1992. Facsimile edition: Gracián, *Oráculo manual y arte de prudencia* [1647]. Zaragoza: Institución Fernanto el Católico, 2001.

Kant, Immanuel. *Critique of Practical Reason and Other Works on the Theory of Ethics*, 4th ed., trans. Thomas Kingsmill Abbott. London: Kongmans, Green and Co., 1889.

Lucian of Samosata. *True History* [2nd century]. Trans. Francis Hickes. London: A. H. Bullen, 1902.

Machiavelli, Niccolò. *The Prince* [1532]. Trans. William K. Marriott. New York: E. P. Dutton, 1958.

Sartre, Jean-Paul. *Being and Nothingness* [1943]. Trans. Hazel E. Barnes. New York: Philosophical Library, 1948.

Scusa l'anticipo ma ho trovato tutti verdi. Ed. A. Bucciante. Turin: Einaudi, 2010.

Swift, Jonathan. *Gulliver's Travels into Several Remote Regions of the World* [1726]. London: George Routledge, 1882.

Swift, Jonathan / John Arbuthnot. *The Art of Political Lying*. New York: Editions Dupleix, 2013.

Tagliapietra, Andrea. *Filosofia della bugia: Figure della menzogna nella storia del pensiero occidentale*. Milan: Bruno Mondadori, 2001.

Webster, Nesta. *Secret Societies and Subversive Movements*. London: Boswell, 1924.

Weinrich, Harald. *Metafora e menzogna: Sulla serenità dell'arte* [Metaphor and Lie: On the Serenity of Art]. Bologna: Il Mulino, 1983.

9. On Some Forms of Imperfection in Art

Augustine. *De civitate Dei. The City of God.* In *The Works of Aurelius Augustine, Bishop of Hippo,* ed. Marcus Dods, vol. 1. Edinburgh: T. and T. Clark, 1871.

Chateaubriand, François-René de. *Itinéraire de Paris à Jérusalem et de Jérusalem à Paris* [1811]. *Itinerary from Paris to Jerusalem.* Trans. Anthony S. Kline. CreateSpace Independent Publishing Platform, 2015.

Croce, Benedetto. *La poesia: Introduzione alla critica e storia della poesia e della letteratura* [1936]. Milan: Adelphi, 1994.

Diderot, Denis. *Oeuvres completes,* vol. 16: *Salon de 1767, Salon de 1769* (Beaux Arts III). Critical edition annotated by E. M. Bukdahl, M. Delon, and A. Larenceau. Paris: Hermann, 1990.

Dumas, Alexandre. *The Count of Monte Cristo* [1844]. New York: Random House / Modern Library, 1996.

Dumas, Alexandre. *The Three Musketeers* [1844]. London: Wordsworth Editions, 1997.

Greimas, Algirdas Julien. *De l'imperfection* [*On Imperfection*]. Périgueux: P. Fanlac, 1987.

John Scotus Eriugena. *De divisione naturae. Periphyseon: The Division of Nature.* Trans. I.-P. Sheldon-Williams and John J. O'Meara. Paris: Bellarmin, 1987.

Leopardi, Giacomo. *Zibaldone di pensieri* [1817–1832]. Critical edition, ed. G. Pacella. Milan: Garzanti, 1991.

Levi-Montalcini, Rita. *In Praise of Imperfection.* Trans. Luigi Attardi. New York: Basic Books, 1988. Levi-Montalcini. *Elogio dell'imperfezione.* Milan: Garzanti, 1987.

Montaigne, Michel Eyquem de. *Essays of Montaigne* [1580–1588]. Trans. Charles Cotton. New York: Edwin C. Hill, 1910.

Moravia, Alberto. *The Time of Indifference.* Trans. Angus Davidson. New York: Farrar, Straus and Young, 1953. Moravia. *Gli indifferenti.* Milan: Alpes, 1929.

Pareyson, Luigi. *Estetica* [1954]. Milan: Bompiani, 1988.

Proust, Marcel. *Pleasures and Days* [1896]. Trans. Andrew Brown. London: Hesperus Press, 2004.

Shakespeare, William. *Hamlet* [1600–1602]. New York: Simon and Schuster, 2012.

Shakespeare, William. *Romeo and Juliet* [1594–1596]. New York: Simon and Schuster, 2004.

Tanizaki, Junichiro. *The Key* [1956]. Trans. Howard Hibbett. New York: Alfred A. Knopf, 1961.

Thomas Aquinas. *Summa Theologiae: Latin Text and English Translation.* New York: McGraw-Hill, 61 vols., 1964–. Repr. New York: Cambridge University Press, 2006.

William of Auvergne. "De Bono et Malo" [13th century; "On Good and Evil"]. Transcription of Latin manuscript: J. Reginald O'Donnell. "Tractatus Magistri Guillelmi Alvernensis *De Bono Et Malo.*" *Medieval Studies* 8 (1946): 245–299.

10. Some Revelations on Secrecy

Ancient and Mystical Order Rosae Crucis (AMORC). *Manuel Rosicrucien.* Paris: Éd. rosicruciennes, 1984.

Baillet, Adrien. *La Vie de Monsieur Descartes.* Paris: Daniel Horthemels, 1691.

Barruel, Augustin. *Mémoires pour servir à l'histoire du jacobinisme,* 5 vols. Hamburg: P. Fauche libraire, 1798–1799.

Brown, Dan. *The Da Vinci Code.* New York: Doubleday, 2003.

Casanova, Giacomo. *The Story of My Life* [1789–1798]. Trans. Stephen Sartarelli and Sophie Hawks. London: Penguin Classics, 2001.

Di Bernardo, Giuliano. *Freemasonry and Its Image of Man.* Trans. Guy Aston and Giuliano di Bernardo. Tunbridge Wells, UK: Freestone, 1989. Di Bernardo. *Filosofia della massoneria.* Venice: Marsilio, 1987.

Eco, Umberto. *Foucault's Pendulum.* Trans. William Weaver. San Diego: Harcourt, Brace, Jovanovich, 1989. Eco. *Il pendolo di Foucault.* Milan: Bompiano, 1988.

Guénon, René. *Perspectives on Initiation.* Trans. Henry D. Fohr, ed. Samuel D. Fohr. Hillsdale, NY: Sophia Perennis, 2001. Guénon. *Aperçus sur l'Initiation.* Paris: Éditions Traditionelles, 1946.

Ibn Khaldun. *The Muqaddimah: An Introduction to History.* Trans. Franz
Rosenthal. Princeton: Princeton University Press, 1994.

Johannes Valentinus Andreae. *Fama fraternitatis* [1614]. In *Manifesti rosacroce:
Fama fraternitatis, Confessio fraternitatis, Nozze chimiche,* ed. G. De Turris.
Rome: Edizioni Mediterranee, 2016.

Luchet, Jean-Pierre-Louis de. *Essai sur la secte des illuminés.* Paris, 1789.

Maier, Michael. *Themis aurea* [1618]. Frankfurt am Main, 1624.

Mazarin, Jules. *The Politicians' Breviary* [1684].

Neuhaus, Henry. *Avertissement pieux et très utile des Frères de la Rose-Croix, à
sçavoir s'il y en a? quels ils sont? d'où ils ont prins ce nom? Et a quelle fin
ils ont espandu leur renommée?* [*Pious and Very Useful Warning about the
Brothers of the Rose Cross; Namely, If There Are Any? What Are They?
Where Did They Take This Name? And to What End Have They Sought
Renown?*]. Paris: au palais, 1623.

Ratzinger, Joseph. *The Message of Fatima.* June 26, 2000. http://www.vatican
.va/roman_curia/congregations/cfaith/documents/rc_con_cfaith_doc
_20000626_message-fatima_en.html.

Simmel, Georg. "The Sociology of Secrecy and of Secret Societies." *American
Journal of Sociology* 11 (1906): 441–498.

Yates, Frances. *The Rosicrucian Enlightenment.* London: Routledge and Kegan
Paul, 1972.

11. Conspiracy

Baigent, Michael, Richard Leigh, and Henry Lincoln.*The Holy Grail.* London:
Jonathan Cape, 1982.

Brown, Dan. *The Da Vinci Code.* New York: Doubleday, 2003.

Chiesa, Giulietto, and Roberto Vignoli, eds. *Zero. Perché la versione ufficiale
sull'11/9 è un falso* [Zero: Why the Official Version about 9/11 Is a
Fraud]. Casale Monferrato: Piemme, 2007.

Gioberti, Vincenzo. *Il gesuita moderno* [1846]. Milan: Bocca, 1942.

Hofstadter, Richard. *The Paranoid Style in American Politics and Other Essays.*
London: Cape, 1964.

Jolley, Daniel, and Karen M. Douglas. "The Social Consequences of Conspiracism: Exposure to Conspiracy Theories Decreases Intentions to

Engage in Politics and to Reduce One's Carbon Footprint." *British Journal of Psychology* 105, no. 1 (2014): 35–56.

Pascal, Blaise. *Lettres provinciales* [1656–1657]. *The Provincial Letters.* Trans. A. J. Krailsheimer. Harmondsworth, UK: Penguin, 1967.

Pipes, Daniel. *Conspiracy: How the Paranoid Style Flourishes and Where It Comes From.* New York: Free Press, 1997.

Polidoro, Massimo, ed. *11/9: La cospirazione impossibile.* Casale Monferrato: Piemme, 2007.

Popper, Karl. *Conjectures and Refutations: The Growth of Scientific Knowledge,* 3rd rev. ed. London: Routledge and K. Paul, 1969.

Popper, Karl. *The Open Society and Its Enemies.* London: G. Routledge and Sons, 1945.

Sède, Gérard de. *The Accursed Treasure of Rennes-le-Chateau.* Trans. Henry Lincoln. Paris: Éditions de l'Oeil du Sphinx, 2013. Sède. *Le trésor de Rennes-le-Chateau* [1967]. Paris: J'ai lu, 1972.

Spinoza, Baruch. *Tractatus Theologico-Politicus* [1670]. *Theologico-Political Treatise.* Trans. A. H. Gosset. London: G. Bell, 1883.

Sue, Eugène. *The Mysteries of the People, Or, History of a Proletarian Family across the Ages.* Trans. Daniel De Leon and Solon De Leon. New York: NY Labor News, 1904. Sue. *Les Mystères de Paris.* Originally serialized in ninety parts in *Journal des débats,* June 1842 to October 1843.

Sue, Eugène. *The Wandering Jew.* London: Routledge, 1879/1880. *Le Juif Errant,* serialized 1844–1845.

William of Ockham. *In libros Sententiarum* [Commentary on the *Sentences* of Peter Lombard].

12. Representations of the Sacred

Alacoque, Marguerite Marie. *The Autobiography of St. Margaret Mary Alacoque* [second half of 17th century]. Charlotte, NC: Tan Books, 1986.

Böhme, Jakob. *The Incarnation of Jesus Christ* [1620]. Trans. John Rolleston Earle. London: Constable, 1934.

Firth, Raymond. *Symbols Public and Private.* Ithaca, NY: Cornell University Press, 1973.

John of the Cross, Saint. *The Ascent of Mount Carmel* [1618]. In *The Complete Works of Saint John of the Cross*, 3 vols., trans. Edgar Allison Peers. London: Burns, Oates and Washbourne, 1934–1935.

Mary Magdalene [Maria Maddalena de'Pazzi]. *I quaranta giorni* [1598]. Palermo: Sellerio, 1996. Selections from *The Forty Days* in *Maria Maddalena de'Pazzi*. Trans. Armando Maggi. New York: Paulist Press, 2000.

Pseudo-Dionysius the Areopagite. *On the Divine Names and On the Mystical Theology.* Trans. C. E. Rolt. London: SPCK, 1920.

Ratzinger, Joseph. *The Message of Fatima.* June 26, 2000. http://www.vatican .va/roman_curia/congregations/cfaith/documents/rc_con_cfaith_doc _20000626_message-fatima_en.html.

Tauler, Johannes. *Sermons* [1300–1361]. Trans. Maria Shrady. Mahwah, NJ: Paulist Press, 1985.

Teresa of Ávila, Saint. *The Book of My Life* [1562]. Trans. Mirabai Starr. Boston: New Seeds, 2007.

William of Ockham. *Summa logicae.* In *Ockham: Philosophical Writings, A Selection,* trans. Philotheus Boehner. Edinburgh: Nelson, 1957.

Index

Index

fireplace, 98
Fire Sermon (Buddha), 122–123
Firth, Raymond, 278
Flagellation of Christ, The (della Francesca), 30
Flame, The (D'Annunzio), 117
Flaubert, Gustave, 221
Fleming, Ian, 61
fluctuating characters, 136–139, 140, 142–143
Fludd, Robert, 228
Fontanelle, Bernard Le Bovier de, 2
forgeries, 183–189, 191, 257
forgery, diplomatic, 188–189
Formaggio, Dino, 25
Forty Days, The (Maddalena de' Pazzi), 272
Foucault's Pendulum (Eco), 238–242
Frankenstein (Shelley), 59
Frazetta, Frank, 69
Freemasons, 231–233, 245, 254
French Revolution, 234, 248
Friedrich, Caspar David, 44, 79
Fuoco greco, Il (Malerba), 121
furor sententialis, 166
Futurists, 65–66

Gaelic, 7
Gale, Megan, 20
Galileo Galilei, 178
Gassendi, Pierre, 12
Gates, Bill, 22
Gaudí, Antoni, 69, 218
G8 conference, 19
generational clash / generations: drug abuse and, 22; giant-dwarf metaphor and, 13; innovation and, 21; need for, 23; in 1968, 18; nonconformity and, 23; in philosophy, 8; requirements for, 19–20; technology and, 21; transgenerational models and, 20–21. See also father-son conflicts; giant-dwarf metaphor; innovation; shoulders of giants
Gesuita moderno, Il (Gioberti), 249
giant-dwarf metaphor, 1, 11; Christianity and, 14; Enlightenment and,

15–16; progress and, 13–14. See also generational clash / generations; shoulders of giants
Gibson, Mel, 48
Gioberti, Vincenzo, 249
Giotto, 34
globalization, 18–19
global warming, 122
Gluckman, Max, 13
God, 266; absolute's identification with, 74–75; associated with light, 31–32; direct experience of, 268–284; ethics without, 95–96; as Great Void, 268–272; representations of, 267–268. See also sacred
good: vs. beautiful, 42; beauty identified with, 50
Goretti, Maria, 279
gossip, 225–226
Gozzano, Guido, 66–67
Gracián, Baltasar, 174, 178, 224
grammar, imperfect tense in, 221
"Grandmother Speranza's Friend" (Gozzano), 66–67
Great Schism, 173
Greek culture, ugliness and, 50–51
Greek fire, 121
Gregory of Tours, 4
Greimas, Algirdas, 196
Gronchi pink stamp, 199
Grosseteste, Robert, 33, 34, 105
Gryphius, Andreas, 57–58
Guénon, Réné, 229
Guercino, 258
Guerrini, Olindo, 64–65
Guevara, Che, 18
Guggenheim, Benjamin, 249
Guimard, Hector, 68
Guinizelli, Guido, 26, 104
Gulliver's Travels (Swift), 180–181

Ham (Biblical figure), 2
Hamlet (Shakespeare), 217
hearth, 98
Hegel, Georg Wilhelm Friedrich, 7, 14, 16, 51, 78

Index   315

Index   317